TOO DARN HOT

Writing About Sex Since Kinsey

A Global City Book
Edited by
Judy Bloomfield, Mary McGrail,
and Lauren Sanders

PERSEA BOOKS
New York

Copyright © 1998 by Global City Press

Persea Books, Inc.
171 Madison Avenue
New York, New York 10016

Library of Congress Cataloging-in-Publication Data

Too darn hot : writing about sex since Kinsey: an anthology / edited
    by Judy Bloomfield, Mary McGrail, and Lauren Sanders.
        p.   cm. — (A global city book)
    ISBN 0-89255-233-6 (alk. paper)
    1. Sex—Literary collections. I. Bloomfield, Judy. II. McGrail,
Mary.   III. Sanders, Lauren.   IV. Series.
PN6071.S416T66   1998   98-5293
306.7—dc21   CIP

Designed by Robert and Rita Lascaro
Printed and bound by Haddon Craftsmen, Bloomsburg, Pennsylvania

First Edition

ACKNOWLEDGMENTS

We would like to thank everyone who submitted work for our anthology, all the people who directed us to writers or writing that appears here, and the writers who donated their work or allowed us to reprint it at a reduced fee.

At Global City Press we are grateful to Linsey Abrams, Rachel DeNys, Diana Estigarribia, Marin Gazzaniga, Laurie Liss, and Susan Thames. We are indebted to Karen and Michael Braziller at Persea Books for their encouragement and editorial insight, and to Paula Bomer for her work on securing permissions.

In addition, we thank the following people for their support and continuous inspiration throughout this project: Ellen and Allen Bloomfield, Erica Bobone, Christine Champagne, Gabrielle Danchick, Marie-Alice Devieux, Rory Devine, Elena Georgiou, Cynthia Kimball, Denis La Breche, Margaret Lewis, Jamie McClelland, Ethan Lowenstein, Ann B. McGrail, Laurie Piette, Susan and Fred Sanders, Taylor Stoehr, Andrea Stover, Benjamin Van der Wel, Beatrice R. W. Williams, The Audio Visual Club at Park East High School, and Dr. John Bancroft, director of The Kinsey Institute for Research in Sex, Gender, and Reproduction.

Finally, a special thanks to Cliff Hahn, Winifred Guillaume, and everyone at Children's Express for generous use of their office space. A very special thanks to Isabel Pipolo, editorial intern extraordinaire.

CONTENTS

V. AN EPILOGUE Let's Talk About Sex

INTRODUCTION

No single event did more for open discussion of sex than the Kinsey Report, which got such matters as homosexuality, masturbation, coitus and orgasm into most papers and family magazines.   —Time, *1953*

On January 5, 1948, a zoologist from Indiana University named Dr. Alfred C. Kinsey published the results of his personal interviews with 5,300 American men. The book was called *Sexual Behavior in the Human Male* and caused an immediate uproar in American society for its frank and nonjudgmental depiction of men's sexual attitudes, practices, and fantasies. At the time, many Americans thought this information to be inappropriate for print; it was better left behind closed bedroom doors or confined to the pages of a few notorious pieces of literature. While published by W. B. Saunders for the scientific community, Kinsey's book nevertheless drew public opposition from psychiatrists, doctors, scientists, politicians, and members of the clergy. A national, more mainstream debate about America's first large-scale "sex survey" followed, providing fodder for articles and cartoons in *Life, Newsweek, The New Yorker, Time,* and other publications. The debate helped put the book on the bestseller list. Almost immediately, American culture registered the impact of Kinsey's book in campaign slogans, pamphlets, and hit songs such as Martha Raye's "Ooh, Dr. Kinsey" and Cole Porter's "Too Darn Hot" with its ironic look at sex and the weather. Clearly, *Sexual Behavior in the Human Male* was no ordinary scientific treatise.

But it was a book whose time had come. A sign that America was ready to end two centuries of silence about sexual behavior. It is difficult for those born after the Second World War to understand just how repressed Americans were in the first half of the century. Despite the risqué reputation of the "roaring twenties," America was still a place where homosexuality and adultery were punishable by law, masturbation was supposed to cause blindness and hairy palms, and premarital sex was considered a sin. Or, as *Harper's* magazine editor Louis Lapham noted in the August 1997 issue of the magazine, before 1948, to most Americans, "sex was something that happened in France."

Into this world stepped Kinsey and his sex book. Yet despite all the fanfare and the book's intriguing title, what became known as "the Kinsey Report" offered anyone who plunked down his $6.50 nothing more than a compilation of charts, lists, and graphs—nearly one thousand pages of them. Five years later, in 1953, Kinsey's second volume, *Sexual Behavior in the Human Female*, prompted even more outraged responses at a time when the idealized woman was still a wife and mother. Nobody wanted to imagine the American housewife seeking out orgasms. But according to the August 31, 1953, issue of *Newsweek*, prepublication reviews of the female volume played "heavy and very hot" in the press: "Sexual discussions and terminology that would be taboo in any other instance rolled off the presses and rolled up circulation." Within a week of these reviews, Democratic Representative Louis B. Heller of Brooklyn called for the post office to bar mailing of the book and for a Congressional investigation of Kinsey for "hurling the insult of the century at women." Meanwhile, in Philadelphia, W. B. Saunders was fielding requests for an unprecedented 250,000 books in advance sales. Americans gobbled up the second Kinsey Report, just as they rushed out to buy the inaugural issue of *Playboy*, which appeared the same year, and would soon gather in front of their television sets and movie screens to see the likes of Jayne Mansfield, Marilyn Monroe, and the first censored rock-and-roll icon, Elvis Presley. The cultural landscape was in a state of upheaval, trading its repressive past for a new explicitness. The ripple effects of this struggle between candor and repression would continue to define America's culture for decades to come.

Even the most extreme attempts to reverse history could not bring back a pre-Kinseyian world. If anything, the pace of change accelerated. By the end of the fifties, rock and roll, originally a slang term for sex, was the most popular music in the country. In 1960, the FDA approved the Pill, and for the first time in history, women could theoretically pursue sex with the freedom men had always taken for granted. By 1967, with America's infamous Summer of Love, the Sexual Revolution was in full swing. Then, in the seventies, the women's liberation movement and the burgeoning gay rights movement continued to challenge traditional society. People were questioning everything about family life, in practice and in print.

In American literature, the seeds of this change had been present for some time. Since the Second World War, a new generation of writers had begun to deal explicitly with sex and sexuality in their work. Writers such as John Cheever, John Updike, Norman Mailer, and Philip Roth began to speak about marriage as a sexual battlefield, uncovering a restlessness in apple-pie America. Simultaneously, Allen Ginsberg, Jack Kerouac, and William S. Burroughs—

the "Beats"—integrated sexual ambiguity, drug use, and an open disdain for the trappings of traditional society into their art. With all of this new writing about sex, one thing had not changed: male voices still defined the discussion. In fact, it wasn't until the 1970s that women began to publish their own stories of sexual liberation and disappointment. Feminist writers such as Kate Millett, Marilyn French, Adrienne Rich, and Audre Lorde exposed the inadequacy of a candor that did not include women. Along the way, Erica Jong in *Fear of Flying* unleashed Isadora Wing, an unapologetic sexual adventuress. No longer would women let men define "sexual behavior in the human female." By the nineties, literature by men and women had expanded to include every aspect of Kinsey's original quest to define and discuss the sexual practices of Americans.

On the occasion of the fiftieth anniversary of the Kinsey Report, we wanted to look at this singular event and its continuing cultural relevance—how writers, poets, and other chroniclers of American culture have given a personal voice to Kinsey's charts and graphs. Over time, words like masturbation, coitus, homosexuality, and orgasm have worked their way into the popular lexicon. People now talk about sex almost casually. On radio and television talk shows, in Hollywood movies, Riot Grrrl rock anthems, tell-all memoirs, in mandatory sex education classes, and sessions in the therapist's office, people are revealing their own sexual histories. Such narratives speak less about the experiential element of sex than about how people have become comfortable expressing their sexual practices and preferences. Kinsey was a pioneer in this area, opening up the first postwar, public dialogue about sex. In a sense, we wanted to see where all of this talk has gotten us.

Just as Kinsey engineered his study by asking questions, we decided to do the same. Our investigation began with a call for submissions of fiction, poetry, and nonfiction exploring America's sexual mores. In selecting pieces, we asked the questions: Is it Kinsey? And what does this mean? Should the pieces be erotic? Analytical? Speak to a particular more or subculture? Should they be multicultural? Must they make direct or indirect references to Kinsey? As the questions multiplied, we realized that a collection of writing surrounding the Kinsey Report could be infinite. We had to limit the scope. Like Kinsey, we wanted to take a nonjudgmental point of view, but we would confine ourselves to cultural documents, not scientific or medical data. Also, we limited ourselves to written material—no paintings, drawings, photographs, or cartoons. We began looking for pieces that spoke about America's specific sexual behaviors and habits in some fresh or interesting way, pieces that might not have been written had there not been a Kinsey Report or the movements of the following five decades. Whenever possible, we tried to find pieces that represented a particular time or era of change. The goal was to include new young writers of today with the pioneers of writing in this area.

The result is a cultural anthology—a collection of poetry, fiction, articles, book reviews, essays, memoir, personal ads, advice columns, sex handbooks, marriage manuals, film scripts, and even a passage from the Bible. In keeping with the hybrid and idiosyncratic nature of the documents collected, we divided the book into five parts—Desire, Society, Body, Ritual, and an epilogue called Let's Talk About Sex. Each part begins with a piece dating back to Kinsey's time period in order to understand some of the cultural forces within which he was operating. Though they may seem quaint, these pieces underscore just how revolutionary Kinsey's work was, and they show how radically American society has changed since then. They also provide an interesting contrast for much of the material that follows.

"Desire" seemed the logical place to start. Tantalizing, irrational, maddening, gratifying, destructive—desire is the catalyst for sexual behavior. The section begins with an excerpt from Herbert Huncke's autobiography, which details his interview with Kinsey, and the profoundly liberating effect of finally disclosing his sexual desires to another human being. In "A Conversation" with Allen Ginsberg and William S. Burroughs, conducted for the film *Heavy Petting* and appearing here in print for the first time, the writers discuss their earliest sexual desires. Offbeat and elegiac, the interview captures the frenetic world of adolescent sexuality. Eve Ensler's "Vagina Monologues" shows the path desire takes in the lives of two very different women. One is traumatized by it, the other emboldened. Desire ends with a collection of personal ads. Princesses seeking frogs, masters seeking slaves, and just plain folks looking for love comprise the found poetry of contemporary sexual desire.

In "Society," desire meets the larger world. This is where rules and regulations enforce particular sexual behaviors, authorizing some while pushing others underground. By exposing the hidden, Kinsey pushed the limit of what could be talked about publicly. In her groundbreaking 1973 essay, "Uses of the Erotic: The Erotic as Power," Audre Lorde claims eroticism as a life force for women. Lisa Palac in her essay, "How Dirty Pictures Changed My Life," talks about her transition from the feminism of Andrea Dworkin and Catharine MacKinnon to career pornographer. Taken together, these essays show society's changing perceptions of women and the erotic. Pieces by Alan Helms, Andy Warhol, and James Earl Hardy highlight the creation of sexual subcultures at different points in post-Kinsey history. In closing, "Society" goes back a few thousand years to the Bible in a section from Leviticus—the original Rules.

The third part, "Body," is perhaps the most obvious. This is where it all happens; the site of pleasure and pain. The body is the direct subject and object of sexuality. This section demonstrates how sexual behavior is affected if you're a mother, if you're getting old, if you're black in a white society, if you have AIDS, or if you're "a man born in a woman's body." Pieces by Mary Gordon, Sharon Olds, bell hooks, Richard McCann, Dan Savage, and others reveal the search to heal, sell, claim, reclaim, or simply understand the workings of the flesh.

In "Ritual" we investigate the prescribed rites of sexuality. The section begins with excerpts from *A Marriage Manual,* first written in the 1930s and subsequently updated, and *The New Joy of Sex,* published in 1991. Different as they are, both pieces celebrate the role of ceremony in a relationship. Other pieces conjure the lure of even the most violent rituals. An excerpt from *Possessing the Secret of Joy* by Alice Walker exposes the practice of female genital mutilation and its power over a woman in search of her identity. In other pieces, rituals are enactments of self-created sacraments—be they sacred or profane. Whether they originate in the world of Catholicism, as in Philip Appleman's poem "A Priest Forever," or in the fevered mind of the young girl portrayed in Dorothy Allison's "Private Rituals," these rites allow their inventors a semblance of control over seemingly uncontrollable impulses.

In conclusion, we thought it would be interesting to find out where we are going in terms of the practice and discussion of sex. With the help of a couple of teenagers, we devised our own sex survey and had the young interviewers question their peers. The outcome, "Let's Talk About Sex," is an uncensored conversation with teenagers on sex and sexuality, giving us a glimpse into a new generation's sexual mores.

This year, The Kinsey Institute for Research in Sex, Gender, and Reproduction is reprinting *Sexual Behavior in the Human Male* to celebrate its fiftieth anniversary. The original Kinsey data—18,216 sex histories, taken from 1938 to 1963, using Kinsey's interview method—are still being used by sex researchers. (Kinsey died in 1956 at age 62.) Beyond that, the Kinsey Report has become a cultural artifact. It continues to prove there is no one sexual norm. To quote Kinsey himself: "There is an abundance of evidence that most human sexual activities would become comprehensible to most individuals, if they could know the background of each other's individual behavior."

Kinsey could not have predicted that fifty years later we would become a nation obsessed with sex. Yet he did recognize a lack of straightforward information about people's sex lives. This lack of information persists today. While the discussion of sex is more open, most of its expression in popular culture is guided not by the desire to enlighten but more to shock and titillate gratuitously, or to sell products. The same was true when Kinsey first took the sexual pulse of America, though in a more veiled manner. Kinsey trusted the public enough to take an unflinching look at sex, regardless of the consequences, and to pass on what he had found. We have tried to do the same.

The forty-seven pieces in this anthology represent an honest look at a wide range of sexual experiences and individual points of view. Throughout the editorial process, we were determined to avoid the banal or superficial in favor of compelling, fresh, and sometimes difficult material. Readers may disagree with some of the choices we made, but we hope they will nonetheless be engaged and entertained without feeling condescended to. Perhaps by addressing sex in a thoughtful yet unexpurgated manner, this book will contribute to the best elements of the discussion begun by Kinsey fifty years ago.

Judy Bloomfield
Mary McGrail
Lauren Sanders

I
DESIRE

Herbert Huncke

from **GUILTY OF EVERYTHING**

One afternoon when I was sitting in Chase's cafeteria I was approached by a young girl who asked if she could join me. She was carrying several books in her arm and was obviously a student. "There's someone who wants to meet you," she told me. I said, "Yes, who?" "A Professor Kinsey."

I had never heard of him and she went on to say, "Well, he's a professor at Indiana University and he's doing research on sex. He is requesting people to talk about their sex lives, and to be as honest about it as possible."

My immediate reaction was that there was some very strange character in the offing who was too shy to approach people himself, someone who probably had some very weird sex kick and was using this girl to pander for him. But I sounded her down.

She obviously knew what the score was insofar as sex, but I didn't know that. I didn't want to shock her but at the same time I wanted to find out exactly what the story was, so I questioned her rather closely about this man. I asked her why he hadn't approached me himself, and she said, "He felt it would be better if someone else spoke with you. He has seen you around, and he thought you might be very interesting to talk to. I'll tell you what I'll do. I'll give you his name and number." At that time he was staying at a very nice East Side hotel. "You can call him and discuss the situation with him." I had nothing else to do, and I said, "Well, I might as well find out what this is all about."

I called Kinsey and he said, "Oh yes, I'd like to speak with you very much." "What exactly is it you're interested in?" I asked him. "All I want you to do," he said to me, "is tell me about your sex life, what experiences you've had, what your interests are, whether you've masturbated and how often, whether you've had any homosexual experiences." "That's all you want?" I said. "That's all I want."

"Well I think it's only fair to tell you," I went on, "and I don't want to be

3

crude—but I do need money." He said, "I'd certainly be willing to give you some money. Would ten dollars be all right?" "It certainly would."

Kinsey wanted me to come up to his place, and I said, "No, I'd rather not do that. I'd rather meet you somewhere first." I did not trust him yet. There was just something about the whole thing that sounded very offbeat to me. I arranged to have him meet me at a bar. "I'll meet you at the bar, but I don't drink," he said. "But I'll buy a drink." "All right, fair enough." "I'll know you when I see you," he told me, "so you sit down and order yourself a drink and I'll be there in a while." We were to meet at a popular bar on the Square, though not the Angler.

I didn't have enough money to buy myself a drink, and I sort of kicked around in front of the place until I saw a cab pull up and a man get out. Kinsey had a very interesting appearance, strictly professorial. His hair was cut very short, slightly gray. He had a round face that was pleasant-appearing, and he was dressed in a suit—obviously a conservative man, I thought.

He walked up to me and said, "I'm Kinsey, you're Herbert Huncke. Let's go in. You'd like to have a drink." I said, "Yes, I'd like to talk to you a few moments before we go to your hotel." He again gave me much the same story the girl had and he assured me that the only thing he was interested in was the discussion, though he did say he wanted to measure the size of the penis. He showed me a card which had a phallus drawn on it. He said he'd like to know the length of it when erect and when soft. Naturally, I was wondering when he was going to get to the point. It was all so strange, and I still did not quite believe him, but I thought, Well, hell, I might just as well go along with him and see what it's all about.

As it turned out, it was a very delightful experience. As I got started rapping to Kinsey about my sex life I sort of unburdened myself of many things that I'd long been keeping to myself. For example, I'd always masturbated, all the way up until I kind of lost interest in sex altogether, around the age of fifty. When I told others of my confessions to Kinsey they all said I was off my rocker, but I must say I was thankful by that time to get it out of my system. I had earned my living from sex at one time and have met all kinds of people, and heard of and had experiences with some very strange fetishes.

I told Kinsey most of these things. In *Huncke's Journal* I describe an interesting experience I had as a young boy, and I spoke to him about this. It tells of a young fellow, about twenty years old, who, after telling me dirty stories and arousing me with pornographic pictures, suggested we go up into a building together. We did, and he suddenly startled me by dropping his pants. There he was with an erection. This thing looked gigantic to me because, being eight or nine years old, it just happened that it was dead in front of my face. I drew back but at the same time I say in all honesty that I was somehow interested. I felt no fear.

He said he wanted to feel me. I was embarrassed. Here was my tiny hunk of flesh and then this gigantic thing standing in front of me. It didn't seem right somehow. Anyway, he did try and convince me that it would be a good idea if I'd allow him to put it up my rectum. I certainly drew the line at that, because I knew it'd be very painful. I assured him I wasn't about to cooperate, and he didn't press the issue. He proceeded to masturbate furiously, and then he ejaculated. That was my first experience with anyone other than children of my own age.

I continued to relate to Kinsey how this was something I would think about when I would masturbate. It would excite me. I had never told anyone about it, however, until I told Kinsey. It was that sort of thing that I unburdened myself of to this man.

As I continued to speak to him he became so adept at his questioning and his approach that there was no embarrassment on my part, and I found myself relaxing. The one thing I could not supply him with was a size to my penis. He finally gave me a card and asked me to fill it out and send it to him later on, which, incidentally, I never did.

Kinsey turned out to be a very intriguing man, a man that I learned to respect and who I began to see quite of a bit of. We met for interviews several times, but I also began to see him outside of his office. He only remained in New York a short time on that first visit. I believe there was some difficulty about the grants that would enable him to continue his research. He had to return to the university; but he did come back, this time with a companion. He was a nice young man, someone who had studied with Kinsey and that Kinsey had taken on as an assistant in his Kinsey Reports.

I believe I was one of the first in New York to be interviewed by Kinsey, and certainly one of the first from Times Square. Kinsey had apparently seen me around the Square and was fairly sure that I'd have information to give, if he could get it from me. He had walked up and down Forty-second Street, and he realized there was action of some sort going on there. Of course, he didn't know too much about the underworld aspect of it, but it was still pretty obvious. One walked by doorways and saw young men in tight pants with their whole profile on display. And there were the many flagrant queens that used to fly up and down the Street, not to mention the more sinister types that could be noticed if one paid attention. I tell you, the area isn't nearly as interesting now as it was back then, just after the war. For one thing, things were not quite as nasty as today. Things were more out in the open, in a manner of speaking. Broadway was lit up bright and sparkling all night long. There was a different, more vibrant feeling then that does not exist today. I told Kinsey about what was happening on the Square.

Kinsey gave me money for the interviews. I wouldn't have accepted anything from him if I hadn't needed it very badly at the time. He told me, "Now, if there's anyone else you know that you think might be interested in being interviewed, by all means send them up. I'll tell you what. For every person you send up from Forty-second Street, I'll give you two dollars. I know you can use the money." "Yes I can."

It was nice to know that when I was uptight I could get two dollars. All I'd have to do is waylay somebody I knew and say, "Hey, man, want to make a couple bucks?" "What do I have to do?" "Well, all you have to do is just sit down and tell this man all there is to tell about your sex life. There's no hanky-panky involved. The man is doing research work on sex." Of course, there was no problem. I sent a number of people I knew up to meet with Kinsey. I think I pretty much made his Times Square study. There were others, of course, who he'd met through me that kind of took over for me. It got to be quite competitive for a while there, what with all the running about for interviewees.

In fact, I introduced [William] Burroughs to Kinsey over at the Angler Bar. Bill [Burroughs], of course, is a very knowledgeable individual. He's been all over the world, and as a young man he had studied medicine in Vienna. The two of them talked the same language. When Kinsey came back to the city the second time he spent more time out and we'd all meet at the Angler. Joan [Burroughs] would come around, and [Allen] Ginsberg and, though I'm not sure, each of them interviewed with Kinsey as well. It was at these long discussions when we all sat around talking with Kinsey that I came to see that Bill is an extraordinary person. I grew to respect him. It was a good crowd, lively and fun to be with, to be sure.

Of course, though, I was seen as the wicked character, always rushing in and out. Say I'd see someone. I'd say, "Excuse me, I'll be back in a little while." I'd go out, rap for a few minutes with someone, or say, "So and so's looking for you," that sort of thing. I'd be introducing various people, and it would go on like that. One night I was very sick and I bumped into Kinsey on the street. I said, "Look, I am really uptight for some money. Can you spare five or ten dollars?" He did, reluctantly. "Now look," he said to me, "I don't want to make a habit of this. I'm in no position to do that, but yes, this one time I'll be glad to help you. Just forget it." When you meet people that understand or are somewhat responsive, it always leaves a good feeling. I've always liked Mr. Kinsey.

Herbert E. Huncke was born in 1915 in Greenfield, Massachusetts. Hitting the road at age twelve, he lived a life on the fringes of American society as a hustler, addict, and petty criminal. In the mid-1940s he met William S. Burroughs and gave him his first shot of morphine. He introduced Jack Kerouac to the term "beat," meaning beaten down to an almost euphoric state of exhaustion. Huncke became part of the intimate circle of Burroughs, Kerouac, and Allen Ginsberg, who all looked to him as a sort of guide to the underbelly of New York City. Although Huncke is better known for appearing in works like Kerouac's On the Road, Burroughs's Junky, and Ginsberg's Howl, he was a prolific writer in his own right. Many of his works, including the autobiography from which this excerpt is taken, are collected in The Herbert Huncke Reader, published in 1997. Huncke died in 1996 in New York City.

Chrystos

I BOUGHT A NEW RED

dress to knock her socks off, spent all day looking for just the right combination of sleeve & drape, so I could actually knock all her clothes off   She met me at the boat dressed so sharp she cut all the boys to ribbons

Over dinner in a very crowded queer restaurant I teased her by having to catch drips of my food with my tongue, staring into her eyes, daring her to lean over & grab my breast or crotch & titillate the faggot waiters   She sat back soaking me up, enjoying my teasing tidbits, for all the world not wanting to fuck me ever   I knew better as she's kept me on my back all night since we met   I began to pout because I wasn't affecting her enough to suit me & she hadn't said a thing about my dress   Just then the waiter brought our dessert, a small cake she'd had decorated to say *Beg Me To Fuck You,* with pink roses all around the edge

I laughed so hard I tore my dress a little   The waiter smirked   I fed her roses from the cake, she licked my fingers so slowly I almost screamed   Near us some blazer dykes were very nervous & offended, so naturally she began to make loud sucking noises   Laughing, we left them to their girl scout sex & went dancing, where she kept her hand on my ass & her thigh between my legs even during the fast ones   Going home she pulled my thigh-top stockings to my knees & played with me   I'd worn no underpants especially for her   We were having such a good time she couldn't park & we laughed as she tried a third time & I blew in her ear almost causing a wreck

Then we started doing it in the front seat of her car, awkward with gear knob & wrong angles, until a cop pulled up

8

& said sarcastically through the open window *Do you need
some assistance parking, Sir?* She flamed as red as my dress
& returned to maneuvering the car instead of me

I was so horny I could barely walk in my matching high
heels & she held my arm as we crossed to her place, pinching my nipple with her other hand & smiling her grin of
anticipation   We necked on the porch to upset her nosy
neighbors, who have twice complained about the noise I
made coming   Then she couldn't get the lock to work &
we giggled as I stood with heels in hand, my stockings full
of runs & a wet spot on the back of my silk dress almost as
wide as my ass   The door popped open so suddenly she fell
forward & I tumbled after her, gasping   I started up the
stairs heading for her bed when she caught hold of my
pubic hair with her hand & pulled me back onto her until I
was kneeling on the stairs as she fucked me from behind &
my dress ripped some more as she took me hard, kicking
the door shut with her foot, taking me out of this world
until I was upside down with my head at the door & leg on
the banister   Heat of her crotch as she came on me, my
dress ripping right up the front as we laughed harder

The next morning her roommate said we were disgusting &
we grinned with pride   The cleaners cannot repair the
sweet dress & looked at me very oddly but I went out giggling & made her a pocket handkerchief with it, sewing
rolled hems & a discreet message along one edge *PLEASE
rip my dress off anytime*

---

*Chrystos was born in 1946, off-reservation, to a Menominee father and an Alsace-
Lorraine/Lithuanian mother. Raised in San Francisco and now living in the Pacific
Northwest, she is a self-educated artist and writer, and an activist for numerous Native
rights and prisoners' causes. Her published books include* Not Vanishing, Dream On, *and*
In Her I Am.

John Updike

WIFE-WOOING

O h my love. Yes. Here we sit, on warm broad floorboards, before a fire, the children between us, in a crescent, eating. The girl and I share one half-pint of French-fried potatoes; you and the boy share another; and in the center, sharing nothing, making simple reflections within himself like a jewel, the baby, mounted in an Easybaby, sucks at his bottle with frowning mastery, his selfish, contemplative eyes stealing glitter from the center of the flames. And you. You. You allow your skirt, the same black skirt in which this morning you with woman's soft bravery mounted a bicycle and sallied forth to play hymns in difficult keys on the Sunday school's old piano— you allow this black skirt to slide off your raised knees down your thighs, slide *up* your thighs in your body's absolute geography, so the parallel whiteness of their undersides is exposed to the fire's warmth and to my sight. Oh. There is a line of Joyce. I try to recover it from the legendary, imperfectly explored grottoes of *Ulysses:* a garter snapped, to please Blazes Boylan, in a deep Dublin den. What? Smackwarm. That was the crucial word. Smacked smackwarm on her smackable warm woman's thigh. Something like that. A splendid man, to feel that. Smackwarm woman's. Splendid also to feel the curious and potent, inexplicable and irrefutably magical life language leads within itself. What soul took thought and knew that adding "wo" to man would make a woman? The difference exactly. The wide w, the receptive o. Womb. In our crescent the children for all their size seem to come out of you toward me, wet fingers and eyes, tinted bronze. Three children, five persons, seven years. Seven years since I wed wide warm woman, white-thighed. Wooed and wed. Wife. A knife of a word that for all its final bite did not end the wooing. To my wonderment.

We eat meat, meat I wrested warm from the raw hands of the hamburger girl in the diner a mile away, a ferocious place, slick with savagery, wild with chrome; young predators snarling dirty jokes menaced me, old men reached for me with coffee-warmed paws; I wielded my wallet, and won my way back. The fat brown bag of buns was warm beside me in the cold car; the smaller bag holding the two tiny cartons of French fries emitted an even more urgent heat. Back through the black winter air to the fire, the intimate cave, where halloos and hurrahs greeted me, the deer, mouth agape and its cotton throat gushing, stretched dead across my shoulders. And now you, beside the white O of the plate upon which the children discarded with squeals of disgust the rings of translucent onion that came squeezed in the hamburgers—you push your toes an inch closer to the blaze, and the ashy white of the inside of your deep thigh is lazily laid bare, and the eternally elastic garter snaps smackwarm against my hidden heart.

Who would have thought, wide wife, back there in the white tremble of the ceremony (in the corner of my eye I held, despite the distracting hail of ominous vows, the vibration of the cluster of stephanotis clutched against your waist), that seven years would bring us no distance, through all those warm beds, to the same trembling point, of beginning? The cells change every seven years, and down in the atom, apparently, there is a strange discontinuity; as if God wills the universe anew every instant. (Ah God, dear God, tall friend of my childhood, I will never forget you, though they say dreadful things. They say rose windows in cathedrals are vaginal symbols.) Your legs, exposed as fully as by a bathing suit, yearn deeper into the amber wash of heat. Well: begin. A green jet of flame spits out sideways from a pocket of resin in a log, crying, and the orange shadows on the ceiling sway with fresh life. Begin.

"Remember, on our honeymoon, how the top of the kerosene heater made a great big rose window on the ceiling?"

"Vnn." Your chin goes to your knees, your shins draw in, all is retracted. Not much to remember, perhaps, for you; blood badly spilled, clumsiness of all sorts. "It was cold for June."

"Mommy, what was cold? What did you say?" the girl asks, enunciating angrily, determined not to let language slip on her tongue and tumble her so that we laugh.

"A house where Daddy and I stayed one time."

"I don't like dat," the boy says, and throws a half bun painted with chartreuse mustard onto the floor.

You pick it up and with beautiful sombre musing ask, "Isn't that funny? Did any of the others have mustard on them?"

"I *hate* dat," the boy insists; he is two. Language is to him thick vague handles swirling by; he grabs what he can.

"Here. He can have mine. Give me his." I pass my hamburger over, you take it, he takes it from you, there is nowhere a ripple of gratitude. There is no

11

more praise of my heroism in fetching Sunday supper, saving you labor. Cunning, you sense, and sense that I sense your knowledge, that I had hoped to hoard your energy toward a more ecstatic spending. We sense everything between us, every ripple, existent and nonexistent; it is tiring. Courting a wife takes tenfold the strength of winning an ignorant girl. The fire shifts, shattering fragments of newspaper that carry in lighter gray the ghost of the ink of their message. You huddle your legs and bring the skirt back over them. With a sizzling noise like the sighs of the exhausted logs, the baby sucks the last from his bottle, drops it to the floor with its distasteful hoax of vacant suds, and begins to cry. His egotist's mouth opens; the delicate membrane of his satisfaction tears. You pick him up and stand. You love the baby more than me.

Who would have thought, blood once spilled, that no barrier would be broken, that you would be each time healed into a virgin again? Tall, fair, obscure, remote, and courteous.

We put the children to bed, one by one, in reverse order of birth. I am limitlessly patient, paternal, good. Yet you know. We watch the paper bags and cartons ignite on the breathing pillow of embers, read, watch television, eat crackers, it does not matter. Eleven comes. For a tingling moment you stand on the bedroom rug in your underpants, untangling your nightie; oh, fat white sweet fat fatness. In bed you read. About Richard Nixon. He fascinates you; you hate him. You know how he defeated Jerry Voorhis, martyred Mrs. Douglas, how he played poker in the Navy despite being a Quaker, every fiendish trick, every low adaptation. Oh my Lord. Let's let the poor man go to bed. We're none of us perfect. "Hey, let's turn out the light."

"Wait. He's just about to get Hiss convicted. It's very strange. It says he acted honorably."

"I'm sure he did." I reach for the switch.

"No. Wait. Just till I finish this chapter. I'm sure there'll be something at the end."

"Honey, Hiss was guilty. We're all guilty. Conceived in concupiscence, we die unrepentant." Once my ornate words wooed you.

I lie against your filmy convex back. You read sideways, a sleepy trick. I see the page through the fringe of your hair, sharp and white as a wedge of crystal. Suddenly it slips. The book has slipped from your hand. You are asleep. Oh cunning trick, cunning. In the darkness I consider. Cunning. The headlights of cars accidentally slide fanning slits of light around our walls and ceiling. The great rose window was projected upward through the petal-shaped perforations in the top of the black kerosene stove, which we stood in the center of the floor. As the flame on the circular wick flickered, the wide soft star of interlocked penumbrae moved and waved as if it were printed on a silk cloth being gently tugged or slowly blown. Its color soft blurred blood. We pay dear in blood for our peaceful homes.

In the morning, to my relief, you are ugly. Monday's wan breakfast light bleaches you blotchily, drains the goodness from your thickness, makes the bathrobe a limp stained tube flapping disconsolately, exposing sallow décolletage. The skin between your breasts a sad yellow. I feast with the coffee on your drabness. Every wrinkle and sickly tint a relief and a revenge. The children yammer. The toaster sticks. Seven years have worn this woman.

The man, he arrows off to work, jousting for right-of-way, veering on the thin hard edge of the legal speed limit. Out of domestic muddle, softness, pallor, flaccidity: into the city. Stone is his province. The winning of coin. The maneuvering of abstractions. Making heartless things run. Oh the inanimate, adamant joys of job!

I return with my head enmeshed in a machine. A technicality it would take weeks to explain to you snags my brain; I fiddle with phrases and numbers all the blind evening. You serve me supper as a waitress—as less than a waitress, for I have known you. The children touch me timidly, as they would a steep girder bolted into a framework whose height they don't understand. They drift into sleep securely. We survive their passing in calm parallelity. My thoughts rework in chronic right angles the same snagging circuits on the same professional grid. You rustle the book about Nixon; vanish upstairs into the plumbing; the bathtub pipes cry. In my head I seem to have found the stuck switch at last: I push at it; it jams; I push; it is jammed. I grow dizzy, churning with cigarettes. I circle the room aimlessly.

So I am taken by surprise at a turning when at the meaningful hour of ten you come with a kiss of toothpaste to me moist and girlish and quick; the momentous moral of this story being, An expected gift is not worth giving.

John Updike was born in 1932, in Shillington, Pennsylvania. He is the author of some forty books, including collections of short stories, poems, and criticism. Updike's novels have won the Pulitzer Prize, the National Book Award, the National Book Critics Circle Award, and recently, for Rabbit at Rest, *the Howells Medal for the most distinguished work of American fiction of the last five years, given by the American Academy of Arts and Letters. "Wife-Wooing" was first published in 1960.*

Eve Ensler

from THE VAGINA MONOLOGUES

The following monologues are selected from Ensler's Off-Broadway performance piece based on interviews with women about their vaginas.

The Flood

Own there? I haven't been down there since 1953. No, it had nothing to do with Eisenhower. No, no, it's a cellar down there. It's very damp, clammy. You don't want to go down there. Trust me. You'd get sick. Suffocating. Very nauseating. The smell of the clamminess and the mildew and everything. Whew! Smells unbearable. Gets in your clothes.

No, there was no accident down there. It didn't blow up or catch on fire or anything. It wasn't so dramatic. I mean, well, never mind. No. Never mind. I can't talk to you about this. What? Jesus, o.k.

There was this boy, Andy Leftkov. He was cute, well I though so. And tall, like me and I really liked him. He asked me out for a date in his car....

I can't tell you this. I can't do this, talk about down there. You just know it's there. Like the cellar. There's rumbles down there sometimes. You can hear the pipes and things get caught there, animals and things and it gets wet and sometimes people have to plug up the leaks. Otherwise the door stays closed. You forget about it. I mean it's part of the house, but you don't see it or think about it. It has to be there though cause every house needs a cellar otherwise the bedroom would be in the basement.

Oh, Andy, Andy Leftkov. Right. Why do you want to hear this story? It's old. It's tired. What's a smart girl like you talking to old ladies about their down there's? We didn't do this kind of thing when I was a girl.

Andy was very good looking. He was a "catch." We were in his car, a white Impala. I remember thinking that my legs were too long for the seat. I have long legs. They were bumping up against the dashboard. I was looking at my big kneecaps when he just kissed me in this "surprisingly take me by control like they do in the movies" kind of way. And I got excited, so excited and well, there

14

was a flood down there. I couldn't control it. It was like this force of passion, this river of life just flooded out of me, right through my panties, right onto the car seat of his white Impala. It wasn't pee and it was smelly, well, frankly I didn't really smell anything at all, but he said, Andy said that it smelled like sour milk and it was staining his car seat. "I was a stinky weird girl" he said. I wanted to explain that his kiss caught me off guard, that I wasn't normally like this. I tried to wipe up the flood with my dress. It was a new yellow primrose dress and it looked so ugly with the flood on it. Andy drove me home without saying another word and when I got out and closed his car door, I closed the whole store. Locked it, never opened for business again. I dated some after that, but the idea of flooding made me too nervous. I never got close again.

I used to have dreams, crazy dreams. Oh they're dopey. Why? I never told anyone these dreams. It was always Burt Reynolds. I don't know why. He never did much for me in life, but in my dreams.... Burt was it. It was always the same general dream. We'd be out, Burt and I.... It was some restaurant like the kind you see in Atlantic City, all big with chandeliers and stuff and thousands of waiters with vests on. Burt would give me this orchid corsage. I'd pin it on my blazer. We'd laugh. Eat shrimp cocktail. They were always huge, those shrimp. We'd laugh more. We were very happy together. Then he'd look into my eyes and pull me to him in the middle of the restaurant and just as he was about to kiss me, the room would start to shake, pigeons would fly out from under the table (I don't know what those pigeons were doing down there), and the flood would come straight from down there. It would pour out of me. It would pour and pour. There would be fish inside it and little boats and the whole restaurant would fill with water and Burt would be standing knee deep in my flood, looking horribly disappointed in me that I'd done it again, horrified as he watched his friends, Dean Martin and the likes swim past us in their tuxedos and evening gowns.

I don't have those dreams anymore. Not since they took away just about everything connected with down there. Moved out the uterus, the tubes, the whole works. The doctor thought he was being funny. He told me if you don't use it, you lose it. But really I found out it was cancer. Everything around it had to go. Who needs it anyway? Highly overrated. I've done other things. I love the dog shows. I sell antiques.

You ask me what it would wear? It would wear a big sign—CLOSED DUE TO FLOODING.

What would it say? It's not like that. It's not like a person who speaks. No, it wouldn't talk, cause it doesn't talk. It stopped being a thing that talked a long time ago. It's a place. A place you don't go. It's closed up, under the house. It's down there. You happy? You made me talk—you got it out of me. You got an old lady to talk about her down there. You feel better now.

(Turns away, turns back)

Actually you're the first person I ever told about that and I feel a little better.

Reclaiming Cunt

I call it cunt. I've reclaimed it cunt. I really like it. Cunt. Listen to it. Cunt C C (ca ca) Cavern, cackle, clit, cute, come-closed c-close inside, inside ca-then u-then cu-then curvy, inviting sharkskin u-uniform, under, up, urge, ugh, ugh, -u-then n then cun-snug letters fitting perfectly together-n-nest, now, nexus, nice, nice, always with depth, always round in upper case, cun, cun-n a jagged wicked electrical pulse-n (high pitched noise) then soft n-warm n-cun, cun, then t-then sharp certain tangy t-texture, take, tent, tight, tantalizing, tensing, taste, tendrils, time, tactile, tell me, tell me cunt cunt, say it, tell me cunt. Cunt.

The Woman Who Loved to Make Vaginas Happy

I love vaginas. I love women. I do not see them as separate things. Women pay me to dominate them, to excite them, to make them come. I did not start out like this. No, to the contrary. I started out as a lawyer, but in my late thirties, I became obsessed with making women happy. There were so many unfulfilled women. So many women who had no access to their sexual happiness. It began as a mission of sorts, but then I got involved in it. I got very good at it, kind of brilliant. It was my art. I started getting paid for it. It was as if I had found my calling. Tax law seemed completely boring and insignificant then.

I wore outrageous outfits when I dominated women. Lace and silk and leather and I used props; whips, handcuffs, rope, dildoes. There was no excitement like this in tax law. There were no props, no excitement, and I hated those blue corporate suits, although I wear them now from time to time in my new line of work and they serve quite nicely. Context is all. There were no props, outfits, in corporate law. There was no wetness. There was no dark mysterious foreplay. There were no erect nipples. There were no delicious mouths, but mainly there was no moaning. Not the kind I'm talking about anyway. This was the key. I see now, moaning was the thing that ultimately seduced me and got me addicted to making women happy. When I was a little girl and I would see women in the movies making love, making strange orgasmic moaning noises, I used to laugh. I got strangely hysterical. I couldn't believe that big outrageous, ungoverned sounds like that came out of women. I longed to moan. I practiced in front of my mirror, on a tape recorder, moaning in various keys, various tones with sometimes very operatic expressions, sometimes more reserved, almost withheld expression. But always when I played it back, it sounded fake. It *was* fake. It wasn't rooted in anything sexual really, only in my desire to be sexual.

But then when I was ten I had to pee really badly once. On a car trip. It went on for almost an hour and when I finally got to pee in this dirty little gas station, it was so exciting, I moaned. I moaned as I peed. I couldn't believe it, me moaning in a Texaco station in the middle of Louisiana. I realized right then that moans are connected with not getting what you want right away, with putting things off. I realized moans were best when they caught you by surprise, they came out of this hidden mysterious part of you that was speaking its own language, that moans were in fact that language.

I became a "moaner." It made most men anxious. Frankly, it terrified them. I was loud and they couldn't concentrate on what they were doing. They'd lose focus. Then they'd lose everything. We couldn't make love in people's homes. The walls were too thin. I got a reputation in my building and people stared at me with contempt in the elevator. Men thought I was too intense, some called me insane.

I began to feel bad about moaning. I got quiet and polite. I made noise into a pillow. I learned to choke my moan, hold it back like a sneeze. I began to get headaches and stress related disorders. I was becoming hopeless when I discovered women. I discovered that most women loved my moaning, but more importantly I discovered how deeply excited I got when other women moaned, when I could make other women moan. It became kind of a passion. Discovering the key, unlocking the vagina's mouth, unlocking this voice, this wild song.

I made love to quiet women and I found this place inside them and they shocked themselves in their moaning. I made love to moaners and they found a deeper, more penetrating moan. I became obsessed. I longed to make women moan, to be in charge, like a conductor maybe or a band leader. It was a kind of surgery, a kind of delicate science, finding the tempo, the exact location or home of the moan. That's what I called it.

Sometimes I found it over a woman's jeans. Sometimes I snuck up on it, off the record, quietly disarming the surrounding alarms and moving in. Sometimes I used force, but not violent, oppressing force, more like dominating, I'm going to take you some place, don't worry, lay back and enjoy the ride

17

kind of force. Sometimes it was simply mundane. I found the moan, before things even started, while we were eating salad or chicken just casual just right there, with my fingers, here it is like that, real simple, in the kitchen, all mixed in with the balsamic vinegar. Sometimes I used props, loved props, sometimes I made the woman find her own moan in front of me. I waited, stuck it out until she opened herself. I wasn't fooled by the minor, more obvious moans. No, I pushed her further all the way into her power moan.

There's the clit moan, the vaginal moan, the combo, clit, vaginal moan. There's the pre-moan, the almost moan, the right on it moan, the elegant moan, the Grace Slick moan, the Wasp moan, the semi-religious moan, the mountain top moan, the baby moan, the doggy moan, the birthday moan, the uninhibited militant bisexual moan, the machine gun moan, the tortured Zen moan, the Diva moan, the twisted toe orgasm moan, and finally, the surprise triple orgasm moan.

After I finished this piece I read it to the woman whom I'd based the interview on. She didn't feel it really had anything to do with her. She loved the piece, mind you, but she didn't see herself in it. She felt I had somehow avoided talking about vaginas, that I was still somehow objectifying them. Even the moans were a way of objectifying the vagina, cutting it off from the rest of the vagina, the rest of the woman. There was a real difference in the way lesbians saw vaginas. I hadn't yet captured it.

So I interviewed her again.

As a lesbian, she said, I need you to start from a lesbian centered place, not framed within a heterosexual context. I did not desire women for example, because I disliked men. Men weren't even part of the equation. She said, you need to talk about entering into vaginas. You can't talk about lesbian sex without doing this.

For example, she said, I'm having sex with a woman. She's inside me. I'm inside me. Fucking myself together with her. There are four fingers inside me, two are hers, two are mine.

I don't know that I wanted to talk about sex. But then again, how can I talk about vaginas without talking about them in action. I am worried about the titillation factor, worried about the piece becoming exploitative. Am I talking about vaginas to arouse people? Is that a bad thing?

As lesbians, she said, we know about vaginas. We touch them. We lick them. We play with them. We tease them. We notice when the clitoris swells. We notice our own.

I realize I am embarrassed listening to her. There are a combination of reasons: excitement, fear, her love and comfortability of and with vaginas and my distancing, terror of saying all this in front of you, the audience.

18

I like to play with the rim of the vagina, she said, with fingers, knuckles, toes, tongue. I like to enter it slowly, slowly entering, then thrusting three fingers inside. There's other cavities, other openings, there's the mouth. While I have a free hand, there's fingers in her mouth, fingers in her vagina, both going, all going at once, her mouth sucking my wet fingers, her vagina sucking my fingers, both sucking, both wet.

Does talking about vaginas ruin the mystery or is that just another myth that keeps vaginas in the dark, keeps them unknowing and unsatisfied?

My tongue is on her clitoris. My tongue replaces my fingers. My mouth enters her vagina.

Saying these words feels naughty, dangerous, too direct, too specific, wrong, revealed, intense, in charge, in your face, alive.

My tongue is on her clitoris. My tongue replaces my fingers. My mouth enters her vagina.

To know women, to love our vaginas, to know them and touch them and be familiar with who we are and what we need. To satisfy ourselves, to teach our lovers to satisfy us, to be present in our vaginas, to speak of them out loud, to speak of their hunger and pain and loneliness and humor, to make them visible so they cannot be ravaged in the dark without great consequence, so that our center, our point, our motor, our dream, is no longer detached, mutilated, numb, broken, invisible, or ashamed.

You have to talk about entering vaginas, she said. Come on, I say, come in.

Eve Ensler's play, The Vagina Monologues, *won a 1997 Obie Award and was nominated for a Drama Desk Award. It was presented in an Off-Broadway run, has toured nationally and abroad, and, in 1998, was published in book form. Ensler's other plays include:* The Depot, Floating Rhoda and the Glue Man, Cinderella Cendrillion, Scooncat, Loud in My Head, Lemonade, Ladies, Reef and Particle, Extraordinary Measures, *and* Necessary Targets.

Allen Ginsberg and
William S. Burroughs

A CONVERSATION

The following interviews were conducted by Obie Benz in December 1986 for his film Heavy Petting.

Q: *I wonder, did you go out on dates?*

Burroughs: Somewhat. That is—you were expected to take someone to a party.

Q: *Well, how would you ask someone for a date?*

Burroughs: Oh, well this was decided for you. That is, you were supposed to pick up so-and-so and take her to this party.

Ginsberg: Who decided? The parents?

Burroughs: Yes.

Ginsberg: At some private school or something?

Burroughs: No, the parents decided, or whoever was giving the party said all right, who's going to bring so-and-so, who's going to bring so-and-so? So it was a compulsory procedure. And the guy'd take them home of course.

Q: *How did you do in that situation?*

Burroughs: Hmmm.

Q: *You had to pick up a girl and take her to a date?*

Burroughs: Go to her house, pick her up, take her to the party. And you were supposed to spend some time with her at the party, of course, and take her home.

Ginsberg: Did you have any problem making conversation?

Burroughs: Not really, no, they're just ready to talk about absolutely anything.

Ginsberg: Were they frightened of you, do you think?

Burroughs: Oh, I don't think so at all.

Ginsberg: Did they think you were cute?

Burroughs: I don't know, they didn't say so. In fact they apparently had a bad opinion of me, 'cause I heard through the sister of Rex Weisenberg "the girls are down on you."

Ginsberg: Oh! What for?

Burroughs: I don't know.

Ginsberg: You never found out?

Burroughs: Well, no, it wasn't any particular thing. It was just my emanations, they felt were not…

Ginsberg: Did you feel bad about it?

Burroughs: No, I didn't feel bad about it.

Ginsberg: Not at all?

Burroughs: Why should I?

Ginsberg: I would have been ashamed of myself if that happened to me. Or humiliated.

Q: *Did you ever try and kiss a girl at night on the doorstep?*
Burroughs: No. Not on the doorstep. Sometimes in the car.

Q: *Can you recall a scene in a car with a girl?*
Burroughs: Oh, I really don't—I prefer not to. *(Laughs.)*

Ginsberg: Were you horny?

Burroughs: No, not really.

Ginsberg: A little interested?

Burroughs: Possibly. Nothing came of it anyway. It was just sort of a dull…contretemps.

Ginsberg: This is high school time we're talking about?

Q: *Yes.*
Ginsberg: High school I had a crush on some young athletic gymnasts. There were three guys, me and two other guys, that used to hang around a lot together, and one of them was sort of a little heavier and the other was a trim, neat looking Jewish boy that later became a doctor and I had a big crush on him. So I used to sublimate it, not say anything, but hang around with him and have sodas with him or walk around town with him. But never said anything.

Q: *Did you ever feel that you could date with boys, or did you ever do anything at that point?*
Ginsberg: No, no, no! I was scared to death of opening my mouth and saying

21

anything that would betray me as the ultimate sissy, you know. But I had all sorts of fantasies of throwing myself on my knees at their feet and begging for love, and being embraced and cherished and comforted. In fact I never did say anything about all that, until I was maybe seventeen or eighteen. And the first person I told was Jack Kerouac, who had a sufficiently accommodating character to be able to receive my private confession and groan a bit, knowing that it meant trouble, but on the other hand not rejecting me, not, you know, not saying, "I don't want to know you anymore," but just sort of take it as a new piece of Dostoevskian juiciness in the drama of our existence.

* * *

Ginsberg: It was an interesting homosexual subculture in the forties to the fifties; on one level, it was a literary world, there were European refugees from Hitler. A world where everything was a *tout comprendre, tout pardonné.* Everything understood, everything pardoned. In the elegant world, I suppose Christopher Isherwood and W. H. Auden and Gypsy Rose Lee and a group of intelligent people lived together in a house in Brooklyn Heights in 1939 through the early forties. And when I was at Columbia in the mid-forties, there was a group of gay young men who dressed well and would go down to the Blue Angel nightclub to hear Edith Piaf or whoever was in town, maybe Marlene Dietrich or some singer or other, or some witty, ditty artist. They dressed well, in Brooks Brothers clothes, and went to hear Wanda Landowska at Carnegie Hall, and went to gay bars. There was one young gentleman that played cello that was Auden's boyfriend for many years.

Then there was one tall, young guy, rather portly, who later became an insurance executive, who went down to Washington and was wandering through the upper corridors of some very good hotel right near the White House, and was accosted, for erotic purposes, by J. Edgar Hoover, no less, and told me about that in 1947. So I always had Hoover's number, although it was very difficult to prove. Like Cardinal Spellman, another gent who was supposed to be a closet queen, and supposedly had young men accompany him on his trips. That was, of course, never breathed in the newspaper, although both of those guys were fervent anti-Communists and heavy moralists and all in favor of all sorts of censorship. Nonetheless, among the underground or elegant gay world, there were many rumors about them, and even, as I say, one or two encounters, particularly with J. Edgar Hoover, the head of the Federal Bureau of Investigation, who lived with an agent, Clive Tolson, for many years, and who insisted that his agents wiped their hands, so there was no sweat on their hands, before they shook hands with him. And had posters of children being accosted by strangers all over the country, in the late forties, saying, never trust a stranger who gives you candy, the strangers coming out from trees and side streets to accost little Lolitas.

He insisted there was no organized crime. In fact, in those years I had the fantasy that the Mafia might have secret movies of J. Edgar Hoover in the basement with some big, hairy Mafia Lothario, and were blackmailing him so he'd lay off organized crime, because he insisted there was no organized crime.

So that was sort of like the amusing subculture gossip in the gay world. There were Turkish baths, which were gay baths. Rare, but interesting. In fact, one of them, I think the Everard, was rumored to be owned by the Police Athletic League, or the Patrolman's Benevolent Association, I've forgotten. Somebody could do some research into that. That was the main one that I knew of in town, in New York. As I said, Burroughs and Kerouac and I once visited there together.

There were gay bars of course. San Francisco was another matter in the fifties. There was a great club called the Black Cat. In the "monkey block." There was a monkey block downtown, North Beach, where the Transamerica Building is now. It was an artists' building with a lot of lofts, and in it, there was a huge cabaret-nightclub-bar called the Black Cat, which was a bohemian assortment of everybody, like freaks, junkies, alcoholics, old newspapermen, young newspapermen, poets, theater people, transvestites. Then it had a gay pianist who sang, dressed in a turtleneck sweater and was bald and played a honky-tonk piano and sang sort of a *louche*, as they say, song. *Louche* was the word, forties and fifties, meaning the French word for off-color. And it was the best bar in San Francisco, and the liveliest, and the wildest, it was a great place to get drunk in, or to have a conversation, or bring a European, sophisticated guest to see some Wild West wisdom.

In New York, as I said, there was MacDougal Street bar which was a basement gay bar where you might find anywhere from *New Yorker* editors to account executives to—second mates from the Merchant Marine, and a few sailors now and then. There was a lesbian bar on Bleecker Street, across from what was then the Flophouse Mills hotel, now the Atrium, an elegant condominium. There was another little basement where dykes, as they were called, hung out. I remember Burroughs talking about a lady who lived in his Greenwich Village brownstone, Louise her name was, liking her a great deal. The lady who was a lesbian, saying she was straightforward, manly and reliable. That was 1944.

And there was another bar on Eighth Street directly across from MacDougal, a street which is like the nerve center of the commercial Greenwich Village. And that was more outrageous where you'd get transvestites and people in perfumed, elegant frilly shirts, or people with make-up on, more effeminate types. Old queens sometimes. Maybe stockbrokers with a little rouge on their face like in German expressionistic films or Bertolt Brecht operas. Or Fritz Lang films. So that was a little more scary to me, 'cause I couldn't connect with anybody actually. It was just so artificially theatrical, the gay life. And I wasn't that much attracted to effeminate. As they say in the personal columns now, "fems." No fems and fatties.

So I'll say—it was very much a suppressed life. You wouldn't want to be caught there by your office mate who dropped in for a drink if he didn't know you were gay. And in those days, they didn't use the word "gay," they used "queen." Or "queer" was the basic word. He's queer. I'm queer. I'm putting my queer shoulder to the wheel. Queer was the right word in those days. And it still is kind of interesting. Gay is charming because it indicates the butterfly gayness of a waving hand. But queer was actually the more American word. What are you, a queer? Or, I'm queer.

William S. Burroughs is the author of Naked Lunch, Junky, Queer, Cities of the Red Night, The Place of Dead Roads, The Western Lands, Interzone, The Cat Inside, My Education, *and* The Letters of William S. Burroughs, 1945-1959. *He died in 1997 in Lawrence, Kansas.*

Allen Ginsberg's signal poem, "Howl," overcame censorship to become one of the most widely read poems of the century. Some recent publications include Selected Poems 1947-1995; Illuminated Poems, *illustrated by Eric Drooke;* Journals Mid-Fifties 1954-1958; Howl Annotated; Cosmopolitan Greetings: Poems 1986-1992; White Shroud Poems 1980-1985; *and* Collected Poems 1947-1980. *Ginsberg died in New York City in 1997.*

Elena Georgiou

TALKIN' TRASH

I want the phone to ring.
I want the sound of your voice
to smack my body as waves hit rock,
grinding down mountains, opening up
secrets hidden between my shoulder blades.

I want you to beg me to let you come
over to wash my hair with rose-water.
When I refuse, I want you to hang up.

I want you to call back when I'm doing my laundry
and whine until I agree to let you be with me,
the next time its washday,
so you can fold it.

I want you to ask me if I miss you.
And when I say: *Yes, I think about you
night and day,* I want you to know
I'm lying.

I want you to tell me you'd buy three bridges,
cross two oceans in a thunderstorm
to make my lie of missing you a reality.

I want to tell you that for a small
part of the Caribbean sea I'd turn into
a hungry anemone that sucks you closer.

I want you to ask me if this is all I want.
I want to tell you, no.

I want you to be my boy, my girl.
I want to paint your toenails gold,
massage your fingers with homemade oil
named after the smell of your neck.

I want to dust my mattress with baby powder,
lie on satin, tie ivory shells around my hips
and prepare myself for your coming.
I want you to call one last time,
ask me to unlock my door,
lie on my bed and wait.

I want to hear your bag drop to the floor,
the drag of your feet move to my bed.

I want to feel the weight of your body
sink the mattress two inches lower.

I want your arms
to come from behind and hold
my breasts in an open prayer.

I want to hear you call on God
and give her credit for making me.

I want to watch you plead: *Lord
have mercy*, as you slide your mouth
from my navel to the back of my knee.

I want you to make me speak in tongues.
I want you to make me reach for things
you swear to me aren't there.

I want you to flip me, hold me
with one arm around my waist,
press your stomach to my spine,
fall and rise with me,
slide into night with me.

And when morning offers the hush of sleep,
I want you to open your tired eyes,
wrap my hair around your fingers,
pull me closer and murmur: *Yes, baby,*
I promise I will be your toy.

Elena Georgiou has been published in various literary journals and anthologies. She is the co-editor, with Michael Lassell. of the forthcoming poetry anthology entitled The World in Us. *She teaches Creative Writing at City College, CUNY, and lives in Brooklyn.*

Celia Bland

AS YOU SPEAK

I watch your hands
and seeing becomes the most intimate
of senses:
how the top flange of the knuckle bends as you
touch your own face.
If I could touch your face
with my tongue I would taste my own seeing, the sight
of your delicate dark eyes,
the curve of your skull,
this flatness where the brain pulses within.
You could die and I would taste it.

I can smell
my wetness rising to my sense
like bread rises on a backporch in Florida
beneath the handkerchief of a dish towel.
I am swaddled in happiness, emanating
a warning scent.

Your shoulders are as broad as a table.
Place the bread on the table, slice it with this knife
I hold here sweating in my palms, the cool blade,
and your long be-ringed fingers
will test its sharp edge, slipping
between my legs, my thighs, a quick dip
of honey for the bread.

I would taste your nipples, the dark hairs
I glimpsed
on your belly, the smooth veins
in your legs, ah, to think that you are a man
and can give me such pleasure! To be such a voice,
a mind, a wit, a companion, and a man as well!
To have a tongue
like a sliced strawberry, and muscles cording your arms —
I follow those blue veins
with the tip
of my knife, dip
into the pinpricks of blood, ah, I can taste it, your death,
your fucking death with me.

Celia Bland's poetry has appeared in The Apalachee Quarterly, Mudfish, Chain, *and* 13th Moon. *In 1996, her work won the* Snake Nation Review's *Editor's Choice Award and the* Brooklyn Journal *Poetry Award.*

Alix Kates Shulman

A STORY OF A GIRL AND HER DOG

Lucky Larrabee was an only child, and unpredictable. At eight, she was still trying to sail down from the garage roof with an umbrella. She never ate ice cream without a pickle. She was afraid of nothing in the world except three boys in her class and her uncle Len who patted her funny. She brought home every stray dog in the neighborhood. She upset the assistant principal by participating in the Jewish Affair.

Naturally her parents worried; but they adored her nevertheless and all the more.

There is little Lucky, wearing red anklets with stripes down the sides and poorly tied brown oxfords while everyone else has on loafers, her hair hanging down in strings, her chin thrust out, absolutely refusing to sing the words, Jesus or Christ. Why? Two Jewish girls in her class will not sing, and though she has never been Jewish before, Lucky has joined them. She says it is a free country and you can be anything you like. I'm a Jew, she says and will not sing Jesus.

Everyone knows she's no more Jewish than their teacher. It is ridiculous! But she insists and what can they do? She is ruining the Christmas Pageant. They'll get her at recess, they'll get her after school, they'll plant bad pictures in her desk, they'll think of something. But it won't work. Incorrigible little fanatic!

Okay. She doesn't have to sing. But will she just mouth the words silently during the program please? No one will have to know.

No, she won't. If they try to make her, she swears she'll hold her breath until she faints instead. Perhaps she'll do it anyway! Perhaps she'll hold it till she's dead! That'll show them who's a Jew and who isn't.

Is something wrong at home, Mrs. Larrabee? Does Lucky eat a good enough breakfast? Get enough sleep? She is very thin. Has she grown thinner? Not

30

meaning to alarm you, but Lucky has been unusually sullen in class lately—doesn't participate in the class discussions as she used to, doesn't volunteer her answers, no longer seems interested in current events, spends too much time daydreaming, picking at scabs, being negative. She doesn't seem to be trying. Her fingernails. Is there any known source of tension at home? The school likes to be kept informed about these matters as we try to keep parents informed about progress at school. Don't you agree, parents and teachers ought to be working closely together in harmony, for the benefit of the child. The only concrete suggestion the school can make at this time is some companionship and diversion for Lucky. Another child perhaps, or a dog. Meanwhile, we'll just keep an eye on her. Thank you so much for coming in. These conferences are always helpful in any case, even if they do no more than clear the air.

As the Larrabees had been half considering buying a dog for Christmas anyway, they decided it would do no harm to seem accommodating and took the step. They waited until a month had elapsed after the Christmas Pageant so Lucky would not suspect a connection, and then, piling into the new family Nash, backing out of the cinder drive, they drove straight out on Main Street beyond the city limits and continued on into the country to buy a dog.

Naturally, Lucky was permitted by the concerned Larrabees to pick out the pup herself, with only one restriction. It had to be a boy dog, they said, because if they took home a girl dog, sooner or later they would have to have her spayed, which would be cruel and unnatural and would make her into a fat, lazy and unhappy bitch, or they'd have to let her have babies. For keeping her locked up during heat (also cruel and unnatural) couldn't be expected to work forever; creatures have a way of eluding their jailers in quest of forbidden knowledge—witness the fate of Sleeping Beauty, Bluebeard's wives, etc., and the unwanted litters of the neighborhood bitches. And if they let her go ahead and have her babies, well, either they'd have to keep the puppies (a certain portion of which could be expected to be females too), generating an unmanageable amount of work, anxiety, and expense, even supposing they had the facilities, which of course they did not. Or they'd have to wrench the pups away from their mother (equally cruel and unnatural as well as a bad example for a child) and worry about finding a decent home for each of them besides. No, no, it could be any pup she chose as long as it was male.

The seven mongrel puppies from which she was permitted to choose one were to her untutored eyes and arms indistinguishable as to sex unless she deliberately looked. So she was perfectly happy to restrict her choice to the four males, though she did feel sorry for the females who, it seemed, were condemned to suffer a cruel and unnatural life or else bring on, like Eve, more trouble than they were worth—particularly since cuddling them in the hollow between her neck and shoulder felt quite as wonderful as cuddling the males. But such, she accepted, was family life.

She chose neither the runt she was temperamentally drawn to but upon whom her father frowned, nor the jumper of the litter over whom her mother voiced certain reasonable reservations, but instead picked from the two remaining males the long-eared thoughtful-eyed charmer who endeared himself to her by stepping across three of his siblings as though they were stepping stones in order to reach her eager fingers wiggling in the corner of the box and investigate them with his adorable wet nose. Curiosity; the quality her parents most admired in Lucky herself. He sniffed and then licked her fingers in a sensual gesture she took for friendship, and although she continued to examine all the pups for a considerable time, picking them up and cuddling them individually, deliberating at length before rendering her final decision, she knew very early the one she would take home. It pained her to reject the others, particularly the runt and a certain female who tickled her neck lovingly when she held her up and was pure when she peeked underneath. But by eight Lucky had already learned through experience that one could not have everything one wanted, that every choice entailed the rejection of its alternatives, and that if she didn't hurry up and announce her selection, much as she enjoyed playing with all the puppies, she'd provoke her father's pique and lose the opportunity to decide herself.

She named the dog Skippy because of the funny way he bounced when he walked. An unimaginative name perhaps, but direct (a quality she instinctively valued) and to her inexperienced mind which did not know that the dog would stop bouncing once it got a few months older, appropriate. Her parents thought she might have selected a name with more flair, but naturally they said nothing.

The day of Lucky's brightening (her word, for no one ever taught her another) seemed like an ordinary late-summer Saturday. Unsuspectingly, she was just finishing a treasured bath, where she had spent a long time sending the water back and forth between the sides of the tub to simulate ocean waves. She was studying the movement of the water, its turbulence, its cresting at the edges and doubling back, trying to imagine how the process could possibly illumi-

32

nate, as her father declared, the mysteries of the ocean's waves and tides; and afterwards when her brain had grown weary of encompassing the continental coasts, which she had never seen, the earth and the moon, she filled her wash-cloth with puffs of air which she could pop out in little explosions into the water sending big bubbles rippling through the bath like porpoises.

Up through the open bathroom window drifted the familiar sounds of her father setting up the barbecue in the backyard and her mother bringing out the fixings on a tray. Next door Bertie Jones was still mowing the lawn while from the Jones's screened-in porch the ballgame droned on. Summer days; dog days.

Lucky climbed reluctantly from the tub, now cold, and examined herself in the mirror. Whistle gap between her front teeth, a splash of freckles, short pro-truding ears, alert: Lucky herself. If she had known what delights awaited her in the next room, she would not have lingered to peel a strip of burnt skin from her shoulder or scratch open a mosquito bite. But she was a nervous child who had never, from the day she learned to drop things over the edge of her high chair for her mother to retrieve, been able to let well enough alone. Three full minutes elapsed before she finally wrapped herself in a towel and padded into her bedroom where Skip, banished from the backyard during dinner preparations, awaited her with wagging tail.

"Skippy Dip!" she cried, dropping to her knees, and throwing her arms around him. She hugged his neck and he licked her face in a display of mutual affection.

She tossed the towel at the door, sat down on the maple vanity bench, made a moué at her freckly face in the mirror, and in a most characteristic pursuit, lifted her left foot to the bench to examine an interesting blister on her big toe, soaked clean and plump in her long bath.

Suddenly Skip's wet little nose, as curious as on the day they had met, delved between her legs with several exploratory sniffs.

"Skip!" Lucky giggled in mock dismay. "Get out of there," pushing his nose aside and quickly lowering her foot, for she did know a little. Skip retreated playfully but only until Lucky returned (inevitably) to the blister. For like any pup who has not yet completed his training, he could hardly anticipate every consequence or generalize from a single instance. You know how a dog longs to sniff at things. When Lucky's knee popped up again, exposing that inter-esting smell, Skip's nose returned as though invited.

Suddenly Lucky felt a new intriguing sensation. "What's this?"

She had once, several years earlier, felt another strange sensation in the groin, one that had been anything but pleasant. She and Judy Jones, the girl next door, had been playing mother and baby in a game of House. As Lucky lay on the floor of that very room having her "diaper" changed by a maternal Judy, the missing detail to lend a desired touch of verisimilitude to the game struck Lucky. "Baby powder!" she cried. "Sprinkle on some baby powder!"

"Baby powder?" blinked Judy.

"Get the tooth powder from the bathroom shelf. The Dr. Lyons."

In the first contact with Skip's wet nose, Lucky remembered her words as if they still hung in the room. She didn't stop to remember the intervening events: how Judy obediently went to the bathroom but couldn't find the Dr. Lyons; how, after finally finding it she could barely manage to get the tin open. Lucky's memory flashed ahead to the horrible instant when the astringent power fell through the air from a great (but not sufficiently great) height onto the delicate tissue of her inner labia and stung her piercingly, provoking a scream that brought her poor mother running anxiously from a distant room.

But the sensation produced by her pal Skippy was in every respect different. It was cool, not hot; insinuating, not shocking; cozy, provocative, delicious. It drew her open and out, not closed in retreat. No scream ensued; only the arresting thought, *"What's this?"* Like the dawning of a new idea or the grip of that engaging question, What makes it tick? If she had had the movable ears of her friend's species, they would have perked right up. *What's this?* The fascination of beginnings, the joy of the new. Something more intriguing than a blister.

She touched Skip's familiar silky head tentatively, but this time did not quite push it away. And he, enjoying the newness too (he was hardly more than a pup), sniffed and then, bless him, sniffed again. And following the natural progression for a normally intelligent dog whose interest has been engaged—the doggie's pink tongue followed his nose's probe with a quizzical exploratory lick.

What would her poor parents have thought if they had peeked in? They would have known better than to see or speak evil, for clearly these two young creatures, these trusting pups (approximately the same ages when you adjust for species), were happy innocents. They would probably have blamed themselves for having insisted on a male pup. They might even have taken the poor animal to the gas chambers of the ASPCA and themselves to some wildly expensive expert who would only confuse and torment them with impossibly equivocal advice until they made some terrible compromise. At the very least, there would have been furious efforts at distraction and that night much wringing of hands.

Fortunately our Adam and Eve remain alone to pursue their pragmatic investigations. The whole world is before them.

The charcoal is now ready to take on the weenies. Mrs. Larrabee kisses her husband affectionately on the neck as she crosses the yard towards the house. She opens the screen door, leans inside, and yells up the stairs, "Dinner."

"Just a minute," says Lucky, squeezing her eyes closed. One more stroke of that inquisitive tongue—only one more!—and Lucky too will possess as her own one of nature's most treasured recipes.

Waves and oceans, suns and moons, barbecues, bubbles, blisters, tongues and tides—what a rich banquet awaits the uncorrupted.

Alix Kates Shulman has written four novels, two books on the anarchist-feminist Emma Goldman, and several children's stories. Her essays and stories have appeared in many periodicals, among them The Village Voice, The Nation, Ms., Atlantic Monthly, The Women's Review of Books, *and* The New York Times Book Review. *"A Story of a Girl and Her Dog" was written in 1975. Shulman divides her time between New York City and Maine.*

Mary Gaitskill

THE BLANKET

V alerie had been celibate for two years when she met Michael, and sex with Michael was like a solid left hook; she reeled and cartoon stars burst about her head. The second time he came to her San Francisco apartment, he walked in with two plastic bags of fruit, extending a fat red tomato in one outstretched hand, his smile leaping off his face. "I brought you things," he said. "I brought you fruit to put on your windowsill, and this." He handed her the tomato and said, "I'm a provider." His voice was full of ridiculous happiness. He was wearing shorts, and one of his graceful legs was scuffed at the knee. He was twenty-four years old.

Valerie was thirty-six. Michael couldn't actually provide for her, but she didn't need him to do that. She loved that he'd gone to the grocery store and roamed the aisles of abundant, slightly tatty and unripe fruit so that he could bring her bags of it. His impulse seemed both generous and slightly inept, which she found sweeter than generosity straight.

Michael himself was a little surprised by his beneficent urges, surprised and pleased by their novelty. It occurred to him that it had something to do with her physicality, although he didn't know quite what. Valerie was pretty, but she was not beautiful. Her arms and neck were fine-boned and elegant, while her hips and legs were curvy, fatty, almost crudely female. She embraced him confidently, but her fingers sought his more delicate places—the base of his head, the knobs of his spine—with a tactile urgency that was needy and uncertain. After their first time together, on the floor of her living room, she'd put on her underpants and stood over him, posing with her hands on her hips, chin lifted, one hip tilted bossily—but she held her legs close together, and her one bent in-turned knee had the tremulous look of a cowed animal. "Woman of the year," he'd said, and he'd meant it.

It was only their second time together when she suggested that they "role-play." "You know," she said. "Act out fantasies."

"*Fantasies?*" The idea was a little embarrassing, yet it also intrigued him;

under the cheesy assurance of it, he felt her vulnerability, hidden and palpitant. Besides, the fantasies were fun. She would be a slutty teenager who's secretly hoping for love, and he would be the smug prick who exploits her. He would be the coarse little gym teacher trying to persuade the svelte English teacher to let him go down on her after the PTA cocktail party. She would be a rude girl with no panties flaunting herself before an anxious student in the library. Feverishly, they'd nose around in each situational nuance before giving in to dumb physicality. Then she'd make them a dinner of meat and salad and a pot of grains, and they'd eat it with their feet on the table.

When he left her apartment, Michael felt as if the entire world loved him. He walked down the street, experiencing everything—scraps of trash, traffic, trotting pets, complex, lumbering pedestrians—as a kind of visual embrace. Once, immediately after leaving her, he went into a bookstore and sat down on a little stepladder to peruse a book, and he was assailed with a carnal memory so pungent that he opened his mouth and dropped a wrinkled wad of gray chewing gum on the page. He stared at it, embarrassed and excited by his foolishness. Then he closed the book on the wad.

For the first week she wouldn't let him spend the night with her, because that was too intimate for her. But he would get in bed with her and hold her, cupping her head against his chest and stroking the invisible little hairs at the base of her spine. "My girlfriend," he would say. "My girlfriend." His chest was big and solid, but under her ear, his heart beat with naked, helpless enthusiasm.

When he held her that way, she felt so happy that it disturbed her. After he left, it would take her hours to fall asleep, and then when she woke up she would feel another onrush of agitated happiness, which was a lot like panic. She wished she could grab the happiness and mash it into a ball and hoard it and gloat over it, but she couldn't. It just ran around all over the place, disrupting everything.

Valerie made a fair living illustrating book jackets, which meant she worked at home, which meant she was pretty susceptible to disruptions anyway. When Michael appeared she had just started a jacket for a novel by a well-known hack, which required that she draw prowling leopards. It should've been an easy job, but she could not bring her sensory apparatus to bear on the leopards. She would draw for minutes and then spend nearly an hour pacing around, listening to overblown love music or obnoxious sex music. Her thoughts were fragmented. Her feelings buzzed and swarmed. She remembered sitting on the edge of the couch, him kneeling on the floor, her underpants dangling from the tip of her high-heeled foot. Finally, the gym teacher had gotten the English teacher to come across! Aggression surged between them in bursts, but he'd paused to bend and press his cheek against her thigh.

The kitchen table became littered with partial leopards.

"It's like I'm so happy I can't feel it," she said to her friend Tanya. "It's just sex, really; I mean, he's too young for us to actually get involved. But the enthusiasm of him—I mean, he's just right there."

"How can he be right there if you're not really involved?"

"We are involved, in a profound, sexually spiritual way. But we're not going to be boyfriend and girlfriend."

"But you like it when he calls you his girlfriend."

"I do." Valerie paused, thinking how she could best explain this apparent contradiction. "It's like another version of the slutty-teenager fantasy. It's real, but only in the erotic realm. I mean, we have feelings for each other, but they can't be permanent."

Michael was a bartender, but he also played bass guitar in a band. The band was a ramshackle affair, perpetuated by the dour perseverance of the lead singer and animated by the disproportionate loudness of the sound system. They were usually just a warm-up act in a good-natured dive, but Valerie was enchanted to think of Michael onstage with his guitar, one hip slung out insouciantly. "I think all twenty-four-year-old boys should play in bands," she said.

It was a condescending thing to say, but he didn't mind. He sensed that the luxury of such minor arrogance was new to her, and that she was trying it out, with a certain brittle excitement, just to see what it felt like. He would imagine her watching him from the audience as he turned away from them all, in private communion with his guitar, aloof and mysterious and secretly delighted in his role of admired object.

During the second weekend of their affair, the band went up to Seattle to play. Valerie thought she'd spend the weekend retrieving her equilibrium, but just hours after he left, she discovered one of his sweaty T-shirts balled up at the bottom of her bed and found she had to listen to loud music while she paced around with the shirt pressed to her cheek.

That evening he called her from the pay phone of a gas station while the rest of the band peed and raided the candy machine.

"I had to tell you this," he said. "When we were driving through Oregon we went past this cornfield, and I was just staring at it and I saw this little white cat walking between the rows. It so much made me think of you. The way it walked was so intrepid and fine."

He heard a quick intake of breath, followed by a soft, tremulous silence. He closed his eyes and took a long, ecstatic drink of grape pop.

Later that night, a beautiful girl threw herself at him. He was standing at the bar after the band's last set, wiping his face with a wet cocktail napkin, when she emerged from the ambient murk. She had long black hair and a fancy little strut that suggested uncomplicated, competent sex. They made out against the wall, and she nonchalantly pressed her pubic bone against him. He was going to suggest that they go to her place, but realized, in the midst of speculating about what she might have in the way of food, that to do so would only increase his longing for Valerie. The girl stuck her hand inside his shirt and circled the rim of his navel with one cold finger. "I can't do this," he said. "I'm in love with this girl in San Francisco." The irritated hoyden slunk off, and he slid to the floor, free to wallow in the thrilling abjection of his love.

The next day he called Valerie and told her what had happened.

"You shouldn't have done that," she said mildly. "That girl was probably really hurt."

"Oh, she was just a groupie," he said. "The point is, I didn't care how beautiful she was. I wanted you."

When they got off the phone, Valerie buried her face in the T-shirt, rubbing it across her lips and cheeks, helplessly nipping at it with her teeth.

His return was a festival of romantic lewdness. At four in the morning, as they lay on the rug in the irradiant caress of the television light, she invited him to sleep with her. At six in the morning, Michael slept like a healthy animal while she lay in a grim ball, tormented by overstimulation. The joy of the previous day seemed unreal, and even if it wasn't, the outsize quality of it was bound to heighten the desolation she would surely feel when the affair was over. Valerie had not had many good experiences with men in her life, and as the sad sacks and malefactors of the past assembled for her mental review, her excitement over this boy began to seem pathetic. But each time she was about to sink into a restful misery, boisterous optimism surged up and kicked her into wakefulness.

When they got up, they had mugs of tea with spoonfuls of honey in them, and then Michael pretended to be a sleazy boss dropping in on an unsuspecting housewife just after her naive husband has left for work. The boss was a terrible malefactor, but in the haven of fantasy, he was safely confined to her script. There was great drama as the poor housewife struggled to resist him, but to no avail: Valerie opened her eyes just in time to be a little startled by the look of almost demented malice on Michael's young face as he ejaculated across her mouth and nose.

They lay in each other's arms for a long time. Then Valerie got up and put on a tape of piano jazz and made them a big pancake breakfast. They ate it on a rickety table on her back porch. It was nice, except the sauciness of the jazz suddenly sounded so self-satisfied that she had to go in and turn it off. "I'm sorry," she said when she came back out. "That music was making me feel like an asshole." Michael laughed. He sat in his boxer shorts, with his long legs spread, exuding succulent boyness just faintly shaded with dim, inchoate cruelty.

They went for a genteel walk, up and down the hills of the Castro and Noe Valley. They admired the flowers with which residents had planted their yards. Michael told her that he had been fat in junior high and that other kids had made fun of him. Then he had lost weight in a dramatic growth spurt during the summer before high school and had returned to school eagerly anticipating what he assumed would be his new social status, only to have the same mean kids call him "Pig Dick" again.

"It made me think that people would just do that to me all my life, no matter what I did," he said. "After the end of that day, I went into a deserted classroom and cried. I mean, I really cried."

Valerie emitted a tender moo and embraced his hips with one arm. "I wish I could've come to you as a visitation from the future," she said. "I would've held you and told you you were handsome."

Michael stopped walking and hugged her against his chest. His heart beat like a proudly flying flag.

They went back to the apartment and had sex while imagining a heartless scene between Michael and the Seattle girl he'd rejected. About halfway through the fantasy, Valerie stopped being a bystander and became the poor girl. She pleaded with him to fuck her, but when he did, she felt a terrible rush of emotional pain that shocked her into tears. Mistaking her shudders for excitement, he became too rough, and she cried out for him to stop. They separated and Valerie turned on her side, just in time to see Michael's expression of impersonal cruelty devolve into confusion and injury. He clasped her wet face in his hands. "Oh," he said, "I didn't mean...I didn't mean it..." They started again and she cried more, but she didn't want to stop.

When they finished, they separated and stared at each other, disoriented and almost shamed. "Well," said Valerie, "and this is only the third week."

"Holy shit," said Michael. "You're right."

Again he spent the night. He slept curled around her from behind, his fore-

40

head butting against her shoulder blades, one hand on her breast. She lay wide awake, withstanding surges of happiness and fear.

The next day she was too physically sensitive for sex. Half joking, he pawed and cajoled her. His aggression ran in a giddy zigzag that grabbed her up and pulled her along, which was fun except that she didn't feel like going anywhere. Like the sleazy boss, he mauled and grabbed, and under his clownishness she sensed the vicious look she had glimpsed the day before. Another time, the look might've excited her, but now it felt like an unfriendly finger poking a tender spot. "I need to be by myself," she said. "Like, for several days."

After he left, it occurred to her that he saw her withdrawal as a squeamish flinch from his carnal might, and that idea so irritated her that she walked around muttering sarcastically for several minutes. She was older than he was! Their fantasy life was her idea! She remembered that she had cried, but the memory seemed to be about someone else; the image of her weeping face was static, as if it were an abstract signifier of something just beyond her vision. She remembered Michael's expression, as it went from malice to tenderness, with a piercing, secretive poignancy that was like a sore tooth. She felt like squirming.

She sat down to finish a jacket cover illustrated with the leafy branches of trees.

He called her the next day. The band had suddenly gotten an out-of-town gig, which meant he would be leaving town for a few days, starting tomorrow. "I know we're having a moratorium," he said. "But I can't go that long without seeing you, and also we have this big cool car that we rented for the trip. We could go for a fun drive in it."

She told him she wanted to see him but that she didn't want to have sex. "I just can't do it now," she said. "I feel too sensitive. Can you respect that?"

He paused, as if savoring an elaborate and slightly absurd delicacy. In a soft voice, he said yes.

"Are you sure? Because I don't want to have some ridiculous scene."

He swallowed voluptuously. "I'm sure."

She noticed his condescension, but it felt to her like another version of his expression, caught between malice and unspeakable tenderness. It felt secret and sweet.

When he got to her house, they cuddled on the couch. They told each other about their lives. Valerie talked about leaving home when she was sixteen. She told him about panhandling and selling jewelry on the street. She described her shiftless older boyfriend, whom she had supported by working as a waitress.

"It sounds rough," ventured Michael.

"Mostly not," she said. "Mostly it was banal. And sometimes it was fun. I would do stuff like go to Las Vegas for a weekend with some guy I'd just met. Even ordinary stuff was fun. Like when I got a job painting and lettering signs at a circus in Montreal. I thought that was really cool."

"That *is* cool," he said admiringly.

"Some bad stuff happened, though. I was raped by this asshole once."

Michael sat up and smiled. "Yeah? What happened? What did he make you do?"

Valerie felt startled, then she realized she wasn't really startled at all. "Are you reacting that way because I had sort of a smiley look on my face when I told you I was raped?"

His smile snagged and lapsed.

"That smile was left over on my face because I'd just told you this other nice stuff. I wasn't smiling about being raped."

He looked down. "I don't know why I did that. I know rape is horrible, but it's the horribleness that gives it a charge. It's like the fantasy thing. Like, right now, some guy is making some girl do something really gross. It's weird."

"Yeah, but I'm not some girl." She spoke gently, not angrily; she felt very aware that she was older than he was. "It wasn't a fantasy. I tried to fight him, and he punched me in the face. It was really bad."

He put his hand on her forearm. "I'm sorry," he said.

"It's okay," she said. "Sometimes I tell people really awful stuff like it's a joke. I don't know why. I'm trying not to do that anymore."

He put his arms around her. "I'm sorry anything bad ever happened to you," he said. His embrace was soft, but muscular underneath. She lay in it, feeling the immense relief she might feel on finally explaining herself to someone who for years had refused to hear her out. She felt upheld by his youth and strength. She felt this even though she knew Michael still didn't quite grasp that she wasn't talking about a fantasy. Even though, really, she hardly knew him at all.

He wished he could roll her up in a ball and hold her. When she'd said, "I'm trying not to do that anymore," it had provoked a storm of monstrous pathos in him. It was the kind of pathos that felt so good he wanted to make it go on forever. It shocked him that someone had hit her, but following close upon the shock was an overwhelming tenderness that made the shock seem like an insignificant segue. He remembered fucking her while she was crying, her legs all the way open; it made him think of eating sweet vanilla pudding while he watched TV.

42

"Let's go for our drive," he said.

He drove them to the Marina and across the Golden Gate Bridge into Marin County. The fog was heavy and wet.

"Right after I moved here, I had a dream," said Valerie. "I dreamed me and my high school boyfriend were lying on a beach in California. The sun was so bright and the sand was like a giant, breathing body. In the dream it was like, finally, I was getting to do the stuff that everybody else did—I was lying on the beach with my boyfriend!"

Distractedly he patted her leg. He was staring helplessly at the inside of his head, at images of Valerie, openmouthed and victimized, her face tear-stained and humiliated and very dear. He thought of the sounds she sometimes made when he was way inside her, deep sounds that came out ragged, like they'd been torn off. On a whim, he took a Mill Valley exit. Without the light from the freeway traffic, it was suddenly very dark.

"Why're you going to Mill Valley?" asked Valerie.

"No reason. Just driving."

"Oh. Anyway, when I woke up I thought at first I'd dreamed about an actual memory, that me and my boyfriend *had* gone to a beach. Then I realized there weren't any beaches where we grew up; it was just a dream. I felt somehow cheated."

He didn't say anything. He was driving up a warren of narrow streets wound around a steep hill. The glimpses of people puttering about behind their windows was soothing to her.

"It probably sounds strange that I felt cheated," she said. "I think it's because since I left home so early, I didn't really have boyfriends my own age. They were always a lot older, and I didn't go on normal dates or to proms or anything."

"That's kind of sad," he said.

"I don't know. I thought proms seemed pretty horrible, actually."

Maybe, he thought, he could bend her over the seat back and pull her pants down. Maybe she would make a lot of those noises. Maybe she would cry again. If she did, he would hold her against his chest and stroke her hair until she breathed gently and evenly. He turned abruptly down a dirt road. She thought it was a very long driveway at first, but then she saw there was no house at the end of it. "Michael," she said, "what are you doing?"

He pulled over and stopped the car. He turned sideways in his seat and leaned against the car door.

He didn't answer her. She remembered the way he had held her and said he was sorry anything bad had ever happened to her. In the dark, she couldn't see his face. "Michael?" she said.

He didn't answer her.

"Michael?"

She was suddenly so scared she couldn't think. She felt her weakness like a burst of nausea; if he wanted to hurt her, there was nothing she could do about it. Indignation rose up against her helplessness, but it was like the voice of a child crying, "But you said! But you said!" over and over again. Her fear took on the flat urgency of a trance. She put her hand in her purse so that she could find the heavy chain necklace she had been meaning to take to the jewelers. She found it and wrapped it around her fist, then carefully withdrew her fist from the bag. He leaned forward. She turned to face him and retracted her fist. Her voice came out in a hoarse growl. "Don't come near me," she said.

His retreat was like a sudden frown. "Valerie?" he said. "What's wrong?"

"Don't come closer."

"Valerie?" There was a short, vibrant silence. "Are you afraid of me?"

His puzzled voice cracked her trance. She relaxed her fist and put the chain back in her purse. "Start the car," she said. "I want to go home."

"Wait a minute—"

"Start the fucking car. I mean now."

He muttered as he pulled out of the dirt road and negotiated the dainty lanes. It dawned on him that if he took his hands off the steering wheel they'd be shaking. "Valerie," he said, "are you really mad at me?"

She didn't answer. He glanced at her. Her profile had the bristling intensity of a trapped rodent. "Shit," he said. "This is really bad."

"You must be a moron," she said flatly. "For three weeks I've been doing it with a moron."

He smarted as though from a blow across the bridge of his nose. "How could you say that to me?" he said.

"I don't want to talk. I just want to go home."

The rest of the drive was an abstract of misery. When he pulled up in front of her apartment they sat in private misery for some moments. "I don't think I can see you anymore," said Valerie finally. "This was just too awful."

"Too awful? What was too awful? Nothing happened! I was only playing, I wasn't going to do anything if you didn't want it."

"You already did something I didn't want." She shoved open the car door and stepped out onto the pavement, then spun back on the first step. "What do you think? You spoiled, stupid, ignorant little shit! I tell you I don't want to fuck, I tell you about being raped, and you set up a rape fantasy? What's wrong with you!"

"I was just doing what we do all the time."

"It's not the same!" But his quiet, injured voice had interrupted her anger, and besides, what he said was true. She sat in the car and stared at the sidewalk. She abandoned her anger. "You were disrespecting me," she said quietly. "For real."

Her small voice and her words hinted at the wonderful pathos that had so gripped him. Again it made him want to roll her in a ball, to see her cry, to split her open, to comfort her. He tried to think of how he might explain this to her. He couldn't. "It wasn't disrespect," he said. "It wasn't."

Her silence was like a tiny, pale feather falling a long distance. For a moment he thought she might put her head on his shoulder. If she did that, everything would be okay.

"The problem is, you're a kid," she said. "Everything's like TV to you. You don't really know anything."

He looked out the window. His cheeks burned. "Valerie," he said. "If you don't say something nice to me, this is going to be really bad."

"Something *nice* to you?"

"Please. Say something nice to me."

His plaintive tone pierced her. Without the anger, her emotions were like blunt, blind, vying shapes, each blotting the others out before she could tell what they were. The fragmentation dazed her, almost hurt her.

"I love you," she said.

He sat up and drew back. "You don't mean that."

"I don't know." Her bewilderment increased. "I think I do."

"You love me?" His voice was astounded and fluting. "You love me!" He opened the car door, bounded out, and jumped up and down in the street, yelling.

It's true, she thought, astounded herself. It's true.

He flew around the car, into the shelter of her open door, and knelt, his arms about her waist. "I love you too," he said. "And I'm going to respect you. I'll sleep here all night and I won't try to do anything."

"Sleep here?" She took his face in her hands and rubbed her nose the length of his. "No way. You'll be after me all night, and I'll never get any sleep."

"I'm not leaving," he said. "If I leave, it'll ruin everything. I'm going away for a week tomorrow, and I've got to stay with you."

45

"See, you're doing it again. You're not respecting my wishes." But her voice was full of shy delight.

"I'll sleep on the floor!" he said. "In the living room!"

"That's ridiculous. It would be much too uncomfortable." She paused. "You can sleep on the bed, but you have to wear your clothes and stay outside the blankets." She felt like a little girl with a rhinestone tiara on her head. She waved her plastic scepter. "You have to promise."

All night, he shivered against her warm, blanketed body. In the light from the window, her sleeping face appeared concentrated and intent. Once she twitched, and the tiny, urgent movement seemed the result of a fierce, private effort she was making deep in her head. He turned away from her so that he could look out the window, his back firmly against hers. His thoughts went forward, then backward, then he fanned them out laterally: a phone call to his mother, a quarrel with the drummer, a newscast about a raped and murdered teenage baby-sitter, the kitchen of that dump in Seattle where he ate hot french fries out of the fryer basket and listened to the cook talk shit about some girl. He imagined scooping up sleeping Valerie and placing her in the middle of his thoughts. He imagined her waking in the thriving garden of his thoughts, confused and possibly frightened. Then he imagined her realizing what he'd done; she put her hands on her hips, she tapped her foot, she fixed him with a fussing eye.

He was cold to the bone by now, but he didn't move even to shut the window. He was respecting her.

"Michael?" She turned and gently groped his back. "What's wrong? You're shaking so—oh, you're cold! Come under the blanket!"

"It's all right. I said I would stay outside the blanket, and I will."

"Don't be silly. Come under the covers." She lifted the blankets, greeting him with her warmth and smell. "Come on. You'll get sick or something."

He hesitated, drawing out the moment.

"Don't you…" She faltered. "Don't you want to?"

"Yes," he said. "I want to." And he did.

Mary Gaitskill is the author of the short story collections Bad Behavior *(1988) and* Because They Wanted To *(1997), in which "The Blanket" appears; the novel* Two Girls, Fat and Thin; *and numerous stories and articles. She lives in New York City and Northern California.*

Erica Jong

from FEAR OF FLYING

The zipless fuck was more than a fuck. It was a platonic ideal. Zipless because when you came together zippers fell away like rose petals, underwear blew off in one breath like dandelion fluff. Tongues intertwined and turned liquid. Your whole soul flowed out through your tongue and into the mouth of your lover.

For the true, ultimate zipless A-1 fuck, it was necessary that you never get to know the man very well. I had noticed, for example, how all my infatuations dissolved as soon as I really became friends with a man, became sympathetic to his problems, listened to him *kvetch* about his wife, or ex-wives, his mother, his children. After that I would like him, perhaps even love him—but without passion. And it was passion that I wanted. I had also learned that a sure way to exorcise an infatuation was to write about someone, to observe his tics and twitches, to anatomize his personality in type. After that he was an insect on a pin, a newspaper clipping laminated in plastic. I might enjoy his company, even admire him at moments, but he no longer had the power to make me wake up trembling in the middle of the night. I no longer dreamed about him. He had a face.

So another condition for the zipless fuck was brevity. And anonymity made it even better.

During the time I lived in Heidelberg I commuted to Frankfurt four times a week to see my analyst. The ride took an hour each way and trains became an important part of my fantasy life. I kept meeting beautiful men on the train, men who scarcely spoke English, men whose clichés and banalities were hidden by my ignorance of French, or Italian, or even German. Much as I hate to admit it, there are *some* beautiful men in Germany.

One scenario of the zipless fuck was perhaps inspired by an Italian movie I saw years ago. As time went by, I embellished it to suit my head. It used to play over and over again as I shuttled back and forth from Heidelberg to Frankfurt, from Frankfurt to Heidelberg:

A grimy European train compartment (Second Class). The seats are leatherette and hard. There is a sliding door to the corridor outside. Olive trees rush by the window. Two Sicilian peasant women sit together on one side with a child between them. They appear to be mother and grandmother and granddaughter. Both women vie with each other to stuff the little girl's mouth with food. Across the way (in the window seat) is a pretty young widow in a heavy black veil and tight black dress which reveals her voluptuous figure. She is sweating profusely and her eyes are puffy. The middle seat is empty. The corridor seat is occupied by an enormously fat woman with a moustache. Her huge haunches cause her to occupy almost half of the vacant center seat. She is reading a pulp romance in which the characters are photographed models and the dialogue appears in little puffs of smoke about their heads.

This fivesome bounces along for a while, the widow and the fat woman keeping silent, the mother and grandmother talking to the child and each other about the food. And then the train screeches to a halt in a town called (perhaps) CORLEONE. A tall languid-looking soldier, unshaven, but with a beautiful mop of hair, a cleft chin, and somewhat devilish, lazy eyes, enters the compartment, looks insolently around, sees the empty half-seat between the fat woman and the widow, and, with many flirtatious apologies, sits down. He is sweaty and disheveled but basically a gorgeous hunk of flesh, only slightly rancid from the heat. The train screeches out of the station.

Then we become aware only of the bounding of the train and the rhythmic way the soldier's thighs are rubbing against the thighs of the widow. Of course, he is also rubbing against the haunches of the fat lady—and she is trying to move away from him—which is quite unnecessary because he is unaware of her haunches. He is watching the large gold cross between the widow's breasts swing back and forth in her deep cleavage. Bump. Pause. Bump. It hits one moist breast and then the other. It seems to hesitate in between as if paralyzed between two repelling magnets. The pit and the pendulum. He is hypnotized. She stares out the window, looking at each olive tree as if she had never seen olive trees before. He rises awkwardly, half-bows to the ladies, and struggles to open the window. When he sits down again his arm accidentally grazes the widow's belly. She appears not to notice. He rests his left hand on the seat between his thigh and hers and begins to wind rubber fingers around and under the soft flesh of her thigh. She continues staring at each olive tree as if she were God and had just made them and were wondering what to call them.

Meanwhile the enormously fat lady is packing away her pulp romance in an iridescent green plastic string bag full of smelly cheeses and blackening bananas. And the grandmother is rolling ends of salami in greasy newspaper. The mother is putting on the little girl's sweater and wiping her face with a handkerchief, lovingly moistened with maternal spittle. The train screeches to a stop in a town called (perhaps) PRIZZI, and the fat lady, the mother, the grandmother, and the little girl leave the compartment. Then the train begins to move again. The gold cross begins to bump, pause, bump between the widow's moist breasts, the fingers begin to curl under the widow's thighs, the widow continues to stare at the olive trees. Then the fingers are sliding between her thighs and they are parting her thighs, and they are moving upward into the fleshy gap between her heavy black stockings and garters, and they are sliding up under her garters into the damp unpantied place between her legs.

The train enters a *galleria*, or tunnel, and in the semi-darkness the symbolism is consummated. There is the soldier's boot in the air and the dark walls of the tunnel and the hypnotic rocking of the train and the long high whistle as it finally emerges.

Wordlessly, she gets off at a town called, perhaps, BIVONA. She crosses the tracks, stepping carefully over them in her narrow black shoes and heavy black stockings. He stares after her as if he were Adam wondering what to name her. Then he jumps up and dashes out of the train in pursuit of her. At that very moment a long freight train pulls through the parallel track obscuring his view and blocking his way. Twenty-five freight cars later, she has vanished forever.

One scenario of the zipless fuck.

Zipless, you see, *not* because European men have button-flies rather than the zipper-flies, and not because the participants are so devastatingly attractive, but because the incident has all the swift compression of a dream and is seemingly free of all remorse and guilt; because there is no talk of her late husband or of his fiancée; because there is no rationalizing; because there is no talk at *all*. The zipless fuck is absolutely pure. It is free of ulterior motives. There is no power game. The man is not "taking" and the woman is not "giving." No one is attempting to cuckold a husband or humiliate a wife. No one is trying to prove anything or get anything out of anyone. The zipless fuck is the purest thing there is. And it is rarer than the unicorn.

Erica Jong is the author of six best-selling novels, including Fear of Flying *(1973), from which this excerpt is taken, as well as many books of poetry, nonfiction, a children's book, and the international bestseller* Fear of Fifty. *Other recent works include* The Devil at Large, *a memoir of her friendship with Henry Miller, and* Inventing Memory: A Novel of Mothers and Daughters. *She lives in New York City and Weston, Connecticut.*

J. D. McClatchy

LATE NIGHT ODE

Horace IV.i

It's over, love. Look at me pushing fifty now,
    Hair like grave-grass growing in both ears,
The piles and boggy prostate, the crooked penis,
    The sour taste of each day's first lie,

And that recurrent dream of years ago pulling
    A swaying bead-chain of moonlight,
Of slipping between the cool sheets of dark
    Along a body like my own, but blameless.

What good's my cut-glass conversation now,
    Now I'm so effortlessly vulgar and sad?
You get from life what you can shake from it?
    For me, it's g and t's all day and CNN.

Try the blond boychick lawyer, entry level
    At eighty grand, who pouts about the overtime,
Keeps Evian and a beeper in his locker at the gym,
    And hash in tinfoil under the office fern.

There's your hound from heaven, with buccaneer
    Curls and perfumed war-paint on his nipples.
His answering machine always has room for one more
    Slurred, embarrassed call from you-know-who.

Some nights I've laughed so hard the tears
    Won't stop. Look at me now. Why *now?*
I long ago gave up pretending to believe
    Anyone's memory will give as good as it gets.

So why these stubborn tears? And why do I dream
    Almost every night of holding you again,
Or at least of diving after you, my long-gone,
    Through the bruised unbalanced waves?

J. D. McClatchy is the author of several poetry collections, including Ten Commandments, Scenes from Another Life, Stars Principle, *and* The Rest of the Way, *and a book of criticism,* White Paper. *He has edited two editions (1990 and 1996) of* The Vintage Book of Contemporary American Poetry. *He is chancellor of the Academy of American Poets and editor of the* Yale Review.

PERSONAL ADS

The following are real personal ads culled from weekly newspapers and magazines, intellectual journals, religious publications, newsletters from professional associations, and web sites.

WOMAN!

A stern voice calls. You tremble painfully. You are at last ready to submit to your feminine side to receive all you want, need and deserve. The MASTER beckons. You respond softly, eagerly. The time is nigh.

ATTRACTIVE
ORAL SPECIALIST

Seeks horny F, 25-50, who craves sensuous oral service. This MWM loves to plse. No reciprocation req. Race unimportant. Buxom figure a def +. Pls be d/d free.

BiWF sks Marilyn Manson type. M/biF. Petite platinum blnd, 27, interested in gothic clubs, tattoos, concerts, role playing & BLACK. Profl. only 20-30. No biM or bpr #s. Serious need only apply.

DOMINANT CEO

SKS SUB F No doormats! U R submissive but PROUD! You dream of belonging to a very experienced but truly caring dominant M. Novices wlcm.

GAY WIFE
WANTED

You are 25-35 pretty, feminine, closeted. No smoking, loves past or present. Be sane. I am 36 GWJM kind & secure. Family life important.

HIV+ Spanish F 5'3 brn/brn 140lbs hlthy emplyd, strong—enjoys movies, pool, hrsbck rid'g skg SWM 6'+ hlthy optimistic, emplyd, sweet, no drugs/alc no convicts/ovrwt men.

HAIRY, UNSHAVED
WOMAN SOUGHT

by very handsome WM, 46, for erotic times. I'm gentle, sane, clean & very oral. I'm educated & normal. I just like hairy women.

MWM, 39, ISO OTHER MEN who would enjoy looking at revealing photos of our wives & girlfriends while having man to man fun. D/D Free. Discretion a must.

Couple sks bi Asian or bi WF for 1st experience. No men, no couples. D/D free. Absolute discretion assured.

WM 48 D/D free ISO woman 18+ D/D free uninhibited married or single love toys/no strings. Come over/have fun/go home/see ya soon? Age (18+)/race open.

SHM, 22, looking for TS Females or couples for oral pleasures & safe sex. I'm Drug & Disease free. I'm in NJ. Love group sex. TV's welcome too.

SUBMISSIVE FETISH
SHE-MALE
European-born, lives as female, tall blonde fetish doll. Seeks submissive total life style with 50+ WM fetishist. Looks spectacular in fetishwear. Committed and expd.

SWM Nudist, 29, 6'2" 250 lbs., seeking SWF Nudist, 28-30, for friendship or better. Interests are bowling, movies, beach, romance, quiet times, must be N/S, D/F, loyal, honest, and sincere.

Tickle Your Feet.
Looking for guys, 18-30 who love having their feet and toes tickled. Ready to pop with laughter. Safe and serious only! Big feet a plus.

I AM A PRINCESS
HAVING SUFFICIENT EXPERIENCES WITH A PRINCE. SEEKS A FROG.

TEDDY BEAR
Straight MWM 47 has wife's permission to find female partner for safe, sensual, romantic encounters. Race not important.

TV NURSE,
60, dominant seeks naughty submissives for over the knee fun.

ASIAN WOMAN
OR COUPLE
sought by handsome, slim 30 yr old SWM for swing clubs, night clubs, travel AND possible relationship. Pls be honest, attrac, slim.

TICKLE OUR FEET
White Couple 40s sks other couple to remove our shoes & tickle our feet until you feel we've had enough.

HERPES.
Seeking SWM 25-35 interested in serious relationship. If you are looking for someone who is easy going and enjoys life then answer my ad.

IT'S A JUNGLE OUT THERE! GUYS!!! THIS HOT LIONESS IS ON THE PROWL!!!!!!!!!!!! MEOW!

MBF, full figured, 27 seeking WM 27-45 for LTR. I'm looking for a confidant paramour who can give this bored wife some excitement in her dull life. Honesty and no game playing.

Oriental Beauty, young (18+), slim long hair, passionate, mysterious, enjoys rock, seeks single Male, attractive, slim, longer hair, kind, fun-loving, stylish, any age, but youthful (18+) looking—inside and out.

Sleeping Single
In A Double Bed?
Want A Friend & Not To Get Wed? In My Mid 40's, A Widow & White For Dancing/Dining Under Moonlight If Your A Man Who Enjoys The Same Give Me Info & Your Name!

SOMEONE SPECIAL

Petite Chinese lady, youthful 39, w/brain, looks, elegance, grt smile & hi IQ, trilingual, ISO attr, smart, considerate & loving gentleman w/success & style, 40-50 yo, marriage-minded.

LET'S DO IT!

You command me to my knees: to undress, to please you, I do. Oh No!! I escape your bonds, capture you, now... SWJNSNRM designer, athletic, 50, look 40, ISO DREAM woman, for LTR, marriage, kids.

AIN'T NOTHIN WRONG WITH
A BIG STRONG WOMAN

Attr aggressive BF lkg for Fem full figrd beaut BF for fshp/fun

BEAUTIFUL GOTH FEMALE seeks "girlfriend". I'm artistic, pierced & tattooed. Into: vampires, incense, cats, independent films, angels, candles, ethnic goods, horror movies, toys.

Bi Fat Fem Bottom submissive full figure TV 350 lbs., 55 yrs old crossdresser seeks M/F couples for adult pleasures.

Exotic, Elegant, Educated Post-Op.

Would love to merge with a cert. Cosmetic Surgeon. Let's enjoy my "designer look" together. Remember, I know how U feel.

DWM, submissive, retired NYPD, goodlooking, seeks white female dominant for OTK and bare-bottom fun, possible LTR.

TOTAL WRECK
SEEKING SAME

An attractive BiSBF, 26 Seeks financially secure, tall (6'0+) single SUB M for P/T Dom/Sub roleplay & P/T vanilla friendship & possible LTR. Pamper, please & spoil me.

Blond Angel—Big blue eyes, pretty, cultured, slim, Ivy League, religious Catholic, single white female, seeks educated, slim, single white Christian male with decent values. 30-45. No drinking, drugs, diseases, games. Let's start something!

WHIPOLOGIST WANTED!

Very handsome, hung, single, fit, healthy, submissive, professional, 38 y.o. male. Seeks very attractive dominant female for her pleasure and her pleasure only. Watch me dance under your whip!

JSF, 72, seeking a lady 65-75 for companionship. I enjoy swimming and bike riding in a health club. Also the movies and visits to the Fulton St. Seaport. My interests are: art, music, knitting, reading.

MALE PONY SEEKING FEMALE
EQUESTRIAN RIDER

Lonely Christian lady, 31, honest, loving, seeks Christian male, 30-35, marriage-minded. Come let us worship the Lord together. Photo a must.

Passive white gentleman, 50 yrs old, healthy, seeks black women for lunch dates.

Generous Tom Selleck/David Hasselhoff look-a-like wanted by SBF, exotic, enchanting cat-shaped eyes. Tigress for love. Can you handle it?

TOP WANTED. Gay male, 50, who is a bottom only, seeking young tops for fun, 18-30 only.

SPANK ME HARD!!
Submissive SWM in need of strict discipline. Ladies, I've been very bad!

DOMINANT FEMALE DESIRED
SJM, 41, 5'7, handsome, built, sane, secure, seeks uninhibited F to worship & share life with.

II
SOCIETY

Don Calhoun

THE KINSEY REPORT

This book review of Dr. Alfred Kinsey's Sexual Behavior in the Human Male *appeared on February 10, 1948, in* Of Politics, *a Socialist journal of culture and politics edited by Dwight MacDonald. The following is a portion of the review.*

Kinds of Experience

In analyzing how total sexual activity is distributed among the various "outlets," the study finds that 92 percent of the male population at one time or another engage in masturbation which leads to orgasm. There is no evidence that, apart from the reactions of other people, masturbation at any age is harmful. This held true, in the survey, even for those highest-rating males who masturbated on an average of 23 times a week. No doubt the most surprising finding with regard to masturbation is that among *married* men who have attended college, 69 percent masturbate *after* marriage. (This is the highest masturbation rate for married men; as we shall see later, the college-educated, professional group are society's most active masturbators.)

Undoubtedly one of the most revealing parts of the study is the analysis of homosexuality. Previous estimates of its frequency have ranged from 5 percent of the population down to one-tenth of one percent. The Kinsey survey finds that "at least 37 percent of the male population has some homosexual experience between the beginning of adolescence and old age." This, we must bear in mind, is *overt* homosexual experience with actual orgasm, and the figure does not include pre-adolescent homosexuality. (This does *not* mean, of course, that 37 percent of American males find their chief—or even an important—sexual outlet in homosexuality; on the contrary, among the males studied, only 6.3 percent of the total orgasms were derived from homosexual contacts, as against 69.4 percent from heterosexual sources.)

From these findings, the authors draw several inferences. The data demonstrate the complete meaninglessness of a dichotomy between "heterosexual" and "homosexual" *persons.* It is, of course, possible to speak of heterosexual and homosexual *experiences;* but inasmuch as at least half of the population have overt experiences of both kinds, the old two-fold classification of people is useless. Hetero-and homosexuality, the authors conclude, can be conceived of only in terms of a continuum, i.e., *how much* heterosexuality and how much homosexuality have entered into the individual's overt or covert behavior? The old stigmatization (or glorification) of homosexuality further breaks down in light of the fact that there is no conclusive evidence that tendencies in either direction are inherited, or that any distinguishable homosexual type exists. It appears that the homosexual as a visibly distinct biological entity is, from the standpoint of science, going to go the same way the so-called Jewish "race" has gone.

The frequency of pre-marital intercourse varies with social level. "Among the males who go to college, about 67 percent has coital experience before marriage; among those who go into high school but not beyond, about 84 percent has such intercourse; and among the boys who never go beyond grade school the accumulative incidence figure is 98 percent." On the basis of the data on extra-marital sex, the authors estimate that approximately half of American married men at some time sleep with women other than their wives. While these figures may or may not be surprising, the data on prostitution are. About 70 percent of American males at one time or another have at least one experience with a prostitute, but in the total American sexual picture prostitution plays a relatively insignificant role. The authors estimate that not more than four percent of all male sexual activity is with prostitutes; most pre-marital and extra-marital intercourse is with non-professionals, and this is true particularly of the upper social and educational groups. The relative unimportance of prostitutes among American men's sexual partners suggests that the forthcoming Kinsey survey of female sexuality may find women not much less sexually active than men.

The most "unnatural" form of sexual activity is generally thought to be intercourse with animals. The behavior of city boys (apart from their visits to the country—or the stockyards) would demonstrate either the existence of the taboo or the absence of opportunity, or both. Among boys raised on farms, however, the Kinsey report finds that about 17 percent experience orgasm as the result of animal contacts after adolescence. Of the rural groups who ultimately go to college, 26 to 28 percent have such experience. In some communities, the authors found incidences of animal intercourse running as high as 65 percent.

Lest I seem to slight the only form of sexual activity which is permitted by the traditional verbal *mores,* let it be reported that the Kinsey study finds that a little less than half of all American male sexual activity consists of intercourse *within* marriage.

Sex, Law, and Science

The Kinsey report is an excellent case study in the relationship between class structure and "ideology." The authors make clear at many points that the legal sex code is largely an embodiment of the *mores* of a minority of the population, the relatively successful middle class; and that to a large extent even with that class the legal code comes much closer to the verbal *mores* than to actual behavior. If all the sexual practices which are forbidden by law were actually punished, the authors estimate, about 5 percent of law-abiding citizens would be supporting the remaining 95 percent in jail. When "law on paper" is compared with "law in action," it is found that apprehension and conviction for any sexual offense depends largely on the class membership of the policeman, judge, etc. Policemen, who generally come from the working class, are lenient with extra-marital intercourse but are likely to haul into court a boy found masturbating. Judges, who are largely of upper class origin, are likely to consider masturbation a minor offense but to deal severely with "fornicators." Kinsey and colleagues make clear that the law in no way embodies the *mores* of the lower classes: the legal restrictions on sex are to the working man simply rather arbitrary and incomprehensible obstructions which one must manage if possible to avoid.

While the methods of science itself, when properly applied, get results which do not embody class bias, the Kinsey report clearly indicates that what passes for the science of sex in popular (and even not-so-popular) culture reflects the *mores* of a minority just as does the legal code. The authors cite, with specific mention of the authorities in question, many instances where experts have put forward as scientific truths statements which the Kinsey study shows to be clearly wrong. They show, furthermore, that the "truths" never rested on much more than common currency and conformity with what the dominant social group wanted to believe and wanted other people to believe.

Kinsey vs. Reich

How do the Kinsey findings square with the much discussed contention of Wilhelm Reich that political and social authoritarianism is maintained by sexual repression? Does the report substantiate or refute Reich's claim? I think the best answer we can give is that the Kinsey findings are not equipped to do either. If one assumes that frequency and promiscuity of sexual experience are signs of good sexual adjustment, then on the basis of the Kinsey findings one would be loath to accept Reich's claim that the subordination of the working classes arises from such frustration. But this is an assumption which neither Reich nor Kinsey makes. Says the senior author of the present study: "It is…quite possible to recognize…many degrees of satisfaction among sexual experiences, and there are admittedly occasions when there is little pleasure accompanying an ejaculation. But we have no statistics on…the various degrees of satisfaction." In other words, the frequency of orgasm and the degree of "orgastic potency" of the individual may be to a large degree independent, and therefore data on frequency of sexual activity throw little light on the basic question of sexual satisfaction and frustration.

Furthermore, the Kinsey findings do not seem to me to demonstrate that the lower classes, as distinguished from the middle, have a full and satisfactory sex life. The lower-class attitude toward sex as reported seems to regard it as a biological inevitability which one should indulge in with as little involvement as possible of one's own ego or that of one's partner. The notion that in sexual relations with a person one really respects the act should be reduced to its barest essentials seems to imply that intercourse is thought of as a dirty and hostile act, an inference which is hardly contradicted by examination of the walls of any public toilet. At the least, Kinsey's findings cannot be taken as a refutation of Reich's theories.

If widely read without distortion, the Kinsey report itself should accomplish some change in the attitudes and behavior of both the guilt-ridden sexual conservative and the exhibitionistic libertine, in whatever class they may be found. One of its most significant contributions, I think, is its demonstration that no type of sexual behavior is so rare that anybody need think himself outside the pale because he practices or has practiced it. There are probably few who will read this article who have not felt that in their sexual history there is some episode which they would rather not have generally known, some "perversion" which in the light of the Kinsey findings may well turn out to be an activity engaged in by the majority of the American people. I am not suggesting, of course, that majority practice, in sex any more than in politics, is the guide to ethical behavior. But the Kinsey study should enable people to view their own sex life, and the sex life of others, in a somewhat more objective light.

Lisa Palac

HOW DIRTY PICTURES CHANGED MY LIFE

"Burn it," I said. The words clinked together like ice cubes. "Burn every last bit of it. Or it's over."

I pointed at the stockpile of hard-core porn that had just slid out of the closet like an avalanche. If looks could kill, my boyfriend would have dropped dead. How could he, Mr. Sensitive Guy, enjoy looking at such disgusting trash? Oh, I was livid. I paced around his tiny one-room apartment, spitting venom, devising his punishment. "Either all this sleazy shit goes or I go."

He looked at me as if he were about to cry; his fingers nervously picked at the edges of his flannel shirt. "I'll get rid of it all, I promise," he whispered. Silence fell around the room like a metal drape. "But first will you watch one—just one—video with me?" The nerve. Here I am threatening to walk, and he's got the audacity to ask me to watch a fuck film before I go. He prattled on about how he just wanted a chance to show me why this stuff turned him on and that it didn't mean he didn't love me and if I didn't like it, he would, as agreed, torch everything in a purging bonfire. I crossed my arms and chewed on the inside of my lip for a minute. If I was going to make him destroy his life's collection of porn, I guess I could allow him one last fling. So that evening we watched *Sleepless Nights*. It was the first dirty movie I ever saw. A seminal film.

I saw that movie when I was twenty years old, and now I'm twenty-nine. Since then I've watched hundreds of X-rated videos, patronized plenty of erotic theaters, put money down for live sex shows, and even run up a few phone-sex bills. Today I make my living making porn. I edit an erotic magazine titled *Future Sex* and recently produced the virtual-reality-based sex CD-ROM program *Cyborgasm*. I've always been a firm believer that if you want something done right, you've got to do it yourself.

Until I sat down and watched an adult film, the only thing I knew about porn was that I shouldn't be looking at it. Growing up female, I quickly

63

learned that girls don't get to look at girlie magazines. Sure, you could take your clothes off for the camera (becoming, of course, a total slut and disgracing your family), but the pleasure is for *his* eyes only. The message to us girls was, Stay a virgin until you get married, procreate, and don't bother finding your clitoris. Whatever you do, stay away from porn, because it's a man's world, honey. Ironically certain strains of feminism gave a similar sermon: Pornography can only exploit, oppress, and degrade you. It will destroy any female in its path, unless you can destroy it first. And if you don't believe this, you've obviously been brainwashed by The Patriarchy.

If the truth be known, the forbidden aspect of pornography made me a little curious. However, I wasn't about to be caught renting a porn video. So when Greg challenged me to watch an X-rated movie, I decided to see for myself what all the fuss was about.

At the time, I thought of myself as an anti-porn feminist. Before that I had identified as a rock-and-roll chick from Chicago. I grew up on the northwest side of the city, not too far from Wrigley Field: the last in a line of four Polish Catholic middle-class kids. My childhood was carved out of a loaf of Wonder bread: I went to church on Sundays, was Cinderella in the kindergarten play, got gold stars in spelling and math, took tap and ballet lessons, forged my troop leader's signature to get extra Girl Scout badges, read all the Judy Blume books (starting with the menstrual manifesto of the sixth grade: *Are You There, God? It's Me, Margaret*), scarfed down Swanson dinners while watching every episode of *The Brady Bunch*, cried when I got caught shoplifting a Bonne Bell Lipsmacker, played doctor with the kids in the neighborhood, and asked my older brothers why they didn't wipe when they peed. It was like, you know, normal.

"But how did you get so interested in sex?" I always get asked. I interpret this question to mean, "What terrible trauma did you experience as a child that made you so perverted?" The answer: I was a corrupted papist.

Catholic school was twelve long years of wool-plaid penance, confessing to empty boxfuls of sin, and silently debating whether Mary stayed a virgin even after Jesus was born. I'd stare up at the crucifix and wonder how much it must have hurt. Then I'd wonder what Jesus looked like naked. Because of my profane thoughts, I always had a fear that I'd become a nun—seriously. That would straighten me out but good. On Career Day, joining the convent was always presented as a fine choice. "But not everyone is chosen to do the Lord's work," the sisters would say, and go on to tell us how one day they just "got the calling" and that was that. "Please don't pick me," I would whisper to myself over and over, bowing my head. "Oh, please, oh, please, oh, PLEASE! Don't make me go!" Needless to say, I never got *that* calling. I chalked it up to the fact that God would never pick someone who mentally undressed his only Son.

Or perhaps I simply inherited a kinky gene. My brothers read *Playboy*. My dad read *Hustler*. I know that because I used to steal peeks at it every time I had the chance. Whenever I'd start to feel bored and like there was nothing to do, I'd find myself thinking, *Maybe I should go look at that* Hustler *magazine again*. My father had a couple of them hidden with his fishing tackle in the basement. On hot summer days when my mom was out mowing the lawn, I'd go downstairs, lie down on the cool concrete floor, and look at those bizarre naked pictures. The one I remember most was of an Asian woman smoking a cigarette out of her pussy. It was the weirdest thing I ever saw. These magazines fascinated me for a long time, and then one day they weren't there anymore. I think my mother found them and threw them out. I didn't look at any more sex magazines until I got to college.

I moved to Minneapolis in the early eighties and enrolled at the University of Minnesota. I really wanted to go to Berkeley, but the family leash would only stretch as far as the land of ten thousand lakes. My career choice: midwife. I applied to the school of nursing. I'd already completed one year of premed at Loyola University in Chicago, but I had to escape from the Jesuits—and my prosaic little existence. In our house, if you were smart, you picked a career that showed it in dollars and cents. Dad looked at college as one long training seminar for the occupation of your choice: business, medicine, or law—the trinity of success. After all, I had to recoup all that college tuition, so forget about majoring in psychology or getting some crummy art degree. If I didn't land a high-paying job when I graduated, I might as well flush my diploma down the toilet. This was the philosophy of the survivors of Operation Bootstrap, the camp that made my dad. I solemnly vowed to rise above my Hallmark-card life and get to know the edges of the world.

Most of my sophomore year was spent either studying, getting wasted, or undergoing some kind of mutation. I went from heavy-metal chick to New Wave punk (albeit about four years late), squeezing into leopard-skin leggings and low-cut sweaters trimmed with ostrich feathers. I spiked my hot-pink hair up with gobs of gel and swam all night in hot-pink heels. I turned on to Joy Division and said "gnarly" a lot. I went to gallery openings. Ronald Reagan bored me and Patti Smith thrilled me. The way things were going, I could handle the tough science it took to get a nursing degree, but I couldn't handle the outfits. White slacks and a tasteful perm were unconscionable. I dropped out and went to art school.

I came out as a film major. My roommate came out as a lesbian. She was the first dyke I ever knew. Suzie was from California and was totally rad. I met her when I was at the U, and we escaped dorm hell together. Together we ate our first mouthfuls of feminism.

I had never heard the word *feminist* before. My mother wasn't a feminist, my older sister didn't call herself a feminist. Yet feminism gave me the words to describe my own experience. I quickly learned that being treated with less respect simply because I was female was called sexism, and it was not okay. Feminism illuminated the offenses that I'd chalked up to being a girl: enduring public comments on the size of my breasts, being paid less for the same work than my male counterparts, putting up with shoddy contraception. This knowledge was power: the power to take control of my life and make my own choices about everything I did.

Armed with our new feminist thinking, Suzie and I resolved to be women, not girls. We tromped on every bit of sexism in pop culture. We marched for pro-choice. We resented having to be constantly on guard against the threat of rape. We mourned the plight of women all across the globe who lived in squalid cages. We turned into pink sticks of dynamite, the crackle and spit of our fast-burning fuse getting louder all the time.

Pornography of course was the big bang. At that time Minneapolis was a hotbed of radical anti-porn politics. Catharine MacKinnon and Andrea Dworkin were teaching a class on porn at the U of M, and they drafted the very first feminist-inspired anti-pornography law, defining pornography as a form of sex discrimination. *The Story of O* was picketed on campus, with flyers denouncing S&M as just another bourgeois word for violence. *Not a Love Story*, a documentary about one woman's adverse experience in the adult business, become a women's studies classic. One woman set herself on fire in Shinder's Bookstore on Hennepin Avenue, a martyr for the right to a porn-free society. The message was clear: This battle was as important as ending the Vietnam War.

Meanwhile the Meese Commission was in full swing, bringing *Deep Throat* star Linda "Lovelace" Marchiano's disturbing testimony of coercion into the living rooms of America and alleging a link between pornography and violence. Women Against Pornography toured the heartland with their slide show, featuring the infamous *Hustler* cover of a woman being fed through a meat grinder. The tenet seemed to be this: Get rid of porn and get rid of all injustice against women. All the battles feminists were fighting could be won by winning the war on porn. So I enlisted.

I didn't have any firsthand experience with porn. I had never watched an adult film, bought an explicit sex magazine, or known anyone who did. Aside from a few stolen glances at my father's collection, the only pornography I saw was in the classroom. This carefully selected group of pornographic images didn't appear very liberating: she's tied up and gagged, with clothespins biting down on her nipples; she's spreading her legs wide open showing pink, his come squirting all over her face. These images were described as inherently degrading and oppressive. No other interpretation was offered. I looked at these images (which were supposedly representative of all porn), added my own experience of being sized up as a piece of ass, and agreed that pornography was the reason women were oppressed. Pornography bred sexism. Like Justice Potter Stewart, I knew pornography when I saw it and I'd seen enough to swallow the rally cries of the anti-porn movement. I chanted and marched and applauded the spray painting of LIES ABOUT WOMEN over Virginia Slims ads and across the fronts of XXX black-veiled bookstores. I learned the slogans like "Porn is the theory and rape is the practice" from older feminists like Robin Morgan.

But soon I began to wonder how it all fit in with what I was doing in my bedroom. I still liked men, even if I didn't like all their piggish behavior. And I liked sleeping with them even more. Since I was fifteen, I used my feminine charms to lure them in. They used their virility to seduce me. Did this constitute sexual objectification? I wasn't sure. I questioned the definition of pornography I'd been handed. Yes, the images I'd seen offended me, but surely there were sexual images that weren't sexist. Where were the erotic alternatives? If the bottom line here was that looking at images of people having sex was wrong, then I hadn't come very far from Catholic school after all. Plus, lumping all men under the heading Sexist Patriarchy seemed a little unfair. The guys I hung out with were caring, respectful, and intelligent—but could they suddenly turn into psychopathic rapists if I waved a porn mag in front of their faces? Underneath it all, I had a lot of questions. And then my boyfriend's porn came tumbling out of the closet.

"Ready?" he said, looking at me with dark eyes full of some corrupt knowledge I didn't yet have. We were both nervous; he was afraid I was going to hate it, leaving him with a mound of prurient ashes and a dead relationship. My fear was more tangled.

"Yeah," my voice cracked like a dry twig. Greg slipped *Sleepless Nights* into the VCR.

Sitting on the floor in the TV room, my mind began churning up shame-filled scenarios: What if my roommate walked in and caught us watching this dirty movie? Or worse, what if I am so turned on by this hideous smut that I become a full-blown porno addict? I could hear the voice: *What a disgusting girl. No one's gonna want you once they find out about this.* Or what if I laugh?

My initial reaction was, *Boy, is this stupid.* Everything was bad, bad, bad: lame script, lousy acting, garish lighting, crippled disco soundtracks, anachronistic garter belts, and repulsive leading men. As a film student I was appalled that the director of this cheap thing didn't even bother with the basics of good filmmaking. The plot was forgettable. I vaguely remember a contrived sex scene on a pool table. I was waiting for the violent rape scene, which never happened. "Is that all?" I asked when it was over. I expected my porno research to yield some kind of groundbreaking vision, the same way that my first glimpses of feminism did.

It's hard to remember exactly what made me want to watch another one. Part of it was like social anthropology, peeling back the layers to see what I could see. And the unladylike act of watching porn was piquantly rebellious. But as we watched other X-rated films, I noticed they suffered from the same plague of filmic badness. I spent my early viewing hours counting the pimples on performers' asses and mimicking the orgasmic fakery of the starlets. Some of the actors looked bored out of their minds; others looked painfully luckless. They fucked in unnatural positions for the sake of the camera. Sometimes they were so unemotional, they reminded me of Spock. Some were so skinny and so young, I felt like shouting "Get out of porn and run for your lives!" I imagined myself in their place; I imagined what my father would think if I did such a thing. Wouldn't all these women rather be doing something else but just don't have the skill or means?

A paradox emerged that I didn't understand. Sometimes I'd see an image of a woman on all fours begging for his cock and think, how humiliating. Other times during scenes like that, the actress's eyes filled up with fire so genuine, and he stroked her hair so tenderly while she sucked him off…it seemed romantic, like an unfiltered moment of pleasure. I began separating the images, recognizing that all of them weren't the same. I began to have flashes of lust.

But I wanted to have what Greg was having. He was getting something out of these movies that I wasn't. The movies didn't turn me off, but they didn't completely turn me on either—he did; his sexual excitement. He was sharing a very intimate part of himself with me and trusting me not to reject him. I wanted to know the side of him he'd so painstakingly hidden from me. Watching him watch the screen, I got turned on by the fact that he was turned on. But this Pavlovian eroticism worried me. While he slipped into erotic wonderland, I stood outside, waiting.

Then I made an important decision: I decided I needed to be alone with pornography. I wondered what might turn me on—if anything. God only knows what could happen to a girl who got turned on by thinking of a naked Jesus. I wanted to perform an experiment, to watch it by myself without him, without talking. I could no longer scrutinize these images from an intellectual distance. I had to get a little dirty.

I made a date with an "all-lesbian" action feature called *Aerobisex Girls*. I tried not to care about the plot. I didn't wonder about the performers' family histories. I didn't think about anything. The movie featured an oiled-up orgy where the women shook with the fury of real, uncontrollable orgasms. I could feel the heat between my legs. As if my erotic imagination was being mapped to the screen, I fingered myself in sync with the women in the film. I opened and closed my eyes, imagining I was part of their scene, replaying certain close-ups over and over. Then my mind began moving back and forth between the real-time video and the frozen frames of cherished erotic memories. I fed the screen with my own fantasies, splicing together an erotic sequence that played only in my head. When I came, it was intense.

Now I knew firsthand what most women don't think about: what men do with all those sex magazines. Guys don't buy *Playboy*, turn to the centerfold, and think *I'd like to marry her,* then turn the page and go grab a burger. No, they masturbate to it. They jerk off. Masturbation is such a big part of every man's life, and to a much lesser extent every woman's, but nobody talks about it. Men do it and don't talk about it, while women don't talk about it and don't do it. This is a fact. Studies like *The Kinsey Report* and *The Hite Report* have documented the high percentage of women who do not masturbate. This statistic is further mirrored in our language: We don't even have the words to describe female self-stimulation. If there is any jerking, wanking, or beating off to be done, it involves a penis, not a clitoris. It's a testimony to how cut off women are from their sexuality, both physically and psychologically.

Despite the fact that seventies feminist liberation honored the female flower and encouraged women to talk more openly about sex, masturbation still remains a taboo. In addition women still aren't given any social encouragement to use erotic pictures to stimulate their sexual imagination. So when it comes to understanding how to use porn, they're in the dark. They don't get what it's for. Men, on the other hand, are very familiar with the concept of stroking, and since they've always had such easy access to sexual material, they can't understand why it's such a big deal for a woman to get off on porn. "So you masturbated to some porno, big deal," they say. "I did that when I was thirteen."

The truth is, I didn't masturbate until I was nearly twenty years old and a vibrator hit me on the head—literally. I was cleaning out a closet in my new apartment, when a battery-operated vibrator fell off a high shelf and bonked me. As if I were a cartoon character, a light bulb went off inside my brain and I decided to give myself a buzz. It was the first time I had an orgasm. Strange but true, I never really thought much about touching myself until then. Try to imagine a guy who doesn't masturbate until an appliance hits him on the head at the age of twenty.

Until this point I never felt in charge of my own pleasure. I was taught that sexual satisfaction was something I lay back and waited for. An orgasm was something my boyfriend gave to me—only he didn't. Although I'd been having penis-in-vagina sex since I was fifteen, I hadn't come from it. I heard plenty about the Big O, but clearly never had the feelings they described in *Cosmo*. I remember one time when an old lover asked me the inevitable question after sex: Did you come? Embarrassingly I said I didn't—ever. "Don't you masturbate to come?" he asked. I was bewildered.

At the beginning of my porn adventures, I was also confused. I was looking for a political theory instead of a sexual experience, and that's why it hadn't been working. Now I had the carnal knowledge that so few women possessed: how to use porn and come. What's important about this isn't just that I learned how to get physically aroused by pornography but that I became sexually autonomous. I was now in complete control of my own erotic destiny. My experience was sexual liberation in action. I now knew how to use my mind to turn a two-dimensional image into a flesh-and-blood erotic response and explore sexual fantasies.

Before I watched porn, my erotic imagination was groggy. I didn't know what a sexual fantasy was; I hadn't really had them. Even when I masturbated, I didn't think about anything except the physical sensations. When I had sex with my lovers, my thoughts were filled only with them, the way they were touching me, the immediacy of the act. And that was good. But there were all these other thoughts that I hadn't explored yet. Pornography dangled sexual fantasy in front of me. It made me aware that my sexual imagination wasn't limited to the heat of the moment or a sensual reminiscence. I could think about anything. I could use anything—books, magazines, videos—for erotic inspiration.

One of my most formative sources of inspiration was a journal titled *Caught Looking*. Written by a group of East Coast feminist activists, this book combined academic refutations of the anti-porn argument with hard-core sex pictures. As its title implied, it gave women the rare opportunity to look at a wide variety of pornographic images. *Caught Looking* confirmed what I had been living: The censorship of pornography is unfeminist. The book represented a whole new breed of women who were reclaiming the power of female sexuality. I felt very much a part of that breed.

Soon I was reading *On Our Backs*, a lesbian sex magazine edited by a woman named Susie Bright. This was pornography created by women for women—how revolutionary! It not only challenged countless stereotypes about lesbian sex being boring and vanilla, but it also defied the myth that women weren't interested in erotic pictures. The magazine ripped apart the notion that porn was only for men. I uncovered Candida Royalle's series of feminist porn videos, *Femme*, and watched every one with fervent camaraderie. Other books, like Nancy Friday's *My Secret Garden*, which detailed women's wide-ranging sexual fantasies, and *Coming to Power*, edited by the lesbian S&M group Samois, further validated my position that female sexuality was a powerful force that could not be politically pigeonholed.

My newfound sexual freedom was sweet, but finding the pornography that waved it along was rare. Wading through the swamp of split beavers and raging hard-ons, I felt by turns critical, angry, depressed, pensive, embarrassed, and bored. I began a relentless search for the right stuff. Often I was surprised at the things that made me wet; things that would no doubt be labeled "male oriented" and "degrading" by any number of good feminist soldiers. But these "good parts" were so few and far between, I spent more time fingering the fast-forward button than anything else. I wanted lots of images that reflected my erotic desires and depicted authentic female sexuality. I scanned for cute guys with long hair, punk butchy women, plots with lots of psychosexual tension, come shots where he doesn't pull out and most of all, genuine female orgasms—most of the actresses' orgasms were so fake, they were laughable.

It seemed the biggest problem with pornography wasn't that it was evil smelling and immoral—it was artificial and predictable. But despite my

71

exhaustive search through all the local dirty bookstores, I came up rather empty-handed. Finally I realized I couldn't wait around any longer for somebody else to give me what I wanted. I had to create it myself.

In 1986 during my senior year in college I created a two-page erotic fanzine called *Magnet School: A Sexographic Magazine*. I felt strongly that the problem with porn wasn't that it was inherently degrading but that it was, for the most part, an erotically retarded genre that needed to get real. I wanted to create something that aroused people sexually and intellectually, where the complexity of human sexuality had a voice. Because I so badly wanted to produce something different, I called it something different. In my first editorial column titled "Yeow!" I did away with those loaded language guns *erotica* and *pornography* and put *sexography* in their place.

Sexography was alternative sexual expression in all its lush and lusty glory. In Issue One, I defined sexography as "absolutely no writing about harlots, no getting off with big orchids, no high heels in bed, no masturbating to Lionel Richie, and no split beavers." (Okay, so I've changed my mind a bit since then.) There were other contenders for a newer, blue title—cliterature, lustography, climaxerox, and even Ovaria—but they didn't have the right egalitarian ring.

Although the Macintosh computer had already made its debut, this 'zine was still a cut-and-paste production. I hammered the first issue out on my typewriter, reprinting text from a Throwing Muses album, daring my best girlfriend to pen a porn story, and pirating any decent hard-core images I could find. I photocopied it for free during the middle of the night at the twenty-four-hour copy center, since I'd made friends with the anarchist punks who worked there. I handed it out in cafés and bars, and of course made distribution rounds to every dirty bookstore in town, telling every dildo clerk about the coming erotic revolution. It was very grassroots.

At the same time I was publishing *Magnet School*, I was completing my senior thesis at art school: a sixteen-millimeter color erotic film called *What You Want*. It was a dark and abstract narrative that dealt with issues of female sexuality, control, and erotic relationships. Basically it was my life turned porn drama with me as the star in a long red wig, since no one else auditioned. Greg and I got naked in a bathtub, toyed with oral sex, and even fabricated a nipple-piercing scene. I had intended deep introspection, but my unpolished direction made it corny. I was disappointed that my best intentions had turned camp because I was trying to make a very important point: Sexual images can be profoundly liberating, rather than oppressive.

During the making of this film we had student critiques in the screening room. Everyone in my class was always very opinionated until I showed my work in progress. Then there was dead silence, followed by, "God; what are your parents going to think?" Well, I wasn't making this film for my parents. I was making it for my peers, and I wanted to know what they thought. At first they were sort of…shocked. They didn't know what to say. The silence was uncomfortable and sometimes hurt me. But outside the classroom my colleagues had a lot to say.

Much to my relief my female friends were extremely supportive. They related to my journey from anti-porn feminism to sexpositive feminism, because many of them were on the same trip. They, too, were fed up with everyone shouting, "Don't look!" when it came to porn. They wanted to see it and they wanted me to show it to them. My friend Bitsy even asked me to invite all the girls over for pizza and porno night.

As we talked, I realized that learning how to use porn is an option most women are never aware of. Too many women only react to pornography as a political debate. Pornography, erotica, sexography, whatever you choose to call it, is a tangled genre with a few razor-sharp sides. This complexity is a reflection of the mystery and depth of our own sexuality, where erotic conflict often makes for excitement. My investigation into the erotic world has resulted in a few mixed feelings. There were images that troubled me, and there still are. But I believe my initial knee-jerk reaction against porn was a result of my own misunderstanding and lack of sensitivity to erotic images.

Pornography as a whole is usually described as offensive. Yet I found that much of what is offensive about porn has to do with interpretations, not sexual acts. Take the controversial example of a woman sucking a man's cock until he comes all over her face. This image can be presented in a very crass and repellent way, or it can be depicted as sensuous and kind. To me the act itself isn't degrading; feeling my lover come all over me can be the most intimate gift. But no matter how artfully presented this image is, it is almost always interpreted as crass and repellent because people refuse to believe there can be other interpretations.

The words *degrading* and *oppressive* are often presented as absolute, objective terms. I found them to be vague and subjective. Was the very act of a woman spreading her legs and wanting sex degrading? Were photographs of her genitals outright demeaning? Why is the image of a woman's sexual appetite seen as oppressive rather than liberating? If we're going to talk about oppressive images of women, we'd better include laundry soap commercials.

The depiction of women as vapid Stepford wives, valued only for their stain-removing talents, is to me completely oppressive.

Another thing that really surprised me as I explored this erotic underworld was the lack of violent porn. I was taught to believe that all porn was violent. However, my own exploration quickly revealed that the majority of commercial porn is rather peacefully formulaic. No knives, no blood, no rape scenes. Instead there was a lick-suck-fuck formula that ended in orgasm, not murder.

Ultimately I felt the anti-porn feminists viewed women as being without sexual self-awareness. Their arguments for the elimination of porn were shaky and flawed. Their claims denied women independence by refusing to acknowledge that women had rich sexual fantasies, powerful libidos, and the power to choose.

I chose to discuss sex in a way my older sister probably never did, particularly with my women friends. We traded vibrator tips, talked about our erotic fantasies—or the lack of them—and shared the secrets of our guilt-ridden, latent masturbatory experiences. We didn't waste time dissing men—we mainly focused on ourselves and figuring out how to power up our own orgasms—although we did agree that the general lack of male nudity was lame. Tits and ass flood our culture, but his bare body is nowhere in sight. We also found it interesting how pornography is usually discussed as the sexual depiction of women, although almost all heterosexual porn features women *and* men. We felt that if porn was going to come of age, not only would the images of women have to change, so would the images of men. Paunchy guys with overgrown mustaches who had little to offer except their big dicks weren't our idea of sexy. We wanted bad boys with angel faces who understood the meaning of seduction. We also wanted them to be a little, well…vulnerable.

Although what we said was significant, how we said it was also important. These conversations didn't take place behind closed doors, but in public. At parties, in cafés, and in living rooms across Minneapolis, we talked about what turned us on. We didn't care who heard us. We had so many questions and we felt so powerful being able to ask them out loud.

Men, on the other hand, were less sure how to act. They were intrigued by my bold sexual independence. It struck a chord with them—they saw their own masculinity reflected in me. In other words, they admired my balls. At the same time they were a bit confused by my overt sexuality. It conflicted with their understanding of feminism. A lot of men my age were raised to believe that if you respected women, you didn't look at naked pictures of them. So if I was a feminist, how could I like pornography? To them the concept of a loudmouthed, sexually self-governing woman was exciting, challenging, and sometimes a bit scary.

Surprisingly, or maybe not, I was never directly attacked by any anti-porn feminists. People often expect me to tell horrifying tales of how I was branded a traitor and was run out of Wimmin's town on a rail. But the truth is the response to my work has always been overwhelmingly positive. I believe it's because more and more women are realizing that erotic images have a necessary place in their lives. Sexual freedom is an integral part of freedom and justice for all. If the basic tenet of feminism is giving women the freedom to choose, then it includes making choices about what we do sexually.

This freedom to go for the erotic gusto, however, exists because of the tremendous gains founding feminists have made. If it wasn't for social and economic battles won during the last few decades, female sexuality would still be chained up in ignorance and silence. The sexual revolution of the late sixties and early seventies paved the way for my generation's erotic liberation.

As a card-carrying feminist, I chose to pursue a career as a pornographer. With eight issues of my homegrown 'zine *Magnet School* completed, I gave in to my crush on California and headed west to San Francisco—Sin City. For two years I worked with my mentor, Susie Bright, as a senior editor at *On Our Backs* and as a freelance journalist.

In 1991 I was hired to edit *Future Sex,* a magazine for women and men that explores the intersection of sex, technology, and culture. I had written about so many aspects of sex, but not this one. What was the link between sex and technology anyway? Was it virtual-reality sex? Digital porn? Fucking robots? While these concepts were certainly futuristic, I hoped they weren't the only things the future of sex had to offer.

The fact that today's young women are able to think more critically about pornography is due in part to technology. The VCR brought a female audience to porn and gave them the unprecedented opportunity to see exactly what it is. Video porn allows both women and men to investigate sexual imagery in a more independent way. Moving X-rated images out of public, often unclean theaters and into the privacy and comfort of the bedroom gave women safe and direct access to this previously off-limits material. In fact women now represent the fastest-growing group of erotic consumers.

I now realize that technology may be this generation's key to taking control of our sexual identities. While computer technology may seem isolating rather than unifying at first, personal computers, modems, camcorders, and a host of other tools offer the potential for unparalleled communication, including erotic communication. In many ways high technology puts the means of production back in everyone's hands. We no longer have to depend on someone else's mass-produced idea of eroticism; we can create our own—easily, cost-effectively, often instantly. Moreover, digital technology gives us the chance to transmit our ideas globally, not just locally.

Today we must also contend with something no other generation had to: AIDS. Since this devastating plague sends the message that sex can equal death, it forces us to talk publicly about sex in a straightforward way in order to save lives. Latex is vogue. Jerking off is in. Safe sex is hot. AIDS is a catalyst for rethinking our relationship to erotica. And the stigma of pornography is slowly being chipped away.

But this new-world pornography will suffer the same pitfalls of the old world if we don't take advantage of the possibilities. A naked babe on a computer screen is just the same old babe, unless we add change. Technology doesn't magically transform—or even replace—erotic traditions. People do. The depth of both female and male sexuality can't be explored if we don't break the mold of prefabricated turn-ons. We've got the power to turn the tired, piston-driven porn formula into a fluid reflection of modern erotic culture. What's hot isn't limited to high heels and big cocks. Gender-bending, multiracial eroticism, bisexuality, and a range of other polymorphous departures from the standard are all a part of the erotic spectrum, but we rarely see them presented as such. That's why the genesis of this new erotic entertainment must be influenced by people with more diverse points of view. And I intend to be influential right from the very start.

Since I watched *Sleepless Nights* almost nine years ago, I've learned a lot about myself and the power of being female. I've learned that the erotic impulse is a part of being human, that it can't be controlled through political warfare or replaced by a silicon chip. I've learned that pornography is a mirror reflecting our rosiest desires, our blackest fears. It catches us looking. And these days I like some of what I see—especially when I've created it.

Lisa Palac lives in Southern California with her husband, Andrew Rice. She is the author of The Edge of the Bed: A Personal History of Sex and Popular Culture.

Gerry Gomez Pearlberg

BLUE MOVIE/MOON WALK

Blue Movie

You turn me on like the star of a blue movie,
five o'clock shadow under a huge blue moon.
Your feminine face all-altar boy, eclipse and allure,
your heart a lunar meadow I've no earthly hope of reaching.

We are in your living room watching blue movies.
I adore the term "blue movies," almost as much as I adore
watching you watch them in the dark, voyeur
of your voyeurism: *I love to watch you watch.*

Raven-haired beauties gyrate on the neon screen.
Outside your window blue-black crows begin to speak.

Your black and white TV's a small blue moon
perfect for blue movies in the five a.m. dark,
for blue corn chips punctuated by glinting grains of salt,
this moment's room a cool cartoon.

Your baby-powdered body smells like blue.
Our pink cunts swerve like submersibles
in their deep-sea denim channels
below smooth lagoons of baby blanket blue.

In just two cycles of the moon
we've made love in countless rooms,
pressed against so many walls and floors
like breathless astronauts sealed to one another,
adrift in pale mystery.

77

Moon Walk

I will follow you to the end of this film strip
as if it were the landing on the moon:
the reasons for the romance
will, of course, be questioned in the end—
there'll be the usual accusations of falsification
and conspiracy. When it's done
we'll each insist the miracle was staged.
But for now, we're glued to one another's sets,
mesmerized by one another's depths
of touch, each moan an icon,
our lonesome flesh carbonated by static,
eerie lighting and alienated costumes,
an ever-more-abstracted world,
accelerated breath, lack
of oxygen, loss of gravity—
and oh the delirious buoyancy, delicious terror
when the safety-cord frays and there's that sudden flash
of something you have always wanted,
hurtling toward you,
impossibly blue.

Gerry Gomez Pearlberg's writings have recently appeared in Apalachee Quarterly, Hers 2, *and* Queer View Mirror 2. *She is the editor of three poetry anthologies, including* Queer Dog: Homo/Pup/Poetry.

Audre Lorde

USES OF THE EROTIC: THE EROTIC AS POWER

There are many kinds of power, used and unused, acknowledged or otherwise. The erotic is a resource within each of us that lies in a deeply female and spiritual plane, firmly rooted in the power of our unexpressed or unrecognized feeling. In order to perpetuate itself, every oppression must corrupt or distort those various sources of power within the culture of the oppressed that can provide energy for change. For women, this has meant a suppression of the erotic as a considered source of power and information within our lives.

We have been taught to suspect this resource, vilified, abused, and devalued within western society. On the one hand, the superficially erotic has been encouraged as a sign of female inferiority; on the other hand, women have been made to suffer and to feel both contemptible and suspect by virtue of its existence.

It is a short step from there to the false belief that only by the suppression of the erotic within our lives and consciousness can women be truly strong. But that strength is illusory, for it is fashioned within the context of male models of power.

As women, we have come to distrust that power which rises from our deepest and nonrational knowledge. We have been warned against it all our lives by the male world, which values this depth of feeling enough to keep women around in order to exercise it in the service of men, but which fears this same depth too much to examine the possibilities of it within themselves. So women are maintained at a distant/inferior position to be psychically milked, much the same way ants maintain colonies of aphids to provide a life-giving substance for their masters.

But the erotic offers a well of replenishing and provocative force to the woman who does not fear its revelation, nor succumb to the belief that sensation is enough.

The erotic has often been misnamed by men and used against women. It has been made into the confused, the trivial, the psychotic, the plasticized sensation. For this reason, we have often turned away from the exploration and consideration of the erotic as a source of power and information, confusing it with its opposite, the pornographic. But pornography is a direct denial of the power of the erotic, for it represents the suppression of true feeling. Pornography emphasizes sensation without feeling.

The erotic is a measure between the beginnings of our sense of self and the chaos of our strongest feelings. It is an internal sense of satisfaction to which, once we have experienced it, we know we can aspire. For having experienced the fullness of this depth of feeling and recognizing its power, in honor and self-respect we can require no less of ourselves.

It is never easy to demand the most from ourselves, from our lives, from our work. To encourage excellence is to go beyond the encouraged mediocrity of our society is to encourage excellence. But giving in to the fear of feeling and working to capacity is a luxury only the unintentional can afford, and the unintentional are those who do not wish to guide their own destinies.

This internal requirement toward excellence which we learn from the erotic must not be misconstrued as demanding the impossible from ourselves nor from others. Such a demand incapacitates everyone in the process. For the erotic is not a question only of what we do; it is a question of how acutely and fully we can feel in the doing. Once we know the extent to which we are capable of feeling that sense of satisfaction and completion, we can then observe which of our various life endeavors bring us closest to that fullness.

The aim of each thing which we do is to make our lives and the lives of our children richer and more possible. Within the celebration of the erotic in all our endeavors, my work becomes a conscious decision—a longed-for bed which I enter gratefully and from which I rise up empowered.

Of course, women so empowered are dangerous. So we are taught to separate the erotic demand from most vital areas of our lives other than sex. And the lack of concern for the erotic root and satisfactions of our work is felt in our disaffection from so much of what we do. For instance, how often do we truly love our work even at its most difficult?

The principal horror of any system which defines the good in terms of profit rather than in terms of human need, or which defines human need to the exclusion of the psychic and emotional components of that need—the principal horror of such a system is that it robs our work of its erotic value, its erotic power and life appeal and fulfillment. Such a system reduces work to a travesty of necessities, a duty by which we earn bread or oblivion for ourselves and those we love. But this is tantamount to blinding a painter and then telling her to improve her work, and to enjoy the act of painting. It is not only next to impossible, it is also profoundly cruel.

As women, we need to examine the ways in which our world can be truly different. I am speaking here of the necessity for reassessing the quality of all the aspects of our lives and of our work, and of how we move toward and through them.

The very word *erotic* comes from the Greek word *eros*, the personification of love in all its aspects—born of Chaos, and personifying creative power and harmony. When I speak of the erotic, then, I speak of it as an assertion of the life-force of women; of that creative energy empowered, the knowledge and use of which we are now reclaiming in our language, our history, our dancing, our loving, our work, our lives.

There are frequent attempts to equate pornography and eroticism, two diametrically opposed uses of the sexual. Because of these attempts, it has become fashionable to separate the spiritual (psychic and emotional) from the political, to see them as contradictory or antithetical. "What do you mean, a poetic revolutionary, a meditating gunrunner?" In the same way, we have attempted to separate the spiritual and the erotic, thereby reducing the spiritual to a world of flattened affect, a world of the ascetic who aspires to feel nothing. But nothing is farther from the truth. For the ascetic position is one of the highest fear, the gravest immobility. The severe abstinence of the ascetic becomes the ruling obsession. And it is one not of self-discipline but of self-abnegation.

The dichotomy between the spiritual and the political is also false, resulting from an incomplete attention to our erotic knowledge. For the bridge which connects them is formed by the erotic—the sensual—those physical, emotional, and psychic expressions of what is deepest and strongest and richest within each of us, being shared: the passions of love, in its deepest meanings.

Beyond the superficial, the considered phrase, "It feels right to me," acknowledges the strength of the erotic into a true knowledge, for what that means is the first and most powerful guiding light toward any understanding. And understanding is a handmaiden which can only wait upon, or clarify, that knowledge, deeply born. The erotic is the nurturer or nursemaid of all our deepest knowledge.

The erotic functions for me in several ways, and the first is in providing the power which comes from sharing deeply any pursuit with another person. The sharing of joy, whether physical, emotional, psychic, or intellectual, forms a bridge between the sharers which can be the basis for understanding much of what is not shared between them, and lessens the threat of their difference.

Another important way in which the erotic connection functions is the open and fearless underlining of my capacity for joy. In the way my body stretches to music and opens into response, hearkening to its deepest rhythms, so every level upon which I sense also opens to the erotically satisfying experience, whether it is dancing, building a bookcase, writing a poem, examining an idea.

That self-connection shared is a measure of the joy which I know myself to be capable of feeling, a reminder of my capacity for feeling. And that deep and irreplaceable knowledge of my capacity for joy comes to demand from all of my life that it be lived within the knowledge that such satisfaction is possible, and does not have to be called *marriage*, nor *god*, nor *an afterlife*.

This is one reason why the erotic is so feared, and so often relegated to the bedroom alone, when it is recognized at all. For once we begin to feel deeply all the aspects of our lives, we begin to demand from ourselves and from our life-pursuits that they feel in accordance with that joy which we know ourselves to be capable of. Our erotic knowledge empowers us, becomes a lens through which we scrutinize all aspects of our existence, forcing us to evaluate those aspects honestly in terms of their relative meaning within our lives. And this is a grave responsibility, projected from within each of us, not to settle for the convenient, the shoddy, the conventionally expected, nor the merely safe.

During World War II, we bought sealed plastic packets of white, uncolored margarine, with a tiny, intense pellet of yellow coloring perched like a topaz just inside the clear skin of the bag. We would leave the margarine out for a while to soften, and then we would pinch the little pellet to break it inside the bag, releasing the rich yellowness into the soft pale mass of margarine. Then taking it carefully between our fingers, we would knead it gently back and forth, over and over, until the color had spread throughout the whole pound bag of margarine, thoroughly coloring it.

I find the erotic such a kernel within myself. When released from its intense and constrained pellet, it flows through and colors my life with a kind of energy that heightens and sensitizes and strengthens all my experience.

We have been raised to fear the *yes* within ourselves, our deepest cravings. But, once recognized, those which do not enhance our future lose their power and can be altered. The fear of our desires keeps them suspect and indiscriminately powerful, for to suppress any truth is to give it strength beyond endurance. The fear that we cannot grow beyond whatever distortions we may find within ourselves keeps us docile and loyal and obedient, externally defined, and leads us to accept many facets of our oppression as women.

When we live outside ourselves, and by that I mean on external directives only rather than from our internal knowledge and needs, when we live away from those erotic guides from within ourselves, then our lives are limited by external and alien forms, and we conform to the needs of a structure that is not based on human need, let alone an individual's. But when we begin to live from within outward, in touch with the power of the erotic within ourselves, and allowing that power to inform and illuminate our actions upon the world around us, then we begin to be responsible to ourselves in the deepest sense. For as we begin to recognize our deepest feelings, we begin to give up, of necessity, being satisfied with suffering and self-negation, and with the numbness which so often seems like their only alternative in our society. Our acts against oppression become integral with self, motivated and empowered from within.

In touch with the erotic, I become less willing to accept powerlessness, or those other supplied states of being which are not native to me, such as resignation, despair, self-effacement, depression, self-denial.

And yes, there is a hierarchy. There is a difference between painting a back fence and writing a poem, but only one of quantity. And there is, for me, no difference between writing a good poem and moving into sunlight against the body of a woman I love.

This brings me to the last consideration of the erotic. To share the power of each other's feelings is different from using another's feelings as we would use a kleenex. When we look the other way from our experience, erotic or otherwise, we use rather than share the feelings of those others who participate in the experience with us. And use without consent of the used is abuse.

In order to be utilized, our erotic feelings must be recognized. The need for sharing deep feeling is a human need. But within the european-american tradition, this need is satisfied by certain proscribed erotic comings-together. These occasions are almost always characterized by a simultaneous looking away, a pretense of calling them something else, whether a religion, a fit, mob violence, or even playing doctor. And this misnaming of the need and the deed give rise to that distortion which results in pornography and obscenity—the abuse of feeling.

When we look away from the importance of the erotic in the development and sustenance of our power, or when we look away from ourselves as we satisfy our erotic needs in concert with others, we use each other as objects of satisfaction rather than share our joy in the satisfying, rather than make connection with our similarities and our differences. To refuse to be conscious of what we are feeling at any time, however comfortable that might seem, is to deny a large part of the experience, and to allow ourselves to be reduced to the pornographic, the abused, and the absurd.

The erotic cannot be felt secondhand. As a Black lesbian feminist, I have a particular feeling, knowledge, and understanding for those sisters with whom I have danced hard, played, or even fought. This deep participation has often been the forerunner for joint concerted actions not possible before.

But this erotic charge is not easily shared by women who continue to operate under an exclusively european-american male tradition. I know it was not available to me when I was trying to adapt my consciousness to this mode of living and sensation.

Only now, I find more and more women-identified women brave enough to risk sharing the erotic's electrical charge without having to look away, and without distorting the enormously powerful and creative nature of that exchange. Recognizing the power of the erotic within our lives can give us the energy to pursue genuine change within our world, rather than merely settling for a shift of characters in the same weary drama.

For not only do we touch our most profoundly creative source, but we do that which is female and self-affirming in the face of a racist, patriarchal, and anti-erotic society.

Audre Lorde (1934-1992) published nine volumes of poetry and five works of prose. The Collected Poems of Audre Lorde *was published in 1997. "Uses of the Erotic: The Erotic as Power" was originally a paper delivered at the Fourth Berkshire Conference on the History of Women, Mount Holyoke College, 1978.*

Alan Helms

from YOUNG MAN FROM THE PROVINCES

The following memoir excerpt covers the early 1960s, a period during which Alan Helms lived a glamorous and promiscuous life in Manhattan.

Back in New York, Cyril Landers, a Canadian producer, got me an apartment at 404 East Fifty-fifth Street, a block-long building with another entrance at 405 East Fifty-fourth. For people in the know, 405 was called "four out of five" because of the many gay tenants who lived there, but the building was better known as a place where celebrities lived: Lucille Ball, Van Johnson, Paulette Goddard and Erich Maria Remarque, Joan Fontaine, Hermione Gingold et luminous al. My next door neighbor was Lotte Lenya; Noël Coward lived on the floor below. Mine was a small studio apartment on the sixteenth floor that looked out to Queens and the Nabisco sign.

Cyril and I had met maybe a year before, and we had begun seeing a lot of each other once I moved into the building. Cyril was my greatest fan and convinced of my eventual stardom. "But of course, dear Alan, there's no question about it. You must simply press on and one day soon we'll see your name up in lights." He loaned me his Jaguar convertible whenever I asked, and invited me to plays and dinners and opening night parties, and fixed me up with visiting English actors and ballet dancers, and introduced me to my own crushes whenever possible (the young Alain Delon, mon Dieu!), and had me to his apartment for afternoon teas with cucumber sandwiches and pastries, and joked a lot about my odd eating habits, and every few weeks he begged to blow me. "It's such a *small* thing for you, and it means *so* much to me." I don't know how often I heard that hustle, yet it never occurred to me to say that, all things considered, dropping my pants for a blow job was in fact a small thing for them, while being pressed into the service of their fantasies was such a large, disorienting, wholly unpleasant thing for me. Though I wasn't easy to get, especially when I didn't desire the other man, anyone who persisted and wasn't downright rude could usually have his way with me if he bided his time, led me into a sense of obligation, persuaded me he cared about the "real whole me," plied me with liquor, then made his pitch. God forbid I should offend anyone, especially a "friend."

On the other hand, the heir to a pharmaceutical fortune whose family paid him to live outside the country had a more straightforward and effective approach. If on one of his rare, brief visits to the States I would come to his suite in the Plaza and have sex with one of the sailors or Marines he picked up in the bar on West Forty-fifth Street where servicemen hustlers hung out, he'd give me a hundred dollars. And he wouldn't touch, just wanted to watch. Those transactions helped with the rent, and it was always a thrill to have sex with a "straight" Marine or sailor, especially when one rolled over on his tight military stomach. If only that neat arrangement had lasted longer, but I arrived at the Plaza one night to find myself paired with Jim Stryker, the principal swoon of the physique magazines. I was so unnerved at confronting one of my major sexual fantasies that I couldn't perform. When I left the Plaza that night, I was toting a bottle of Seagram's in lieu of my usual fee.

One day in the elevator at 404, a neighbor introduced me to Noël Coward. "You must come for drinks this evening, dear boy," so I did, and Noël and I struck up a friendship that I still recall with immense pleasure. It was the kind of relationship I loved at that time: considerate attention from a bright, famous, older rich man who didn't paw me, the kind of friendship I had with Bill Inge. Noël invited me to lunches and dinners, sometimes just the two of us, and he invented the nickname "Alan Upstairs" as a sign of his affection. He also encouraged my acting ambitions, which was one reason he frequently called to invite me down for a drink. "Alan Upstairs? You must drop everything and come down im-*meed*-yutly. There's someone I want you to meet." The someones turned out to be Gielgud, the Lunts, Garland, Olivier, Dietrich—people known by a single name like Noël himself, the most celebrated denizens of the world I longed to inhabit. I served mostly as decoration and appreciative audience on those occasions, but I didn't care, for such times were always a guaranteed thrill. Noël was always on with his friends, delighting in their company and extremely amusing, for he was a great performer and the most effortlessly, brilliantly witty person I've ever known. When he was well-matched, as with Gielgud, the exchanges were vertiginously hilarious. I had a front row seat on the aisle for the best private theater in town. Seeing Noël on these occasions, I had no trouble crediting the story that he'd written *Private Lives* in four days propped up in a sickbed in Singapore, and "Someday I'll Find You" while stalled in a cab in midtown Manhattan.

Back upstairs to my apartment, for a fuzzy year taken up with auditions and modeling and weekends in the Hamptons, voice lessons with Katharine Hepburn's coach, dinners with Noël and Bill Inge and some of the *West Side Story* crowd and the devoted Cyril, and lots of parties and plays and ballets and the gym and sex and more sex and still more sex until it was invading my dreams—all those coal black eyes and crystal blue eyes, hazel eyes glinting green in sunlight, curly hair and wavy hair, straight hair tousled and falling over the eyes, smooth white skin or black or dusty brown or olive skin, firm loins and muscled asses, firm chests with apricot nipples, bunches of pubic hair and the musky smells of crotch, the veins in calves and biceps and the tracery of veins on the inside of thighs and forearms, thick wrists circled with wispy hair, swollen lips and gleaming teeth parted in gasps and abandoned moans, flat saltlick stomachs and the curious dints running up and down the spine, the mysterious kneecaps and delicate hinges of arms and legs, the pliant ledges, sockets, mounds, clefts, and crevices of sex, and more sex, and still more sex.

Promiscuous? That's a hard word to define in a culture in which the average sexual experience now lasts all of two minutes (*The Harper's Index Book*, 1987, page 28). Besides, I was twenty-three or so and at the height of my sexual powers, such as they were. I didn't have a lover during most of this period, so there wasn't that to slow me down, and there was no AIDS to slow anybody down. And though I've said I didn't have a large libido, a lot of the sex I had came from lust manufactured in my head. That is, if you're weak in the self-acceptance department, then whatever your medium of exchange for acceptance, you can't get enough of it. Ask a diffident billionaire if he's got enough money.

It was tricky though, given my psychology. The guy had to turn me on enormously, convey that he wanted me a lot but not in a needy or cloying way, and then be able to lose himself in the sex. Then it was transcendent— like going through door after door into new worlds of sensual experience in which the boundaries of the self fell away, my mind was cleansed of the clutter of mentation, and I was open to the experience of melding with another, if not The Other. Then I could never get enough of it. My personal problems aside, the really good stuff we keep going back to for more, right? I've never known anybody to say "Beethoven's Ninth? Thanks but I've heard it."

Alan Helms lives in Boston, where he is a professor of literature at the University of Massachusetts. He has taught and written about Walt Whitman's poetry for more than a decade and is currently at work on a novel entitled Damaged Goods. Young Man from the Provinces *was published in 1995.*

Amudha Rajendran

HARRY

He drums fingers on her stomach.
She lies flat.
His hand moves to cup a breast.
She cups his hand.
Feel better? She asks.
His cheek rubs against hers.
I hope you feel better, she says, I tried.
He lifts an elbow for a kiss.
Been a long day at work.
She had to sit on him for an hour.
He was still grouchy.
He moves to part her knees.
Tum hurts, she says in a voice invented to distract.
It's baby-talk.
OK? he asks.
She snuggles.
Wrong word, he thinks. She can't snuggle—
her body's more plane than curve—she's sexy, not plush.
Not that she's that sleek. She's malay.
He's been on business planes to Hong Kong, Tokyo.
He's seen the jet capped girls.
But she's fluent. And she cooks chili shrimp.
Watches sports. Likes to dress for him.
And she has the look. Pressed.
She's more plane than curve.
She's got pudding texture. Tapioca sheen.
She locks her leg around his waist.
He holds her foot.
This little piggy—he starts. She isn't listening.

For dinner tomorrow? she asks.
He pulls her heel. If your feet were bound...chik!
I could just snap off a toe!
Oh, she says, let's sleep.
He watches her settle.
In the evening your eyes are...he decides they're raisins,
or pomegranate seeds.
Flirt! she grits. She's got this english.
Then, tickling him: Harry likes asian girls!
Her voice makes time go slow like Tai-chi.
In Japan, he's seen club girls with blunt hair-do's
squat in shortie kimono.
He thought they looked raw, like their food.
And he knows a little cantonese.
In China, the hookers wear mandarin collar.
Hard to tell apart from other girls.
Ha-ad to tell ap-aat! He does a chinese.
Does it for Charlie Chan.
Harry likes asian girls—
he thinks they're poignant.
Plums in Osaka.
Rice fields in Beijing.

Amudha Rajendran is a South Indian writer who grew up in Queens, New York. She writes fiction and poetry, and holds a Master's degree in poetry from New York University. She has been published in FEED, Arude, *and* Western Humanities Review.

Scarlot Harlot

SEX! MASSAGE! GIRLS!

Feminism Circa the '70s

In 1976 I organized a women's writers' group, dedicated to improving women's images. The "great artists" were mostly men. History was told from a man's point of view. Women were silenced and anonymous, but we would change all that. Together we would tell our secret stories! And I would find a place for my weird self.

Feminism was almost perfect for me…except for the fact that I was bisexual and couldn't stop fucking men. Of course, women had to attack me for that. I understood. Women had been so oppressed. And maybe I should stop fucking men? My comrade, anti-porn heroine Macha Womongold *(Pornography: A License to Kill)*, introduced me to some strategies to fight the patriarchy. Macha taught me about the goddess and about how proud I could be of everything female. Macha was even arrested for some obstreperous anti-porn activism. I admired her, but my feminist angst manifested itself in different ways.

For example, occasionally I'd don a few little lacy black things and jill off to my whore image in the mirror. And once, compelled by a passionate curiosity, I dressed up in my sexiest lingerie to dance on amateur night at the Golden Banana in Peabody, Massachusetts. Get over it or get into it, I advised myself. I never told my friends. They might not like it, but I didn't care. Cavorting publicly in lace and garters seemed bad (in the context of the patriarchy), but couldn't I explore that role and write poetry about my findings?

Maybe not. How was I to fit my talents and interests into the scheme of society? My college career had been a bust. My political beliefs conflicted with my masturbatory practices. I was a good girl in a bad girl's psyche.

Or vice versa. Anyway, the blizzard of '78 was the last straw. I moved to San Francisco to find my fate.

Sex! Massage! Girls!

September 1978—San Francisco was like a different country, I thought.

Everything was wonderful, except for the fact that my boyfriend broke up with me. I didn't know anyone and my friends were all back home. I had no job, and the bills were due on my credit cards. In fact, I felt desperate and low and confused and horrible about myself. I look back in wonder at this cross-roads, but it was certainly the lowest point in my quasi-torrid life. It's odd, how the most desperate circumstances can lead to one's salvation.

Besides, San Francisco had fabulous shops and I needed furniture and a new vintage wardrobe.

I had heard that once you agreed to sell it, there was no turning back. I couldn't resist. I took the dare.

A Woman's Last Resort

I took a job at a very seedy massage parlor. I figured they must be selling sex, because they certainly weren't selling ambiance. I was immediately enamored of my friendly, beautiful co-workers, and my first trick was handsome and sweet. After work, I rushed home to look in the mirror.

Now there's a prostitute, I told myself. I hadn't changed. I looked back across that line that had separated me from the old me, the good girl. The line had disappeared.

Prostitutes' issues and images became the center of my life. I'm not say-ing I loved the tricks or the work. It can be fun, especially if you like things like skydiving or hang gliding. But what I liked was getting this insider's view, this secret story to tell. The silence of prostitutes became overbearingly loud. Suddenly, I was surrounded by mute and righteous women and brazen, sexual women and poor women, and junkies and addicted women, and young women who couldn't fight back against rape, and women of other races, and mothers, and women who used to be men, and women who used to be secretaries, and wild, curious women who needed money, just like me.

My new discoveries gave me excuses and revelations:

Other women still wear high heels, bras and lipstick. They walk around in fetish gear for free, sexualizing themselves at every opportunity, and I'm sup-posed to not get paid to play this role. It's all whoring just the same.

All my life I'd been trading sex for approval and for relationships with boyfriends. A lot of women trade sex for some advantage, or for basic survival. This is part of life and I have a right to look square into it.

Jeffrey Masson may be able to brag about having sex with thousands of women. His conquests are not stigmatized. But I'm supposedly promiscuous. I hate that word.

First the patriarchy socializes me to be a sex object, then it sics its flunky cops and rapists on me. I won't be terrorized by these envoys.

Carol Leigh, aka Scarlot Harlot, has been working as a prostitute, activist, and artist in the Bay Area since the early 1980s. She has coordinated a street outreach program through the San Francisco Coalition on Prostitution, providing condoms and health and safety information to street workers. She has written, performed in, and produced videos on prostitutes' issues, and has received numerous awards for her documentaries, including three awards from Visions of US at the American Film Institute. She's a member of the Bay Area Sex Worker Advocacy Network (BAYSWAN). This essay appeared in a longer version on the BAYSWAN web site, http://www.bayswan.org, in 1994.

Andy Warhol and Pat Hackett

from POPism: THE WARHOL '60s

P aul [Morrissey] thought the Factory should be more under control, more like a regular office. He wanted it to become a real moviemaking-moneymaking business enterprise, and he never could see the point of having all the young kids and old kids hanging around all the time for no particular reason. He wanted to phase out the drop-in, lounging habits of the past few years. This was inevitable, really—we'd gotten to know so many people all over town that our small circle had expanded to hundreds and hundreds, and we just couldn't have the all-day-all-night "open house" anymore, it had gotten too crazy.

Paul turned out to be a good office manager. He was the one who'd talk to business people, read *Variety*, and look around for good-looking or funny (ideally, both) kids to be in our movies. He'd dream up theories to throw out to the interviewers—for instance, he had a whole presentation about how similar our organization was to the old M-G-M star system. "We only believe in stars, and our kids are actually very similar to the Walt Disney kids, except of course that they're *modern* children, so naturally they take drugs and have sex."

Most things Paul told the newspapers looked outrageous in print. At first, it was only a comment here and there, but by the end of the next year, interviews about us were full of his quotable spiels. The early Factory style had come out of Pop Art, where you didn't talk, you just did outrageous things, and when you spoke to the press, it was with "gestures," which was more artistic. But now that style was all played out—everyone was ready for some articulation, and Paul was nothing if not articulate.

To make the Factory into more of the "business office" he had in mind, Paul put partitions up around one-third of the floor space, dividing the loft into little cubicles. The intention was to let people know that the Factory was now a place where actual business was conducted—typewriter/paper clip/manila envelope/filing cabinet business. It didn't exactly work out the way he'd envisioned it, though: people started using the cubicles for sex.

Meanwhile, we were becoming the target for some very aggressive attacks on drugs and homosexuality. If the attacks were done in a clever, funny way, I enjoyed reading them as much as anybody. But if someone in the press put us down, without humor, on "moral grounds," I would think, "Why are they attacking *us*? Why aren't they out there attacking, say, Broadway musicals, where there are probably more fags in any one production than there are at the whole Factory? Why aren't they attacking dancers and fashion designers and interior decorators? Why *us*? when all I have to do is turn on my TV to see hundreds of actors who are so gay you can't believe your eyes and nobody bothers *them*. Why us, when you could meet your favorite matinee idols from Hollywood who gave out interviews all the time on what their dream girls were like and they'd all have their *boyfriends* with them?"

Naturally, the Factory had fags; we were in the entertainment business and—That's Entertainment! Naturally, the Factory had more gays than, say, Congress, but it probably wasn't even as gay as your favorite TV police show. The Factory was a place where you could let your "problems" show and nobody would hate you for it. And if you worked your problems up into entertaining routines, people would like you even more for being strong enough to say you were different and actually have fun with it. What I mean is, there was no hypocrisy at the Factory, and I think the reason we were attacked so much and so vehemently was because we refused to play along and be hypocritical and covert. That really incensed a lot of people who wanted the old stereotypes to stay around. I often wondered, "Don't the people who play those image games care about all the miserable people in the world who just can't fit into stock roles?"

When kids we knew would have nervous breakdowns or commit suicide, people would go, "See? See? Look what you did to them! They were fine until they met *you!*" Well, all I can say to that is, if a person was "fine" when they met us, then they stayed fine, and if they had bad problems–sometimes nothing and no one could fix them up. I mean, there's always been an awful lot of people out there on the streets talking to themselves. It wasn't like someone was issuing me newborn babies with good chemicals and letting me raise them.

And there were a lot of sexually straight people around the Factory, too, anyway. The gay thing was what was flamboyant, so it got attention, but there were a lot of guys hanging around because of all the beautiful girls.

95

Of course, people said the Factory was degenerate just because "anything went" there, but I think that was really a very good thing. As one straight kid said to me, "It's nice not to be *trapped* into something, even if that's what you are." For example, if a man sees two guys having sex, he finds out one of two things: either he's turned on or he's turned off—so then he knows where he stands in life. I think people should see absolutely *everything* and then decide for themselves—not let other people decide for them. Whatever else it did, the Factory definitely helped a lot of people decide.

This was the summer I met Candy Darling.

Most people would probably think of the following year, '68, as the time we were getting involved with the drag queens who were around downtown, because it wasn't until then that they first cropped up in our movies, when Paul used Jackie Curtis and Candy in *Flesh*. Of course we'd had Mario Montez in a few of our early films, but since Mario only dressed up as a woman for performances—out in the world, he would never be in drag—he was more like a show business transvestite than the social-sexual phenomenon the true drags were.

As late as '67 drag queens still weren't accepted in the mainstream freak circles. They were still hanging around where they'd always hung around—on the fringes, around the big cities, usually in crummy little hotels, sticking to their own circles—outcasts with bad teeth and body odor and cheap makeup and creepy clothes. But then, just like drugs had come into the average person's life, sexual blurs did, too, and people began identifying a little more with drag queens, seeing them more as "sexual radicals" than as depressing losers.

In the sixties, average types started having sex-identity problems, and some people saw a lot of their own questions about themselves being acted out by the drag queens. So then, naturally, people seemed to sort of want them around—almost as if it made them feel better because then they could say to themselves, "I may not know exactly what I am, but at least I know I'm not a drag queen." That's how in '68, after so many years of being repelled by them, people started accepting drag queens—even courting them, inviting them everywhere. With the new attitude of mind-before-matter / where-your-head-is-at / do-your-own-thing, the drags had the Thing of Things going for them. I mean, it *was* quite a thing, it took up all of their time. "Does she tuck?" the other queens would ask Jackie about Candy, and Jackie would say something oblique like "Listen, even Garbo has to rearrange her jewels."

Candy herself referred to his penis as "my flaw." There was always that ques-

tion of what to call the drags—"him" or "her" or a little bit of both. You usually just did it intuitively. Jackie I always called "him" since I'd known him
before he went into drag, and Candy Darling and Holly Woodlawn were "her"
because they were already in it when I met up with them.

But if in '68 the drag queens were incorporated into the fun of the general freak
scene, in '67 they were still pretty "queer." One hot August afternoon during
that Love Summer of '67, Fred and I were out walking around the West Village
on our way to pick up some pants I was having made up at the Leather Man.
There were lots of flower children tripping and lots of tourists watching them
trip. Eighth Street was a total carnival. Every store had purple trip books and
psychedelic posters and plastic flowers and beads and incense and candles, and
there were Spin-Art places where you squeezed paint onto a spinning wheel and
made your own Op Art painting (which the kids loved to do on acid), and pizza
parlors and ice cream stands—just like an amusement park.

Walking just ahead of us was a boy about nineteen or twenty with wispy
Beatle bangs, and next to him was a tall, sensational blonde drag queen in very
high heels and a sundress that she made sure had one strap falling onto her
upper arm. The two of them were laughing, and as we turned onto Greenwich
Avenue, where the hustlers leaned against the wall, we saw the blonde throw
her head back and say loud, for all the cruising fags to hear, "Oh, just look at
all these Green Witches." Then the boy happened to turn around. He recognized me and asked for my autograph on the paper bag he had from the
English clothes boutique Countdown. I asked him what was in the bag.

"Satin shorts for the tap-dancing in my new play, *Glamour, Glory, and Gold.*
It opens in September; I'll send you an invitation. My name's Jackie Curtis."

I was taking a closer look at the blonde. She was much more attractive from
a distance—up close, I could see that she had real problems with her teeth,
but she was still the most striking queen around. Jackie introduced the blonde
as "Hope Slattery," which was the name Candy was using in those days—her
real name was Jimmy Slattery and she was from Massapequa, Long Island.

At some point much later on, after I'd gotten to know both of them very
well, Jackie told me how he and Candy had gotten together:

"I met her in practically the same spot that we met you—right by Sutter's
ice cream parlor—and I told her, 'There's something, uh, different about
you.' And she said, 'I draw attention because I'm like women on the screen.'
And I looked at her and thought, 'Now, *please.* Just *who* is this one like on the
screen?...' Because, Andy, she was a mess. Before she started taking care of her-

self a little, she looked like the maid in *Dinner at Eight*. Her teeth…Her teeth…" Jackie shook his head in a let's-not-think-about-her-teeth gesture. "To be truthful, she looked more like the fists of Señor Wences than anything else—a blond wig on a fist with lipstick and two button eyes…. Señor Wences? On 'The Ed Sullivan Show'? Anyway, we went into Sutter's and bought a napoleon. She bit into it and her one gold tooth fell out. We stood there staring at it in the palm of her hand, laughing hysterically and going, 'Oh, my God, oh, my God…' I thought to myself, 'This woman is incredible.' I walked her back to where she was staying—the Hotel Seventeen on Seventeenth Street between Third Avenue and Stuyvesant Park, a quiet street with little buildings and lots of window boxes and trees. I was so naive, I didn't recognize all the classic signs that she was dodging her bill there—even when I saw that they were holding her stuff down in the lobby. When she saw that, she turned right around on her high heels and ran across the street. When I caught up with her, she was peering into some guy's ground-floor windows. A dog came out to the bars, and she was going, 'Isn't that dog pret-ty? Pret-ty dog, pret-ty dog…' And I thought to myself, 'She's trying to convince that *dog* that she's a real woman!' Meanwhile she didn't know how to get her stuff back—she'd crawled out of her window and she was ashamed. They knew her scene, and she really was scared.

"Candy touched me so much because I saw myself in her—I was so up-in-the-air myself. I wrote *Glamour, Glory, and Gold* right away and put her in it that fall."

When you hear a person say they're from New York City, you expect them to be really hip and all that. So when Jackie talked about himself as being "naive," it was hard to believe, because after all, he'd grown up on Second Avenue and Tenth Street—the upper Lower East Side–living with his grandmother, Slugger Ann, who owned a bar there.

I said to him, "Come *on*, Jackie, how can you talk about 'naive' when you grew up in the East Village?"

"Yeah, well," he said, giving me a look, "that's not exactly Greenwich Village, you know."

I saw his point. For a kid, the West Village street scene was a lot farther away than just the few blocks in physical distance.

Jackie and Candy hung around together for the rest of the summer, and Slugger Ann even gave Candy a job as a barmaid. "My grandmother," Jackie said, "did not know that Candy was no genetic female. And she certainly did not know Candy would come to work in a slip! But having her there did draw in some new customers—a few fairies from the West Village who couldn't believe she really had a job."

Getting a job in a bar was a dream come true for Candy. She wanted to be the kind of woman you'd find in a diner on Tenth Avenue "slinging hash"— that was maybe her favorite fantasy. Either that or a female whore that men slapped around and treated like dirt. Or even a lesbian—she liked that, too. Anything but a man.

Candy didn't want to be a perfect woman—that would be too simple, and besides it would give her away. What she wanted was to be a woman with all the little problems that a woman has to deal with—runs in her stocking, runny mascara, men that left her. She would even ask to borrow Tampaxes, explaining that she had a terrible emergency. It was as if the more real she could make the little problems, the less real the big one—her cock—would be.

Eric once told me that he'd known Candy from way back in '64. "I used to see her and Rona walking around Bleecker Street. They rode in on the train together from Massapequa and they'd pretend to be girl friends—lesbians." Rona was another Max's girl. "Candy was going to this German doctor on Seventy-ninth and Fifth that we all went to," he said. "It was like a dating agency there—everybody knew everybody. Candy was just starting to sprout little rosebuds underneath her blouse from the hormones he was giving her."

The Beatles' *Sgt. Pepper* music was the main strain you heard all through the summer; you'd hear it playing absolutely everywhere. And the Sgt. Pepper jacket was the general uniform for the boys at this point—the high-collar military jacket with red epaulets and piping that they wore with stovepipe pants— nobody was wearing bell-bottoms anymore. As for hair, lots of the boys had theirs Keith Richard-style—spiky and all different lengths....

Andy Warhol was an artist, filmmaker, writer, rock producer, and publisher. A leading figure of the Pop Art movement, he used his canvasses of dollar bills, soup cans, disasters, and celebrities to erase the distinction between high and popular culture. His career shaped and encompassed the underground scene of drugs, sex, and punk rock, much of which transpired at his Manhattan loft known as the Factory. Warhol died in 1987.

Pat Hackett was one of Warhol's closest confidantes for many years. In addition to co-writing POPism, *she is the editor of* The Andy Warhol Diaries *and co-author of the screenplay for* Bad, *Warhol's cult movie classic.*

James Earl Hardy

from B-BOY BLUES

In the novel B-Boy Blues, *Mitchell Crawford, a twenty-seven-year-old black gay journalist who lives in the Fort Greene section of Brooklyn, New York, meets the hip-hop lovin', street-struttin', crazy crotch-grabbin' B-boy of his lustful dreams: Raheim Rivers, a twenty-one-year-old homeboy from Harlem who is a bike messenger. At first their relationship revolves around sex, but soon Mitchell realizes Raheim is more than a lean, mean sex machine. He's intelligent responsible, and very affectionate. But Mitchell still doesn't know much about the kind of life Raheim leads as a "ruffneck." In the following excerpt, chapter twenty-four of the novel, he gets an eye-opening view of it when Raheim and his homiez, D. C. and Angel, take him to a "B-boy bash."*

From the moment I walked into the third-floor apartment in the six-story housing project, it was obvious what a "B-boy bash" was. Every single person was (or, like me, came with) a B-boy. And, if you didn't fall into either category, don't even try to bum-rush the show. When we arrived, two guys who looked like B-boys were being escorted to the stairs and then thrown down them by a rotund bouncer who accused them of being "wannabees." It was not a cute scene.

But in the somewhat dark, musky-hot (where was the air-conditioning?), incense-maryjane-smelling, loftlike living room were a good seventy brothas who were the real thing. Ranging in age from fourteen to forty, all were in some state of banjeedom: unlaced boots or sneakers, droopy pants, exposed undergear, shirtless chests, cabled necks, goldcapped teeth and adorned fingers, and backwards or sideways tilted caps. Some looked like they'd just escaped in their jailhouse-striped gear. Others were carrying wooden canes, as if they were in some sort of fraternity (I would later find out that they were). Like they do in the bars and clubs, most were standing against the walls (there was nowhere to sit), posturing and posing, staring at no one or no one thing in particular but trying to outman each other. And even those that danced had to do it with cool. Their feet never left the ground, their bodies strutted back and forth in a rockabilly motion, their hands were glued either to their sides or their dicks, their heads swayed up and down but stayed cocked, and their faces remained expressionless, as if they weren't enjoying what they were doing.

This is a party? I asked myself, surveying the scene. *Seems more like a Narcissists Anonymous meeting.* I also thought of the title of a recent Aretha tune: "What You See Is What You Sweat."

As was the case almost anyplace we went, Raheim knew just about everybody. It took us a good half hour to get in the party, because folks were stopping him all around us (and, of course, he didn't introduce me to any of them). Raheim had on his usual, get-loose party gear—a black tank that says COOLEY LOVE, black jean shorts, white boxers with clubs (visible since his pants were way off his waist), and black boots. But he added an extra item to this ensemble: a white head rag with black polka dots. I was surprised when he came out of the bathroom with this on. He had never worn one before—at least in my presence. He really looked like a gangsta. I didn't question it; I figured the reason for it would be revealed when we got to the party, and it was. At least two dozen other fellas were sporting their own head rags, one in the style of an American flag. I laughed, wondering how ex-prez George Bush would've felt about someone wearing that treasured symbol on their head.

After the boyz and I found a spot of our own for the evening Raheim grabbed my arm: "Le's dance, Baby. This my song." Of course, it was "That's the Way Love Goes." We hit the floor and people gave us room. Raheim was always surprised that I knew all the latest dances and could keep up with him. In fact, he'd gag when I'd slide in and under his legs and over his head. He had a lot of energy (not to mention stamina) and could dance all night. If he wanted to, I didn't mind. And after the triumphs of that night—beating D.C. three times but also gaining his respect—I was more than ready.

No matter the song, no matter the style (house, dance, rap, reggae), we jumped and humped and bumped. No, let's say we sexed it up. I ground my behind into him with such a vengeance that Raheim claimed he came (talk about dirty dancing). But at three different times during the night, he worked this same groove with other people—two of those times with one person I didn't know and didn't care for. I remembered him from Gay Pride Day. Like then, this ho, who was a lighter version of me, ignored me, as if I wasn't stand-

101

ing right in front of him, his hands all over Pooquie. Uh-huh, as the song he shook his hips to declared, he was down with O. P. P. And Raheim, while he wasn't exactly returning the attention, once again allowed it to go on. I felt like a fool. I also felt like wringing that trollop's neck with Raheim's shirt, which I was holding. Angel must have sensed that I wasn't pleased. He asked me whether I wanted to dance. I said no. He told me not to worry, that Raheim only had eyes for me.

"David still on his shit, but Raheim ain't havin' none o' dat again," he explained, sippin' on gin and juice. "You think he get da message it's ova…"

"What do you mean, 'get the message it's over'?"

He looked as if I had just caught him with his hand in the cookie jar. "I uh, uh…maybe Raheim should tell ya…"

"Oh, no, Angel, finish what you start," I demanded, preventing him from walking away by holding on to his arm. "Were they…are they involved?"

Seeing no way out, he confessed. "Dey was…las' summa."

My blood began to boil. I went to the bathroom to cool off. What the fuck is his problem? He gets bent out of shape if I so much as shake hands with his boyz, but he flaunts his ex right in front of my face, gyrating and pulsating as if they were still together. By the time I waited on line and splashed cold water on my face, I decided that I wasn't going to be overly jealous like him. But then I walked back into the room and almost lost it. David, wearing black sneakers and a black bodysuit that seemed to be glued to his frame, was now imitating me, throwing his big ass all up in Pooquie's dick. Raheim would kill me if I came out of the house looking like that, but that is obviously what he likes— he was holding on to David's waist, enjoying the ride. I wanted to cut in and cut them both up.

What made the whole thing even worse was that they and the two dozen other couples on the floor were groovin' to Buju Banton's "Boom Bye Bye"— a song which encourages folks to kill homosexuals. How can a room full of faggots even allow a song like that to be played at a party? I wanted to find the host and voice my concern. But that would've done no good—he was one of those going wild on the floor. And what a queen! There were, to my surprise, many there—big bad boyz you'd never think would say "Miss Thing" or "Miss Honey" but who acted as if they invented those phrases, not to mention the limp wrist and vogueing. The concept seemed weird to me: why have all that body, all that bass, and act like that? All of these children had their eyes on the more "masculine" fellas in the house. But there certainly seemed to be more "man-on-man" pairings, which made me giggle at a question Anderson asked me years ago: "How do you know if someone is a, uh, top or bottom?"

Anyway, this death-dancing scene, along with the gross popularity of the *n*-word (Raheim and his boyz caught themselves several times before saying it at my house but joined their peers in the nigga chanting as soon as we arrived), was a bit too much self-hatred for me. I wanted to leave. But I just stood near one of the four giant speakers that were in each corner of the room, out of Raheim's view, not being banjee or queenie at all. After two more monotonous-sounding reggae records, the deejay finally cut me some slack by mixing Whitney and Chaka's versions of "I'm Every Woman"—and I had to do a double take. Raheim was doing the electric slide with David and company, mouthing all the words to the song, pointing to himself and slapping his chest *e-ver-y-time* the divas declared they were every woman. *Now* that was a sight worth seeing. *You're* every woman, it's all in *you*, hunh, Raheim? I couldn't help but laugh out loud.

Then one of my songs came on—the dope house mix of "Ain't 2 Proud 2 Beg" by TLC—and I wanted to dance. I peeked over to see if Raheim and David had resumed fuckin' each other and they had. Now that heifer had his hands inside Pooquie's boxers, which, like his pants, were so low you could see his pubic hair and a good chunk of his ass. Raheim also had a handful of David's butt. I didn't want to make a scene, and I knew I would if I went over to them and butted in (pun intended). I searched for the other boyz, but they were both occupied: Angel was shaking it with one of the only other Latino fellas at the party, and D. C. had some cute, chocolate muscle boy who was shorter than him up against a wall, just workin' it. So, I just bopped in place.

"Wha's up?"

For a second I thought it was Pooquie, because of the bass-boomin' voice. But my eyes focused up—way up—on a B-boy, maybe thirty, who had been steppin' with seven other frat boyz earlier in the evening. One wouldn't know there are gay and bisexual men in fraternities, since most are in the closet. Babyface, who is a Kappa, and Adam, who is Sigma, say some frats do use homosexual activity as an undercover rite of passage to promote "true brotherhood bonding," but won't accept those who identify themselves as gay. I certainly didn't expect to see any at this party. And, to be taller than Pooquie and just as built, this guy was not clunky on his feet at all. It takes a lot of skill and flexibility to do those moves—especially with a cane—and he was doing them with ease.

He had a clean head, which a Chicago Bulls cap barely sat on top of. His eyes were glassy and gray. His goatee was shaped in a box with, no hair between his chin and rosy lips. His nose was broad just like his shoulders. His legs were long and sleek. His red tee was over his left shoulder, and his black-and-red Spandex clung to him nicely. His nipples were sharp. It looked like he had on no underwear. His thang was hangin' kind of low and, judging by the outline in his pants, was *big*. His high-top black-and-red Air Jordans were unlaced.

As B. D. would say, he was tall, light, and lovely. And he made me nervous.

"Hi," I mouthed.

He nodded at the floor. "Dance?"

"Uh, no, no thanks," I said, wishing he'd go away. He was tempting me. I continued bopping.

He moved in, down and closer. "Ya sure? Looks like ya do ta me…"

"Well, I'd like to but…I'm here with my man."

He grinned, showing a gap in his upper front teeth that was very sexy. "Uh-huh, an' where he be?"

My heart sank as my eyes fell on Pooquie and David. "He's…he's dancing"

"She-it, he dancin', leavin' a fine lil' thang like you by yo'self?" He checked me out from head to toe. "You wearin' dem shorts, small fry…" I felt out-dressed in a light brown blouse, sandals, and brown shorts which, of course, couldn't hide my ass. Hmmmm, that line sounded familiar. Do all these B-boys use it?

I smiled. "Thank you, but…"

"You wanna dance, baby, so c'mon…I ain' gon' hur'cha."

He grabbed my arm and took me to the floor. I didn't put up a fight. Hell, if Raheim can dance with whomever he wants, why can't I?

At first I wouldn't let him touch me. At least if Pooquie saw us, he wouldn't be able to say that I was flirting. But it just became a natural thing for him to do. Our bodies blended into each other's well. I allowed him to slide his hands along my waist, then my legs, while I held on to his shoulders, tracing the brand on his arm, curious as to what it felt like. He smiled and whispered: "If ya like da way dat feels, I got somethin' else for ya." I asked what frat he was in. The Q-Dogs: Omegas. By the time the song went off, I had my arms around his neck while he rocked us, enjoying the feel of my rump. Yes, it was turning me the fuck on and he knew it. "Oh yeah, baby…," he groaned, grinning up a storm. I blushed.

It figures that "Rump Shaker" was coming on next—and that Raheim would appear out of nowhere.

He jerked the guy away from me, knocking me against the wall and causing folks around us to run for cover. "Nigga, wha'tha *fuck* you think you doin'?"

The fella threw up his hands, pointing at Raheim. "Motha-fucka, wha'da fuck you think *you* doin'?"

Raheim got all up in his face, putting his hands on his hips. "You ain' got *no* fuckin' bizness puttin' yo' hands where they *ain'* s'pose ta be!"

"Nigga, pleeze, you got a claim on ev'ry *bitch* in da fuckin' place?" He pushed Raheim.

Their hands went up and they went for theirs, rumbling and tumbling to the ground, tussling on the floor right in front of me, fists flying and falling on hard flesh. Up against the wall, I couldn't watch. I ran out of the room against the traffic running to see the fight. I bumped into D. C.

"Wha'da fuck's goin' on?" he asked, the vodka so strong I could smell it on his breath.

I was hysterical. *"Raheim is fighting in there!"*

He took off. "Aw she-it!"

I kept moving along, shaking, ending up outside the apartment in the hallway. I was distraught, as the four or five people chatting in the hall could see. One fella approached me and asked if I was all right. I told him I would be. He gave me his handkerchief so I could wipe my face. I thanked him.

A few minutes later, the guy I danced with came out. He held some tissue up to his eye. Was it black? He bent down to face me as I sat on the top step of the stairs.

"When you wan' a real man an' not some fuckin' chump, le'me know, small fry," he said, dropping a card in my lap. "I know how ta trea'cha." He puckered up and tried to kiss me, but I moved my head away. He snickered, mouthed a kiss, rose, and strode down the stairs. After he had gone, I tore up the card and threw it toward the open window.

Five minutes later, Raheim appeared with D. C. and Angel. He was nursing a bloody nose. I freaked out.

I got up and ran to him. "Oh my God, Raheim, are you all—"

"Don' fuckin' touch me!" he shouted, pulling away and heading for the stairs. I looked at D. C. and Angel. They both shrugged. Not wanting to wake up the whole building, I just followed him down. When we got outside, I placed my hand on his shoulder. He knocked it away.

I was dumbstruck. "Raheim, what's wrong with you?"

He threw his arms up, causing me to jump back. "Wha's wrong wit *me?* Wha'tha fuck is wrong wit *you?* Throwin' yo' shit 'round, all up in some motha-fucka's face an' causin' all shit ta go down. *Day-am,* I can' take yo' ass *no* fuckin' place wit'out you playin' me..."

I squinted. I noticed the bruise on his left cheek. "What?"

He paced. "I ain' bring yo' ass out here ta dance wit any nigga you want. Was you gonna go home wit him an' shit?"

"Oh, I see..." I tried to calm down but couldn't. The words came out angry. "I'm supposed to stand against a *fuck*ing wall and wait for you to finish danc-ing with whoever the *fuck* you want to, even your *fuck*ing ex, and then when you snap your fingers, dance when *you* want?"

Raheim turned to Angel and put his left hand in his face. "Motha-fucka, you got a *big* fuckin' mouth."

Angel threw up his hands. "Yo, man, I ain' mean ta tell, swear ta God."

Raheim was not moved. "*Shut up,* motha-fucka."

"Raheim, don't blame him," I interjected. "You have only yourself to blame. He didn't do anything and I didn't do a damn thing wrong. You did all of this to yourself."

That's when he came for me.

D. C. jumped in front of him. "Yo Brotha Man, now, don' do dis shit, a'right. Dey gon' call da fuckin' cops."

He was screaming at the top of his lungs as D. C. pushed him toward the Jeep. Smoke was coming out of his ears. *"Get offa me, man! I don't give a fuck! You betta stay outa my fuckin' face, you hear, bitch? I fuck you up! You got a whole lota fuckin' mouth..."*

I was afraid. When Angel touched my shoulder, I screamed and started trembling. I walked around in a circle, feeling lost, unaware that folks were watching, snickering. Raheim said he was going to fuck me up. He called me a bitch. A *bitch.* My whole body went numb.

After walking around the corner with Raheim, D. C. came back up to us. He grabbed Angel and they huddled together. After their little talk, they approached me.

D. C. was somber. "Uh, we gon' git you a cab."

They weren't going to take me home. I didn't hear anything else they said.

I didn't say anything. D. C. went into the street and hailed one just like that. Angel opened the door for me. I got in. He closed the door. D. C. gave the driver money and told him where to go. Good thing—I couldn't talk. The cab took off.

Before I knew it, I was home. I got out. It felt like I was in a trance. I don't remember taking out my key. I don't remember opening the downstairs door. I don't remember walking up the stairs to my apartment. I don't remember getting into bed.

But, still clutching Raheim's shirt, I do remember crying myself to sleep.

James Earl Hardy is the author of B-Boy Blues, 2nd Time Around, *and* If Only For One Nite. *He has also written two nonfiction titles—a biography of Spike Lee and a portrait of Boyz II Men—and is featured in* Shade: An Anthology of Fiction by Gay Men of African Descent. *His work has appeared in* Essence, Emerge, Newsweek, Entertainment Weekly, Vibe, *the* Washington Post, New York Newsday, *and* OUT. *He lives in New York City.*

Sandra J. Chu

UNMARKED

For a year, the mailman delivered
brown papered magazines. And even though she disclaimed them,
they help me keep up with the guys in the office, I knew
my mother and I were going through a sexual crisis at the same time.
After tennis practice I'd slide them
out of their sheaths, masturbate on the couch, taking care
not to wrinkle them with my sweat.
I liked the letters. And the photo stories showing sex
in elevators, on airplanes and in offices. I calculated orgasms
to arrive before I had to make dinner, eager for them, but moaning
only as I thought I should. While I stayed home, my faster girlfriends
were having sex. They giggled, used words like *quick, wet,* and *hurt.*
No one said *orgasm.* Then as strangely as they had appeared,
my mother's subscriptions stopped. I had to find back issues hidden
beneath her bed, or interleaved between *Time* and *The Smithsonian*
on her nightstand. Soon, even those were gone.
Years later, I packed for college. For a joke she gave me a *Playgirl.*
Its pages seemed so chaste, so unnecessarily guarded and romantic.

Sandra J. Chu was a recipient of A. Magazine's *honorable mention for poetry in 1995.
Her work has been published in the* Asian Pacific American Journal, Washington Square
Literary Review, Cream City Review, Chachalaca Literary Review, *and will be anthol-
ogized in* Drive, She Said. *Chu lives in Princeton, where she teaches English and is the
Associate Director of Admissions at the Princeton Day School.*

Jenifer Levin

LOVE AND DEATH & OTHER DISASTERS

Disease, health! Spirit, nature! Are those contradictions? I ask, are they problems? No...the recklessness of death is in life, it would not be life without it....Death is a great power. One takes off one's hat before him, and goes weavingly on tiptoe...Reason stands simple before him, for reason is only virtue, while death is release, immensity, abandon, desire. Desire, says my dream. Lust, not love. Death and love—no, I cannot make a poem of them, they don't go together. Love stands opposed to death. It is love, not reason, that is stronger than death....And with this—I awake.   Thomas Mann, *The Magic Mountain*

Michael stumbled into bed with them early morning, the way he did most Sundays. Callie had been used to it for years. The Oedipal complex didn't require a male father and female mother, she knew—just a couple of adults sharing intimacy would do. Kids had extraordinary radar for it. One wet unguarded kiss, one groan of passion through a bedroom door, and they'd be there like white on rice.

This time, though, she and Pat hadn't even got around to it. They hadn't, in fact, for weeks, though both had at times been willing. A waste of Pat, Callie knew. Pat who was strong and soft-butch handsome in her way, who could be smart and tender. But something in them, between them, had lately conjured uncertainty. Maybe all the stuff with Lu, Callie'd speculated in therapy. No shit, her shrink replied.

Groggy-eyed now, the kid disturbed nothing, just tumbled over a mess of sheets in the dark and wedged himself firmly between the fully clad two of them.

"Callie."

"What, Mike?"

"Mom Lu's dying."

"I know she's dying, honey."

109

"No, no, I had a dream." He was half conscious but insistent, his breath a pastiche of sleep, toothpaste, spit. "She's dying *now.*"

Then he slept while something inside Callie burned stark awake, and she stayed that way until the digital clock blinked 6:00 A.M. in green, a lightening gray sky began to shimmer through blinds, and the phone drilled once, twice, stopped—a signal. When ringing resumed she was up and at it, not even bothering to say hello, knowing that, with the weird synchronicity that evolves among those holding long, exhausting vigils, Françoise would understand it was she who'd answered, Callie, and simply begin talking. And, of course, she did. The tones were hushed, husky, accented. Once Callie'd loathed them. Now, though, they were just inescapably familiar: Françoise's voice and the terrifying news it conveyed merely what she'd learned to hear, listen to, stop hating over time.

Cabbing to the hospice she was, as usual, plenty hurt and scared. She took it out on Freud this time. Repeating the personal mantra hotly, silently: Eros and Thanatos, Eros and Thanatos, Eros, Eros, well fuck you, buddy! Fuck you and your fucking Eros! When what I need is agape. When what I need is love. When what I really need is an extra thirty bucks for cab fare today.

When what *she* needs is time.

Which was it in the proverbial nutshell, anyway. The whole trouble with Lu, both BC and AC—before and after cancer—there was never enough time. Not for her. Or for anyone else.

On fouled winter sleet the taxi veered alarmingly close to a bike messenger who turned once, giving them the finger, then sped through a red light. Torn vinyl pricked her thighs. Exhaust clouding out like breath around all the closed windows made her think of that hazy half-dream time after sex and before blessed sleep—shit, she was tired—and she shut her eyes longingly.

Once, she and Lu had had a glimpse of the leisurely passionate serenity they'd always promised each other but had never really delivered—years ago in Provincetown, early autumn. A fading hint of summer on the wind, cloudless sky, seagulls circling briny morsels near the shoreline. They'd found their deserted, forbidden spot, spread one old blanket underneath and another half over, spent the entire day fucking in the dunes. At Lu's instigation and insistence. Callie had been surprised. Because, of course, she was usually the one wanting, Lu the one withholding. Yes, what her shrink called that tired old good cop/bad cop crap had got set in stone early on between them.

This time, though, was different. And they'd both sensed it in a single electric touch of lips and tongues. The touch diffused, spread, widened in a caress that amazed in its softness and strength, and then the slow thoughtless peeling off of clothes, pressing together of more and more skin, until everything felt like one big aching cunt and they were all over each other in a sweet, sweet urgency. It wasn't finished after the first time but happened again. And again. The blankets shifted. Sand got in their hair. And something that had always been there blocking their way to one another, a thing the unmovable stone difference had always seemed writ large on, fell away. They looked at each other fearlessly, caressed and begged and fucked deep, deep inside. Once that afternoon, Callie on her back—which, she'd freely admit, was her favorite place to be when Lu was around—she'd looked up delirious, raw-eyed, to see her lover's face stripped and naked, staring down. Big, charismatic Lu who attracted everyone but had somehow chosen her. Athlete's body, scholar's mind. Lu worked hard at both. All that long, well-muscled flesh trapped hers beneath, the thick, fatless thighs and broad, broad shoulders—a body that almost always made Callie feel impoverished by comparison, self-conscious and flabby. But not today. The words had spilled out of her then, sans thought or reason, crazy, whispered.

"God, Lu. Give me a baby."

"Yes," Lu breathed, "okay," and put her whole hand inside.

Later, showered and dressed, after a cafe dinner, strolling the shadowy, empty town lanes in chillier twilight, they'd discussed logistics. Arthur's sperm, Callie decided. He was a mutual friend and had already volunteered, not to mention the lucky fact that his horror of anal penetration, of oral sex, of sharing bodily fluids—or, for that matter, of ever engaging in any sort of intimacy at all—had left him fat, alone, anxious to baby-sit, and HIV-free. Near Commercial Street, the first fallen leaves brushed their shoes. They paused short of a pool of lamplight and hugged. She could feel her legs still wobbly from the day's emotion and orgasm. They shivered against Lu's stronger, longer ones. Feeling it too, Lu smiled teasingly.

"Did the earth shake, little rabbit?"

"Oh shut up, Lu," she purred, but they were already moving apart.

Michael's birth, his first years, had brought them together again in that fierce, timeless cocoon of borderless protective love, had seemed to close all the gaps between them. For a while.

Time betrayed her again. The cab stopped at the right place much too soon. And the driver turned, unexpected kindness in his eyes.

"Visiting someone?"

111

"Yes."

"Uh-huh. Well, good luck."

"Thank you," she said, "thanks a lot." Truly grateful.

Handing over the money, though, she noticed how gingerly he took it, pinching the edge of the wad so that their fingers would not clumsily meet. The kindness in his eyes was fear, she saw; her own brief gratitude, anger.

"It's not contagious, pal."

"What's that?"

"Cancer. I mean, as far as we know. Although some distinguished experts say the jury's still out. Anyway, let's hope they're wrong—or we're all up shit's creek, huh? Keep the change."

Balding wheels squealed away, and she turned to face the rain, the building, the music, surprised at how pissed off she really, really was.

Lu liked the place. Very civil, she'd told her wryly a while back, very *Bardo,* very *Magic Mountain,* I mean très spiritual, Callie love, this Land of Just Enough Morphine. That day she'd managed a smile. Now, though, she was ashy and expressionless at a window, acknowledging no one. Jello and water untouched on a tray. Callie sat close by.

After a while the head turned with effort to face her. The eyes were still fully conscious Lu, though, trying to speak more clearly than the whispers.

"This is probably it."

"Uh-huh. You don't have to talk, love."

"Mmmm. It's gone, Cal. My sense of humor."

"Well, that's okay."

"Maybe not."

Lu was smaller than her now, she realized. Trying to describe to Pat the increasing physical devastation encountered each visit, the growing unrecognizability and continual subtle deforming of this once-powerful woman whom she'd loved as much as her life, words failed. She'd only been able to whimper, Well, it's interesting. Adding immediately, I mean, if that kind of thing interests you. And Pat, bless her, sensitive in a wordless way, had received both pain and sarcasm with a quiet, intelligent grace.

Today something else thumped inside Callie, in her throat and chest. There was a faint scent of vomit in the room, and she felt herself sweat suddenly, forcefully, caught up by a sheer nauseous wave of terror that almost sent her to the floor in a dead faint. Every once in a while it'd hit her like this, but today was the worst. When stuff in the room—plants and flowers, wall hangings, books and sheets and bottles of medicine—stopped reeling, she blinked away tears while her shirt clung wetly to panicked flesh. Her hands shook.

Lu ignored her. Then, after a few minutes, the head stopped bobbling, pain lines around mouth and eyes relaxed, and she sighed, leaned back almost comfortably in the armchair, and turned to face Callie with a calm, calm affection.

"Better, Cal. The drugs kicked in. Now we can talk."

"Huh," Callie croaked, "can you spare some for me?"

They shared a soundless laugh.

"Françoise called, Lu."

"Yes. I asked her to."

She had, it seemed, sent Françoise home to the kids late last night. With instructions that, if she was still alive by morning, Callie ought to visit.

First Callie found her ego blossoming at this news, and it killed her that, sick as she was, Lu could still touch her this way. She'd chosen to spend the time with her and not Françoise. Then other things occurred, unpleasantries: this was Françoise's mess more than hers. Why should she, Callie, be here on such precious time with that big clock in the sky tick-tick-tocking away? After all, it was another woman and her children Lu had opted for in the end

What was it the bitch had said, at some gallery opening, the first time they'd met? *I find you very attractive.* Well, not surprising. Plenty of dykes thought that about Lu, but Françoise had had the gall to say it to her face, with Callie watching. And that was that—nine years down the drain. She'd seen the writing on that ever-crumbling wall of dyke monogamy quite clearly. Like most rotten things it was unfair, etcetera. She'd been left loveless, with half the earning power and more of the bills, having to salve Michael's confused anguish five days out of seven while Lu stepped easily into Françoise's dramatically more solvent life, continued career success, and a burgeoning circle of friends. What she'd never forgive Lu for was walking out on the kid, though, and into the arms of Françoise's conveniently waiting little brood. Then turning around and demanding weekend visits, making sure she kept a few talons in the flesh, making sure the boy still loved her. Rendering every Monday—the day after tearful return—some hot new hell. *Mom, Françoise's kids have a boat!*

Then, just a few months after meeting Pat, the ominous phone calls began, the news. Lu. Cancer. Which could gnaw up so many more unspoken lives than that of just its victims. They'd learn, over the months—all of Lu's families past and present would learn—to be humble in its presence. Watch it draw and quarter what they loved. Then watch it whip around unpredictably, crush their human quarrels and inflicted romantic cruelties and mutual bitternesses to less than squat beneath its deranged juggernaut hooves.

"I've already said good-bye to Françoise," Lu said, answering the unspoken. "But you and I, we've still got work to do."

"You're incorrigible, Lu. Says who?"

"Callie, it's me, your Lu. Your Lu. For a little while longer. Let's talk. Tell me things. How's Pat? Has she stopped making love to you yet?"

"Sometimes I really hate you, Lu."

"Hmmm." She nodded tiredly. "Listen, Callie, come with me. Come lie down with me for a while."

The place was set up perfectly for the frail and weak: short, bridgeable distances between surfaces to lean against, sit in, lie on, between armchairs and medicines and bed.

Flesh, Callie thought. How changeable it is. How easy to love or to shrink from.

Lu's strength was so completely, so astonishingly gone, ruined by what ate her insides, a creeping, awesome immensity of illness. A savage stalking disease in the face of which, Callie thought, you couldn't help but be afraid. You'd want to kneel down before it, supplicate, sob helplessly in an admiring sort of terror and fascination at its surefire, dauntless ability to strip so much away. Immortally replicating cells. They consumed, those cells—they were the ultimate consumers, in fact, giving nothing in return. Little demigods. Even so, they could not take everything. Lu's eyes were still warrior eyes, Callie saw, searching her face with embarrassing boldness and a shrewd, shrewd knowledge, as they lay side by side deep in pillows.

"So. Is it lesbian bed death, Callie? Not this—excuse the pun. Why don't you and Pat fuck anymore?"

"Is that any of your business?"

"I want you to be happy."

"Pretty late in the day for that, Lu—don't you think?" The words were out before she'd had a chance to stop them. Raw hands clutched her cheeks. Rage sparked out of the warrior eyes staring back at her with one last angry effort.

"Why don't you fight for what you want, Callie? I mean, you're always conceding defeat before the battle. It's as if you don't even desire victory. I've tried to save Michael from that."

Bitch, Callie thought, what else have you tried to save him from?

On the other hand, Lu was right.

114

"Maybe I'm afraid." She sighed. "Maybe fighting's not my way."

"Go to hell, love. You don't have that right. Fear's beside the point. You're a dyke, you have to fight. It's not a privileg—it's a duty."

That was the morning things changed between them again—the strangest morning of Callie's life, the last one of Lu's. Callie'd never fucked with her eyes before. But lying very close it was clear to her that eyes were what they had connecting them, and that was all they had. The pain was going to come back soon—maybe they were both afraid. Maybe that was why a strange bright willingness possessed them. It spun them up in the suffering arms of disease and of light; for a while made them just the same, no longer quite two people lying side by side on a bed, but one inseparable entity. The entity had no energy left to move or undress, only to see. Fully clothed, they put hands between each others' legs in a strange slow-motion kind of fever. Callie squirmed, white-hot sweating and afraid. This arousal, revulsion, terror, whatever, couldn't be physical, she thought. But it surely felt that way.

"Think of me loving you, Callie. Imagine me fucking you."

"Goddamn you, Lu."

"Imagine me fucking you. Hold on tight. But don't move. Don't come. Not yet."

Fuck you, Lu, Callie thought. You're the ultimate control freak. But the swell of something terrible started up at the core of her—wet, dangerous, waiting to explode.

"God, I hate you, Lu. I hate your fucking guts."

"Yes, Callie, that's good," she whispered, "say the truth. Then let me go."

"I mean, *fuck* you for having and leaving us. *Fuck* you for getting cancer. *Fuck* you and *fuck* you for dying. *Fuck* you for letting me go."

The hot, wet, dangerous swell went up her spine into her head, expanded in her throat and heart and cunt, and tingled down into her toes, but she didn't move, just swelled hot and bright with it, kept it inside, and she could feel her lover doing the same, could feel her feeling it too. Then the weight of deeds between them fell utterly away. For a flickering moment they were there without flesh, blood, or bone—inside something that was and was not them, but contained them like bottled essence of fireflies, burning. Callie rode the swell, struggled wildly when it almost escaped, kept it inside. She pressed against lost flesh, tired bones.

"There," Lu gasped. "Yes, there, like so."

They stayed that way, bright-lit, sweating, and breathless, waiting for some last searing, inevitable wave of the demigods' pain. It would pick one of them up this time with its awesome, superior strength—arrogantly, pitilessly. Flay her alive and take all away except a subtle fierce burning in the eyes. Then it would take that too with an unendurable scream, until whatever was left lay there withered and broken, a mass of suffering flesh. Until warrior heart stopped beating, and will and action ceased.

Before that, Lu managed one more thing. Leaning even closer, whispering into an ear, "Forgive me, love, for everything. But I just don't believe in endings." Then Callie pulled back from the pain and the light. And knowing, left her alone.

Michael practiced roller-blading all the next weekend under Pat's watching gaze. When a screw came loose they mended it together. Callie let them bond. Intermittently she was on the phone with Françoise, or family, or Arthur, or some of Lu's old friends, making memorial service arrangements. The boy came in to ask questions or to cry sometimes, and she held him.

Pat was quiet, doing things around the house. She busied herself with Michael mostly and let well enough alone. Callie noticed her for the first time in months: a womanish, boyish presence that might—just might—promise tenderness and delight.

"You've got a cute ass, Pat," she said that night, in their room, "don't *you* drop dead on me any time soon."

"I wasn't planning to, honey."

"Prove it."

Half-naked, Pat wheeled around, enraged. Then grabbed her roughly, tears and warning in her eyes. "You're the one with something to prove tonight, lady. I mean, I know it's bad timing. But things are rough all over. Wake up, you! Wake up."

They rubbed each other into a frenzy on the bed, blessedly uninterrupted by the patter of little feet, and fell asleep naked. Hours later Callie woke to see Michael standing there in pajamas Lu'd given him, staring.

"You're naked."

"Uh-huh."

"Do you and Pat do sex?"

"Yes, Mike."

"Like Françoise and Mom Lu? I mean, yucchy kisses? When I grow up I'll have a wife. We'll make babies. I'll put my penis in her vagina."

"Yes, my love. And a lucky girl she'll be."

"I miss her," he said, and sobbed. She and Pat threw on robes, then cuddled him together until dawn. He finally slept.

"Yaaaah," Callie whispered. "Screw philosophy. Dying sucks."

"Or maybe," said Pat, "we just need to learn how."

The three of them rocked back and forth.

"Pat," she said, "lover, woman, who are you?"

"Not Lu, honey. But funny you should ask. I thought you never would." She smiled, half hero, half shadow in the dark. "Stick around some, doll—we will see."

Jenifer Levin is the author of four novels, the most recent of which, The Sea of Light, *was a Lambda Literary Award finalist. Her first book,* Water Dancer, *published when she was twenty-six, was nominated for the PEN/Hemingway Award, and helped establish her among the few contemporary uncloseted lesbian novelists to be published in and receive serious critical attention from the literary mainstream. "Love and Death & Other Disasters" is the title story from her collection published in 1996.*

LEVITICUS 18

The Lord spoke to Moses, saying: Speak to the Israelite people and say to them:

I the LORD am your God. You shall not copy the practices of the land of Egypt where you dwelt, or of the land of Canaan to which I am taking you; nor shall you follow their laws. My rules alone shall you observe, and faithfully follow My laws: I the LORD am your God.

You shall keep My laws and My rules, by the pursuit of which man shall live: I am the LORD.

None of you shall come near anyone of his own flesh to uncover nakedness: I am the LORD.

Your father's nakedness, that is, the nakedness of your mother, you shall not uncover; she is your mother—you shall not uncover her nakedness.

Do not uncover the nakedness of your father's wife—it is the nakedness of your father.

The nakedness of your sister—your father's daughter or your mother's, whether born into the household or outside—do not uncover their nakedness.

The nakedness of your son's daughter, or of your daughter's daughter—do not uncover their nakedness; for their nakedness is yours.

The nakedness of your father's wife's daughter, who was born into your father's household—she is your sister; do not uncover her nakedness.

Do not uncover the nakedness of your father's sister; she is your father's flesh.

Do not uncover the nakedness of your mother's sister; for she is your mother's flesh.

Do not uncover the nakedness of your father's brother; do not approach his wife, she is your aunt.

Do not uncover the nakedness of your daughter-in-law; she is your son's wife; you shall not uncover her nakedness.

Do not uncover the nakedness of your brother's wife; it is the nakedness of your brother.

Do not uncover the nakedness of a woman and her daughter; nor shall you marry her son's daughter or her daughter's daughter and uncover her nakedness: they are kindred; it is depravity.

Do not marry a woman as a rival to her sister and uncover her nakedness in the other's lifetime.

Do not come near a woman during her period of uncleanness to uncover her nakedness.

Do not have carnal relations with your neighbor's wife and defile yourself with her.

Do not allow any of your offspring to be offered up to Molech, and do not profane the name of your God: I am the LORD.

Do not lie with a male as one lies with a woman; it is an abhorrence.

Do not have carnal relations with any beast and defile yourself thereby; and let no woman lend herself to a beast to mate with it; it is perversion.

Do not defile yourselves in any of those ways, for it is by such that the nations which I am casting out before you defiled themselves. Thus the land became defiled; and I called it to account for its iniquity, and the land spewed out its inhabitants. But you must keep My laws and My rules, and you must not do any of those abhorrent things, neither the citizen nor the stranger who resides among you; for all those abhorrent things were done by the people who were in the land before you, and the land became defiled. So let not the land spew you out for defiling it, as it spewed out the nation that came before you. All who do any of those abhorrent things—such persons shall be cut off from their people. You shall keep My charge not to engage in any of the abhorrent practices that were carried on before you, and you shall not defile yourselves through them: I the LORD am your God.

III
BODY

Hugh Hefner

EDITORIAL

Playboy, Volume I, Number I

f you're a man between the ages of eighteen and eighty, *Playboy* is meant for you. If you like your entertainment served up with humor, sophistication and spice, *Playboy* will become a very special favorite.

We want to make clear from the very start, we aren't a "family magazine." If you're somebody's sister, wife, or mother-in-law and picked us up by mistake, please pass us along to the man in your life and get back to your *Ladies Home Companion.*

Within the pages of *Playboy* you will find articles, fiction, picture stories, cartoons, humor, and special features culled from many sources, past and present, to form a pleasure-primer styled to the masculine taste.

Most of today's "magazines for men" spend all their time out-of-doors— thrashing through thorny thickets or splashing about in fast flowing streams. We'll be out there too, occasionally, but we don't mind telling you in advance—we plan on spending most of our time Inside.

We like our apartment. We enjoy mixing up cocktails and an *hors d'oeuvre* or two, putting a little mood music on the phonograph, and inviting in a female acquaintance for a quiet discussion on Picasso, Nietzsche, jazz, sex.

We believe, too, that we are filling a publishing need only slightly less important than the one just taken care of by the Kinsey Report. The magazines now being produced for the city-bred male (there are two—count 'em— two) have, of late, placed so much emphasis on fashion, travel, and "how-to-do-it" features on everything from avoiding a hernia to building your own steam bath, that entertainment has been all but pushed from their pages. *Playboy* will emphasize entertainment.

Affairs of state will be out of our province. We don't expect to solve any world problems or prove any great moral truths. If we are able to give the American male a few extra laughs and a little diversion from the anxieties of the Atomic Age, we'll feel we've justified our existence.

Hugh Hefner is the founder and publisher of Playboy *magazine. This editorial is reproduced by special permission of* Playboy *magazine. Copyright © 1953 by* Playboy.

Maxine Kumin

ROLE REVERSALS

The Lactating Father

Forbidden from childhood
to look on the ones that fed me
I drew them on paper the color
of bean curd, drew mounds of
pink ones and purples, the nipples
like loved eyes sleeping
or slyer pretending their slumber

never believing my own
plain shelf would erupt
with such riches, such
mild and marvelous opals.
Now milk leaks out of my melons
into the rooting mouth of
this child I sired and suckle.

The Female Phallus

Don't touch it. Pee leaning forward.
Wash without really looking.
Tuck it in gently, your baby
bird, pink perishable wren
lest it rise up shooting from the hip
and poison the sweet fumble
of you chaste relationship.

Procreate cautiously. Think of
England as you lie down to love.
Consider the lilies, review a recipe—
anything to blur this fitting of hand
as it were to glove.

Male Menarche

Let us rejoice in it
stain the world with it
marshall a band for it
admire the hue
of this full-bodied wine
this burgundian dew
that flows as we enter
the gates of manhood.
Every lad front and center.
All sing: blood is good.

Maxine Kumin has published twelve volumes of poetry, as well as novels, short stories, and essays on country living. She was awarded the Pulitzer Prize for Poetry in 1973 and has been a poetry consultant for the Library of Congress and Poet Laureate of New Hampshire. Her Selected Poems 1960-1990 *was published in 1997. Kumin lives on a farm in central New Hampshire.*

Mary Gordon

SAFE

I.

The morning starts with a child's crying. By arrangement I ignore it; by arrangement, my husband, who does not see the morning as I do—the embezzler of all cherished wealth, thief of all most rare and precious—gets the child and brings her to me. Still asleep, I offer her my breast, and she, with that anchoritic obsession open only to saints and infants, eats, and does not think to be offended that her mother does not offer her the courtesy of even a perfunctory attention, but sleeps on. There is a photograph of the two of us in this position. My eyes are closed, the blankets are around my chin. My daughter, six months old, puts down the breast to laugh into the camera's eye. Already she knows it is a good joke: that she is vulnerable, utterly, and that the person who has pledged to keep her from all harm, can do, in fact, so little to protect her. Is a person, actually, who can swear that never in her life has she awakened of her own accord. Yet, miraculously, she feels safe with me, my daughter, and settles in between my breast and arm for morning kisses. This is the nicest way I know to wake up. I have never understood people who like to be awakened with sex: what one wants, upon awakening is something gradual, predictable, and sex is just the opposite, with all its rushed surprises.

I carry my daughter into the bathroom. My husband, her father, stands at the mirror shaving, stripped to the waist. How beautiful he is. I place my cheek on his back and embrace him. The baby plays at our feet. In the mirror I can see my arms, my hands around his waist, but not my face. I like the anonymity. I take my nightgown off and go into the shower. Every time I take a shower now, I worry about the time when water will be rationed, when I will have to wash in a sink in cold water. My mother knew a nun who, after twenty-five years in the convent, was asked what gift she would like to celebrate her silver jubilee. She asked for a hot bath. What did that mean about the twenty-five years of her life before that? All her young womanhood gone by without hot baths. I would not have stuck it out.

I step out of the shower and begin to dry myself. I see the two of them look-

126

ing at me: man and child, she in his arms. She stretches out her arms to me in that exaggerated pose of desperation that can make the most well-fed child suggest that she belongs on a poster, calculated to rend the heart, urging donations for the children of a war zone or a famine-stricken country. I take her in my arms. She nose-dives for my breast. My husband holds my face in both his hands. "Don't take your diaphragm out," he says. Just ten minutes ago, I fed my child; just last night I made love to my husband. Yet they want me again and again. My blood is warmed, then fired with well-being. Proudly, I run my hands over my own flesh, as if I had invented it.

II.

The baby is predictable now. We know that she will want a nap at nine-fifteen, just after we have finished breakfast. I put her in her crib and wait until I hear her even breathing. Does she dream? What can she dream of, having lived so little? Does she dream of life inside my body? Or does she dream for the whole race?

My husband is in bed waiting for me. Deep calls to deep: it must have been sex they were talking about. I want him as much as ever. Because of this, because of what I feel for him, what he feels for me, of what we do, can do, have done together in this bed, I left another husband. Broke all sorts of laws: the state's, the church's. Caused a good man pain. And yet it has turned out well. Everyone is happier than ever. I do not understand this. It makes a mockery of the moral life, which I am supposed to believe in.

All the words of love, of sex and love, the simple words; have, take, come, now, words of one syllable. Behind my eyes I see green leaves, high, branching trees, then rocks that move apart and open. Exhausted, we hold each other, able to claim love. The worst thing about casual sex is not being able to express love honestly afterward. One feels it, but knows it to be false. Not really love. Yet, is it not inevitable to love one who has proffered such a gift?

We drift into sleep, knowing the baby's nap will not last long. She cries; the day begins for real. I am taking her into the city to see an old lover.

III.

Of all the men I have been with, M—— found me consistently, astonishingly, pleasing. We had five months together in a foreign city, London, where he was almost the only one I knew. I was married then, to my first husband, who did not praise, who thought of me as if I were colonial Africa: a vast, dark, natural resource, capable, possibly, of civilization. As it turns out, I did not want his

127

civilization—a tendency colonialists have discovered to their sorrow.

M—— is, as they say, well bred, but with him the phrase has real meaning. Only centuries of careful marriages could have produced, for example, his nose. There are no noses like it in America, which got only the riffraff for its settlers, or those who must fear beauty as a snare. His nose is thin and long, the nostrils beautifully cut, the tip pointed down slightly to the full, decisive lips. He is the blondest man I have ever been with—this, in combination with his elegant, well-cut clothes, made him a disappointment naked. Really fair men always look foolish without their clothes, as if they ought to know better.

M—— likes to pretend that I have been married so many times he can't keep track. In letters, he tells me he imagines me inviting the milkman, the postman, the butcher into bed to thank them for their services. I write that there are no milkmen in America, the postman is a woman, and I buy meat in the supermarket. Don't quibble, he replies, suggesting my gynecologist, my lawyer, the man who does my taxes.

It is all praise, it is all a reminder of my power, and I thrive on it, particularly as we spoke last time we saw each other openly, about the pleasures of friendship without the intrusions of sex. I was newly married then, and he took no small pride in the court adviser/Dutch uncle tone he spoke in when he warned me against the dangers of infidelity. I told him he needn't worry; I had learned my lesson; I wanted to have a child. And besides my husband made me happier than I had ever been. So then you're safe, he said, as safe as houses. I didn't like the image: I knew the kind of houses that were meant: large and wide and comfortably furnished: it made me see myself as middle-aged, a German woman with thick legs and gray bobbed hair.

It is with a high heart that I ride down on the bus on a spring morning. The countryside is looking splendid: frail greens against a tentative blue sky, the turned earth brown and ready. M——'s nose is not his only benefice: his manners, too, are lovely. They are courtly, and I dream of my daughter meeting him at Claridge's one day for tea, when she is twelve, perhaps, and needing flattery. I look at her in my arms, proud of what I have come up with. This rosy flesh is mine, this perfect head, this soft, round mouth. And of course, I think we make a charming picture, rightly observed and I count on M——for the proper angle.

The city pavements sparkle and the sun beams off the building glass. We get a taxi in a second—I am covered over with beneficence, the flattering varnish of good luck. But my luck changes and we are stuck in traffic for forty-five minutes. M—— hates lateness—he thinks it is rudeness—and I know this will get the day off to a bad start.

He is waiting for me in the sculpture garden of the Museum of Modern Art. He does not look pleased to see me, but it is not his way to look pleased. He says he hates his first sight of people he loves: they always expect too much from his face and it makes him feel a failure.

I apologize nervously, excessively, for being late. He steers us silently toward the cafeteria. I am wearing the baby in a front pack sling, when I take her out and give her to M—— to hold, she screams. He asks me what she likes to eat. "Me," I say, but he is not amused. "Get her some yogurt," I say, feeling foolish.

"And you?" he asks.

"Oh, anything," I say.

"You always say that," he says, frowning, "and you always have something specific in mind. You've lost an earring."

He looks at the baby. "Your mother is always losing earrings in the most extraordinary places, at the most extraordinary times." She looks him squarely in the eye and screams. He moves off with a shudder.

Finally, the yogurt pleases the baby, and her good temper is restored. I ask M—— about his visit, and he is noncommittal, uninformative. I begin to fear that he has crossed the ocean to see me. He wants to talk about the past, our past; he keeps bringing up details in a way that makes me know he thinks about me often. He keeps taking my hand, squeezing it in studied, meaningful patterns of pressure, but I keep having to pull my hand away to take things from the baby, or to hold her still. Besides, I don't want to hold his hand. Not in that way. I begin to feel unsettled, and start chattering, diverting much of my foolish talk to the baby, a habit in mothers I have always loathed.

"I've got us theater tickets for tonight," says M—— "And you must tell me where you would most like to have dinner."

I look at him with alarm. "I can't possibly go to the theater with you. I have to get home with the baby. You should have said something."

"I thought you'd know that's what would happen. It's what we always did."

"I never had a baby before. Or a marriage, not a real one. Surely you must know we can't go on a *date*."

"Obviously I don't know anything about you any more. Come on, let's look at the pictures."

I try to put my arms though the sling, but it is a complicated arrangement if one is trying to hold the baby at the same time, and I know she will not go with M——. He stands behind me, helping me to put my arms through the straps. His hand brushes my breast, but instead of moving his hand away, he cups my breast with it.

I am covered over in panic. For the first time in my life, I am shocked by a man's touch. I understand for the first time the outraged virgin, for I am offended by the impropriety of such a gesture, indicating, as it does, radical misunderstanding of my identity. He cannot have free access to my body, not just because it is mine, but because it stands for something in the world, for some idea. My body has become symbolic. I laugh at the idea as soon as it occurs to me, and M—— looks hurt, but I continue to laugh at the notion of myself as icon. My actual virginity I gave up with impatience and dispatch; an encumbrance I was eager to be rid of. Now, fifteen years later, I stand blushing.

We try to look at pictures, but it is no good, the baby cries incessantly. Besides, we really do not want to be together any more. He puts me in a taxi and tries to embrace me, but the baby is strapped to me and all he can manage is a chaste and distant kiss on the cheek. It is the first time I have disappointed him; and I feel the failure all the way home. The baby falls asleep the minute she gets on the bus; she was crying from exhaustion. I do not know what I was thinking of, making this expedition. Or I know precisely what I had been thinking of, and cannot now believe I was so foolish.

IV.

It is evening. My husband and I are going to dinner at our favorite restaurant. The girl who is taking care of the baby is a girl I love. Seventeen, she is the daughter of a friend, a woman I love and admire, a woman of accomplishment whose children are accomplished and who love her. E—— is beautiful, a beauty which would be a bit inhuman if she understood its power, and were it not tempered by her sweetness and her modesty. I know her well; she lived with us in the summer. I was relieved to be unable to assume a maternal role with her; I believed, and still believe, that she sees me as a slatternly older sister, good at heart but scarcely in control. She plays the flute; she gets my jokes; she speaks perfect French; she does the dishes without being asked. The baby adores her. We can leave telling her nothing but the phone number of the restaurant. She knows everything she needs to know.

It is not a good dinner. I want to tell my husband about M—— but cannot. It is not his business; spouses should never be able to image their fears of their beloved's being desired by another. And I may want to see M—— again.

I am distracted, and my husband knows me well enough to know it. We are both disappointed for we do not have much time alone. We do not linger over after-dinner drinks, but come home early to find E—— in the dark, crying. My husband leaves her to me; he has always said that a woman, however young, does not want to be seen in tears by a man who is not her lover. In the car, I ask her what is wrong.

"It's R——," she says, her first boyfriend, with whom I know she has broken up. "It's awful to see him every day, and not be able to talk to him."

"Mm," I say, looking at the dark road.

"It's just so awful. He used to be the person in the world I most wanted to see, most wanted to talk to, and now I rush out of classes so I don't have to pass him in the halls."

"It's hard."

"Was it like that for you? First loving someone, then running away from the sight of them?"

"Yes, it happened to me a lot." I conjure in my mind the faces of ten men once loved. "Do you think people can ever be friends when they fall out of love with each other?"

"I suppose so. I've never been able to do it. Some people can."

She looks at me with anguish in the dark, cold car. "It's such a terrible waste. I can't bear it, I don't think. Do you think it's all worth it?"

"I don't think there's an alternative," I say.

"What a relief it must be that it's all over for you."

So this is how she sees me: finished, tame, bereft of possibilities. I kiss her good-night, feeling like that German woman with thick legs. Lightly, E—— runs through the beam of the headlights over the grass to her house. I wait to see that she is in the door.

Her urgent face is in my mind as I drive home, and M——'s face and the face of ten loved men. I realize that I am old to E——, or middle-aged, and that is worse. The touch of M——'s hand on my breast gave me no pleasure. That has never happened to me before.

I have never thought of myself as old; rather I fear that I am so young-seeming that I lack authority in the outside world. I feel the burdens of both youth and age. I am no longer dangerous, by reason of excitement, possibility—but I cannot yet compel by fear. I feel as if the light had been drained from my hair and skin. I walk into the house, low to the ground, dun-colored, like a moorhen.

My husband is in bed when I return. I look in at the baby. Under her yellow blanket her body falls and rises with her breath. I wash my face and get into my nightgown. It is purple cotton, striped; it could belong to a nun. I think of the nightwear of women in films whose bodies glow with danger: Garbo, Dietrich, Crawford. Faye Dunaway, who has a baby and is not much older than I. I see my husband is not yet asleep. He takes me in his arms. I ask, "Do you ever think of me as dangerous?"

He laughs. "Let me try to guess what you've been reading. *Anna Karenina? Madame Bovary? Vanity Fair?*"

"I'm serious. I'll bet you never think of me as dangerous."

He holds me closer. "If I thought of you as dangerous, I'd have to think of myself as unsafe."

I pull him toward me. I can feel his heart beating against my breast. Safe, of course he must be safe with me. He and the baby. Were they unsafe, I could not live a moment without terror for myself. I know I must live my life now knowing it is not my own. I can keep them from so little; it must be the shape of my life to keep them at least from the danger I could bring them.

In a few hours, the baby will awaken, needing to be fed again. My husband takes my nightgown off.

Mary Gordon is the best-selling author of the novels Final Payments, The Company of Women, Men and Angels, *and* The Other Side. *She has published a book of novellas,* The Rest of Life; *a collection of stories,* Temporary Shelter, *in which "Safe" is collected; a book of essays,* Good Boys and Dead Girls; *and a memoir,* The Shadow Man: A Daughter's Search for Her Father. *She teaches at Barnard College.*

Sharon Olds

NEW MOTHER

A week after our child was born,
you cornered me in the spare room
and we sank down on the bed.
You kissed me and kissed me, my milk undid its
burning slip-knot through my nipples,
soaking my shirt. All week I had smelled of milk,
fresh milk, sour. I began to throb:
my sex had been torn easily as cloth by the
crown of her head, I'd been cut with a knife and
sewn, the stitches pulling at my skin—
and the first time you're broken, you don't know
you'll be healed again, better than before.
I lay in fear and blood and milk
while you kissed and kissed me, your lips hot and swollen
as a teen-age boy's, your sex dry and big,
all of you so tender, you hung over me,
over the nest of the stitches, over the
splitting and tearing, with the patience of someone who
finds a wounded animal in the woods
and stays with it, not leaving its side
until it is whole, until it can run again.

Sharon Olds is the author of many volumes of poetry, including Satan Says; The Dead and
the Living, *which was the Lamont Poetry Selection for 1983 and winner of the National
Book Critics Circle Award;* The Father; *and* The Wellspring.

Rita Dove

ADOLESCENCE—II

Although it is night, I sit in the bathroom, waiting.
Sweat prickles behind my knees, the baby-breasts are alert.
Venetian blinds slice up the moon: the tiles quiver in pale strips.

Then they come, the three seal men with eyes as round
As dinner plates and eyelashes like sharpened tines.
They bring the scent of licorice. One sits in the washbowl,

One on the bathtub edge; one leans against the door.
"Can you feel it yet?" they whisper.
I don't know what to say, again. They chuckle,

Patting their sleek bodies with their hands.
"Well, maybe next time." And they rise,
Glittering like pools of ink under moonlight,

And vanish. I clutch at the ragged holes
They leave behind, here at the edge of darkness.
Night rests like a ball of fur on my tongue.

Rita Dove served as Poet Laureate of the United States and Consultant in Poetry at the Library of Congress from 1993 to 1995. She has published six poetry collections, among them Thomas and Beulah, *which won the Pulitzer Prize in 1987, and most recently* Mother Love. *She is also the author of a book of short stories and the novel* Through the Ivory Gate.

Richard McCann

JAIME'S HAIR

A year later I found myself at a crowded party in a pine-paneled beach cottage, lying on a narrow bed beside a man named Paul—a friend of a friend, a model up from New York for the weekend—who was pressing his ear to the fluted pink edge of a conch shell so he could hear the ocean sound of his own head. "Oh," I kept thinking as I watched him, "he has Jaime's hair." I didn't know if I wanted to tell him this, since he wouldn't have known that Jaime was the man I had lived with all the difficult years before. In truth, I didn't know if those years were really over, and I didn't know if I would ever want to say to anyone again, "You sure have beautiful hair."

I first saw Jaime in a piano bar when I was thirty and he was thirty-four. I stood in a corner watching him while he talked and drank with some Latin guys I used to know. I would love to touch his hair, I thought—thick and black, with a faint trace of silver at each temple, barely noticeable, like a premonition.

That was what desire was like in those days, in case no one remembers— sudden and absolute, so that the sharp blue electric arc of wanting leapt quickly from the pole of impulse to the opposite pole of action. The next night we met for dinner in a rooftop restaurant that has long since gone out of business. When he leaned over the table toward me, I touched his hair.

Over the next ten years, of course, I often had the opportunity to run a hand through his hair. At night sometimes, when making love, or afterward, shampooing each other in the shower. Or in the morning, when we sat at our breakfast table, hurriedly eating his cereal before work. I'd come up from behind him and touch him on the head, and then, because he was an attorney who appeared often in courtrooms, I'd say, "Before you leave, don't forget to comb your hair!"

In the months after his diagnosis, I suppose I was thinking mostly of the time that would come when he would be sick and I would be the one to wash

135

and cut his hair. For a long time, I was afraid of everything that was evidence of the physical life we shared: our razors lying side by side on the porcelain sink; toothbrushes nestling in a water glass smeared with handprints; black hair strung into greasy knots that I sometimes pulled up while snaking the drain of the tub. At night when I lay beside him, I was afraid of the things his body was emitting or sloughing off—like his cum puddling on his belly after he jacked off, or like the nightsweats that soaked the sheets in which we slept. My self-diagnosis, looking back?—A fear of nail trimmings; a fear of mitosis, of cells dividing and failing....

What could I have said to him? Our language had always been touch—a late-night language, with its own grammar of pleasure and consolation, its inflections of sorrow. We had never located a bright corridor of words that would allow us to move with ease toward one another.

I remember driving home one night from signing the power-of-attorney and the document that would one day give me the right to decide when Jaime would die.

"Well," said Jaime after miles and miles. "Well. There."

"That's right," I said. "There."

In the last months of his life, I was afraid of the time when he would be neither here nor there. By then his body has sloughed off almost everything, including the things he most needed: he weighed less than one hundred pounds, and his skin bruised and bled each time the visiting nurse held his arms to hoist him from his bed onto the toilet. By then his meals were delivered by an agency of care-givers—I just had to put the food on a plate and carry his tray up the stairs. Most nights he raged at the health aides who came to flush his heplock and to bathe him with damp towels scented with cologne. The aides were women from far away—from Nigeria, for instance, and Haiti—and sometimes when I was lonely I sat with them in the TV room, watching them while they addressed greeting cards to families back home or while they fiddled with their elaborately plaited and coiled hair.

An ambulance took him to the hospital. I know what people saw that scared them when they glanced into his room while passing down the corridor to the coffee machine—his face like a taut mask stretched on a skull; matchstick arms and legs affixed to a torso swollen with fluids; jaundiced skin almost the color of mahogany. When he was awake, we watched TV or flipped through magazines. But when he slept, I was desperate to study his body. "Where are you taking us?" I wanted to ask it—or someone.

The last day he lived he had three seizures, one after the other, and when they were finished, it seemed he had at last sloughed off everything—except for his rages and their subsequent exhaustions. "Don't touch me, you cocksucker!" he yelled at the orderly who was tying him to the bed.

He looked at me as I stood there. "What do you think you are doing?" he said. "Just what the fuck do you think you're doing now?"

I didn't know what to tell him, although I knew it was wrong to restrain him when he was leaving his life behind. I said I was keeping an eye on him, as I had always done. But he said he didn't believe it. He shook his head—*No, no.*

"Calm down," I said.

I put my hand on his forehead. "Please calm down," I said. "I've come to comb your hair."

Richard McCann is the author, most recently, of a volume of poetry, Ghost Letters, *and the editor of the anthology* Things Shaped in Passing: More "Poets For Life" Writing from the AIDS Pandemic *(with Michael Klein). His fiction and poetry appear in such magazines as* The Atlantic, Esquire, *and* Ploughshares, *and in numerous anthologies, including* The Penguin Book of Gay Short Stories, Men On Men 2, Men On Men 5, *and* Survival Stories: Memoirs of Crisis. *He lives in Washington, D.C., where he co-directs the graduate program in creative writing at American University.*

bell hooks

SELLING HOT PUSSY

Representations of Black Female Sexuality in the Cultural Marketplace

Friday night in a small midwestern town—I go with a group of artists and professors to a late night dessert place. As we walk past a group of white men standing in the entry way to the place, we overhear them talking about us, saying that my companions, who are all white, must be liberals from the college, not regular "townies" to be hanging out with a "nigger." Everyone in my group acts as though they did not hear a word of this conversation. Even when I call attention to the comments, no one responds. It's like I am not only not talking, but suddenly, to them, I am not there. I am invisible. For my colleagues, racism expressed in everyday encounters—this is our second such experience together—is only an unpleasantness to be avoided, not something to be confronted or challenged. It is just something negative disrupting the good time, better to not notice and pretend it's not there.

As we enter the dessert place they all burst into laughter and point to a row of gigantic chocolate breasts complete with nipples—huge edible tits. They think this is a delicious idea—seeing no connection between this racialized image and the racism expressed in the entry way. Living in a world where white folks are no longer nursed and nurtured primarily by black female care-takers, they do not look at these symbolic breasts and consciously think about "mammies." They do not see this representation of chocolate breasts as a sign of displaced longing for a racist past when the bodies of black women were commodity, available to anyone white who could pay the price. I look at these dark breasts and think about the representation of black female bodies in popular culture. Seeing them, I think about the connection between contemporary representations and the types of images popularized from slavery on. I remember Harriet Jacobs's powerful *exposé* of the psycho-sexual dynamics of slavery in *Incidents in the Life of a Slave Girl*. I remember the way she described that "peculiar" institution of domination and the white people who constructed it as "a cage of obscene birds."

Representations of black female bodies in contemporary popular culture

138

rarely subvert or critique images of black female sexuality which were part of the cultural apparatus of 19th-century racism and which still shape perceptions today. Sander Gilman's essay, "Black Bodies, White Bodies: Toward an Iconography of Female Sexuality in Late Nineteenth-Century Art, Medicine, and Literature," calls attention to the way black presence in early North American society allowed whites to sexualize their world by projecting onto black bodies a narrative of sexualization disassociated from whiteness. Gilman documents the development of this image, commenting that "by the eighteenth century, the sexuality of the black, male and female, becomes an icon for deviant sexuality." He emphasizes that it is the black female body that is forced to serve as "an icon for black sexuality in general."

Most often attention was not focused on the complete black female on display at a fancy ball in the "civilized" heart of European culture, Paris. She is there to entertain guests with the naked image of Otherness. They are not to look at her as a whole human being. They are to notice only certain parts. Objectified in a manner similar to that of black female slaves who stood on auction blocks while owners and overseers described their important, salable parts, the black women whose naked bodies were displayed for whites at social functions had no presence. They were reduced to mere spectacle. Little is known of their lives, their motivations. Their body parts were offered as evidence to support racist notions that black people were more akin to animals than other humans. When Sarah Bartmann's body was exhibited in 1810, she was ironically and perversely dubbed "the Hottentot Venus." Her naked body was displayed on numerous occasions for five years. When she died, the mutilated parts were still subject to scrutiny. Gilman stressed that: "The audience which had paid to see her buttocks and had fantasized about the uniqueness of her genitalia when she was alive could, after her death and dissection, examine both." Much of the racialized fascination with Bartmann's body concentrated attention on her buttocks.

A similar white European fascination with the bodies of black people, particularly black female bodies, was manifest during the career of Josephine Baker. Content to "exploit" white eroticization of black bodies, Baker called attention to the "butt" in her dance routines. Phyllis Rose, though often condescending in her recent biography, *Jazz Cleopatra: Josephine Baker in Her Time,* perceptively explores Baker's concentration on her ass:

> She handled it as though it were an instrument, a rattle, something apart from herself that she could shake. One can

139

hardly overemphasize the importance of the rear end. Baker herself declared that people had been hiding their asses too long. "The rear end exists. I see no reason to be ashamed of it. It's true there are rear ends so stupid, so pretentious, so insignificant that they're good only for sitting on." With Baker's triumph, the erotic gaze of a nation moved downward: she had uncovered a new region for desire.

Many of Baker's dance moves highlighting the "butt" prefigure movements popular in contemporary black dance.

Although contemporary thinking about black female bodies does not attempt to read the body as a sign of "natural" racial inferiority, the fascination with black "butts" continues. In the sexual iconography of the traditional black pornographic imagination, the protruding butt is seen as an indication of a heightened sexuality. Contemporary popular music is one of the primary cultural locations for discussions of black sexuality. In song lyrics, "the butt" is talked about in ways that attempt to challenge racist assumptions that suggest it is an ugly sign of inferiority, even as it remains a sexualized sign. The popular song, "Doin' the Butt," fostered the promotion of a hot new dance favoring those who could most protrude their buttocks with pride and glee. A scene in Spike Lee's film *School Daze* depicts an all black party where everyone is attired in swimsuits dancing—doing the butt. It is one of the most compelling moments in the film. The black "butts" on display are unruly and outrageous. They are not the still bodies of the female slave made to appear as mannequin. They are not a silenced body. Displayed as playful cultural nationalist resistance, they challenge assumptions that the black body, its skin color and shape, is a mark of shame. Undoubtedly the most transgressive and provocative moment in *School Daze,* this celebration of buttocks either initiated or coincided with an emphasis on butts, especially the buttocks of women, in fashion magazines. Its potential to disrupt and challenge notions of black bodies, specifically female bodies, was undercut by the overall sexual humiliation and abuse of black females in the film. Many people did not see the film so it was really the song "Doin' the Butt" that challenged dominant ways of thinking about the body which encourage us to ignore asses because they are associated with undesirable and unclean acts. Unmasked, the "butt" could be once again worshipped as an erotic seat of pleasure and excitement.

When calling attention to the body in a manner inviting the gaze to mutilate black female bodies yet again, to focus solely on the "butt," contemporary celebrations of this part of the anatomy do not successfully subvert sexist/racist representations. Just as nineteenth-century representations of black female bodies were constructed to emphasize that these bodies were expendable, contemporary images (even those created in black cultural production) give a similar message. When Richard Wright's protest novel *Native Son* was made into a film in the 1980s, the film did not show the murder of Bigger's black girlfriend Bessie. This was doubly ironic. She is murdered in the novel and then systematically eliminated in the film. Painters exploring race as artistic subject matter in the nineteenth century often created images contrasting white female bodies with black ones in ways that reinforced the greater value of the white female icon. Gilman's essay colludes in this critical project: he is really most concerned with exploring white female sexuality.

A similar strategy is employed in the Wright novel and in the film version. In the novel, Bessie is expendable because Bigger has already committed the more heinous crime of killing a white woman. The first and more important murder subsumes the second. Everyone cares about the fate of Mary Dalton, the ruling class white female daughter; no one cares about the fate of Bessie. Ironically, just at the moment when Bigger decides that Bessie's body is expendable, that he will kill her, he continues to demand that she help him, that she "do the right thing." Bigger intends to use her then throw her away, a gesture reinforcing that hers is an expendable body. While he must transgress dangerous boundaries to destroy the body of a white female, he can invade and violate a black female body with no fear of retribution and retaliation.

Black and female, sexual outside the context of marriage, Bessie represents "fallen womanhood." She has no protectors, no legal system will defend her rights. Pleading her cause to Bigger, she asks for recognition and compassion for her specific condition.

> Bigger, please! Don't do this to me! Please! All I do is work, work like a dog! From morning till night. I ain't got no happiness. I ain't never had none. I ain't got nothing and you do this to me…

Poignantly describing the lot of working-class poor black women in the 1940s, her words echo those of poet Nikki Giovanni describing the status of black

141

women in the late 1960s. The opening lines to "Woman Poem" read: "You see my whole life is tied up to unhappiness." There is a radical difference, however. In the 1960s, the black female is naming her unhappiness to demand a hearing, an acknowledgment of her reality, and change her status. This poem speaks to the desire of black women to construct a sexuality apart from that imposed upon us by a racist/sexist culture, calling attention to the ways we are trapped by conventional notions of sexuality and desirability:

> ...it's a sex object if you're pretty and no love or love and no
> sex   if you're fat get back fat black woman be a mother
> grandmother   strong thing but not woman gameswoman
> romantic woman love needer man seeker dick eater sweat
> getter fuck needing love seeking woman

"Woman Poem" is a cry of resistance urging those who exploit and oppress black women, who objectify and dehumanize, to confront the consequences of their actions. Facing herself, the black female realizes all that she must struggle against to achieve self-actualization. She must counter the representation of herself, her body, her being as expendable.

Bombarded with images representing black female bodies as expendable, black women have either passively absorbed this thinking or vehemently resisted it. Popular culture provides countless examples of black female appropriation and exploitation of "negative stereotypes" to either assert control over the representation or at least reap the benefits of it. Since black female sexuality has been represented in racist/sexist iconography as more free and liberated, many black women singers, irrespective of the quality of their voices, have cultivated an image which suggests they are sexually available and licentious. Undesirable in the conventional sense, which defines beauty and sexuality as desirable only to the extent that it is idealized and unattainable, the black female body gains attention only when it is synonymous with accessibility, availability, when it is sexually deviant.

Tina Turner's construction of a public sexual persona most conforms to this idea of black female sexuality. In her recent autobiography *I, Tina* she presents a sexualized portrait of herself—providing a narrative that is centrally "sexual confession." Even though she begins by calling attention to the fact that she was raised with puritanical notions of innocence and virtuous womanhood which made her reticent and fearful of sexual experience, all that follows contradicts this portrait. Since the image that has been cultivated and commodified in popular culture is of her as "hot" and highly sexed—the sexually ready and free black woman—a tension exists in the autobiography between the reality she presents and the image she must uphold. Describing her first sexual experience, Turner recalls:

> Naturally, I lost my virginity in the backseat of a car. This was the fifties, right? I think he had planned it, the little devil—he knew by then that he could get into my pants, because there's already been a lot of kissing and touching inside the blouse, and then under the skirt and so forth. The next step was obvious. And me, as brazen as I was, when it came down to finally doing the real thing, it was like: "Uh-oh, it's time." I mean, I was scared. And then it happened.
>
> Well, it hurt so bad—I think my earlobes were hurting. I was just dying, God. And he wanted to do it two or three times! It was like poking an open wound. I could hardly walk afterwards.
>
> But I did it for love. The pain was excruciating; but I loved him and he loved me, and that made the pain less— Everything was right. So it was beautiful.

Only there is nothing beautiful about the scenario Turner describes. A tension exists between the "cool" way she describes this experience, playing it off to suggest she was in control of the situation, and the reality she recounts where she succumbs to male lust and suffers sex. After describing a painful rite of sexual initiation, Turner undermines the confession by telling the reader that she felt good. Through retrospective memory, Turner is able to retell this experience in a manner that suggests she was comfortable with sexual experience at an early age, yet cavalier language does not completely mask the suffering evoked by the details she gives. However, this cavalier attitude accords best with how her fans "see" her. Throughout the biography she will describe situations of extreme sexual victimization and then undermine the impact of her words by evoking the image of herself and other black women as sexually free, suggesting that we assert sexual agency in ways that are never confirmed by the evidence she provides.

Tina Turner's singing career has been based on the construction of an image of black female sexuality that is made synonymous with wild animalistic lust. Raped and exploited by Ike Turner, the man who made this image and

143

imposed it on her, Turner describes the way her public persona as singer was shaped by his pornographic misogynist imagination:

> Ike explained: As a kid back in Clarksdale, he'd become fix-
> ated on the white jungle goddess who romped through
> Saturday matinee movie serials—revealing rag-clad women
> with long flowing hair and names like Sheena, Queen of the
> Jungle, and Nyoka—particularly Nyoka. He still remem-
> bered *The Perils of Nyoka,* a fifteen-part Republic Picture
> serial from 1941, starring Kay Alridge in the title role and
> featuring a villainess named Vultura, an ape named Satan,
> and Clayton Moore (later to be TV's Lone Ranger) as love
> interest. Nyoka, Sheena—Tina! Tina Turner—Ike's own
> personal Wild Woman. He loved it.

Turner makes no comment about her thoughts about this image. How can she? It is part of the representation which makes and maintains her stardom.

Ike's pornographic fantasy of the black female as wild sexual savage emerged from the impact of a white patriarchal controlled media shaping his percep-tions of reality. His decision to create the wild black woman was perfectly com-patible with prevailing representations of black female sexuality in a white supremacist society. Of course the Tina Turner story reveals that she was any-thing but a wild woman; she was fearful of sexuality, abused, humiliated, fucked, and fucked over. Turner's friends and colleagues document the myriad ways she suffered about the experience of being brutally physically beaten prior to appearing on stage to perform, yet there is no account of how she coped with the contradiction (this story is told by witnesses in *I, Tina*). She was on one hand in excruciating pain inflicted by a misogynist man who dom-inated her life and her sexuality, and on the other hand projecting in every per-formance the image of a wild, tough, sexually liberated woman. Not unlike the lead character in the novel *Story of O* by Pauline Réage, Turner must act as though she glories in her submission, that she delights in being a slave of love. Leaving Ike, after many years of forced marital rape and physical abuse, because his violence is utterly uncontrollable, Turner takes with her the "image" he created.

Despite her experience of abuse rooted in sexist and racist objectification, Turner appropriated the "wild woman" image, using it for career advance-ment. Always fascinated with wigs and long hair, she created the blonde lioness mane to appear all the more savage and animalistic. Blondeness links her to jungle imagery even as it serves as an endorsement of a racist aesthetics which sees blonde hair as the epitome of beauty. Without Ike, Turner's career has soared to new heights, particularly as she works harder to exploit the visual representation of woman (and particularly black woman) as sexual savage. No longer caught in the sadomasochistic sexual iconography of black female in erotic war with her mate that was the subtext of the Ike and Tina Turner show, she is now portrayed as the autonomous black woman whose sexuality is solely a way to exert power. Inverting old imagery, she places herself in the role of dominator.

Playing the role of Aunty Entity in the film *Mad Max: Beyond Thunderdome,* released in 1985, Turner's character evokes two racist/sexist stereotypes, that of the black "mammy" turned power hungry and the sexual savage who uses her body to seduce and conquer men. Portrayed as lusting after the white male hero who will both conquer and reject her, Aunty Entity is the contemporary reenactment of that mythic black female in slavery who supposedly "vamped" and seduced virtuous white male slave owners. Of course the contemporary white male hero of *Mad Max* is stronger than his colonial forefathers. He does not succumb to the dangerous lure of the deadly black seductress who rules over a mini-nation whose power is based on the use of shit. Turner is the bad black woman in this film, an image she will continue to exploit.

Turner's video "What's Love Got To Do With It" also highlights the convergence of sexuality and power. Here, the black woman's body is represented as potential weapon. In the video, she walks down rough city streets, strutting her stuff, in a way that declares desirability, allure, while denying access. It is not that she is no longer represented as available; she is "open" only to those whom she chooses. Assuming the role of hunter, she is the sexualized woman who makes men and women her prey (in the alluring gaze of the video, the body moves in the direction of both sexes). This tough black woman has no time for woman bonding, she is out to "catch." Turner's fictive model of black female sexual agency remains rooted in misogynist notions. Rather than being a pleasure-based eroticism, it is ruthless, violent; it is about women using sexual power to do violence to the male Other.

Appropriating the wild woman pornographic myth of black female sexuality created by men in a white supremacist patriarchy, Turner exploits it for her own ends to achieve economic self-sufficiency. When she left Ike, she was broke and in serious debt. The new Turner image conveys the message that happiness and power come to women who learn to beat men at their own game, to throw off any investment in romance and get down to the real dog-eat-dog thing. "What's Love Got To Do With It" sung by Turner evokes images of the strong bitchified black woman who is on the make. Subordinating the idea of romantic love and praising the use of sex for pleasure as commodity to exchange, the song had great appeal for contemporary postmodern culture. It equates pleasure with materiality, making it an object to be sought after, taken, acquired by any means necessary. When sung by black women singers, "What's Love Got To Do With It" called to mind old stereotypes which make the assertion of black female sexuality and prostitution synonymous. Just as black female prostitutes in the 1940s and 1950s actively sought clients in the streets to make money to survive, thereby publicly linking prostitution with black female sexuality, contemporary black female sexuality is fictively constructed in popular rap and R&B songs solely as commodity—sexual service for money and power, pleasure is secondary.

Contrasted with the representation of wild animalistic sexuality, black female singers like Aretha Franklin and younger contemporaries like Anita Baker fundamentally link romance and sexual pleasure. Aretha, though seen as a victim of no-good men, the classic "woman who loves too much" and leaves the lyrics to prove it, also sang songs of resistance. "Respect" was heard by many black folks, especially black women, as a song challenging black male sexism and female victimization while evoking notions of mutual care and support. In a recent PBS special highlighting individual musicians, Aretha Franklin was featured. Much space was given in the documentary to white male producers who shaped her public image. In the documentary, she describes the fun of adding the words "sock it to me" to "Respect" as a powerful refrain. One of the white male producers, Jerry Wexler, offers his interpretation of its meaning, claiming that it was a call for "sexual attention of the highest order." His sexualized interpretations of the song seemed far removed from the way it was heard and celebrated in black communities. Looking at this documentary, which was supposedly a tribute to Aretha Franklin's power, it was impossible not to have one's attention deflected away from the music by the subtext of the film, which can be seen as a visual narrative documenting her obsessive concern with the body and achieving a look suggesting desirability. To achieve this end, Franklin constantly struggles with her weight, and the images in the film chronicle her various shifts in body size and shape. As though mocking this concern with her body, throughout most of the documentary Aretha appears in what seems to be a household setting, a living room maybe, wearing a strapless evening dress, much too small for her breast size, so her breasts appear like two balloons filled with water about to burst. With no idea who shaped and controlled this image, I can only reiterate that it undermined the insistence in the film that she has overcome sexual victimization and remained a powerful singer; the latter seemed more likely than the former.

Black female singers who project a sexualized persona are as obsessed with hair as they are with body size and body parts. As with nineteenth-century sexual iconography, specific parts of the anatomy are designated more sexual and worthy of attention than others. Today much of the sexualized imagery for black female stars seems to be fixated on hair; it and not buttocks signifies animalistic sexuality. This is quintessentially so for Tina Turner and Diana Ross. It is ironically appropriate that much of this hair is synthetic and man-made, artificially constructed as is the sexualized image it is meant to evoke. Within a patriarchal culture where women over forty are not represented as sexually desirable, it is understandable that singers exploiting sexualized representations who are near the age of fifty place less emphasis on body parts that may reflect aging while focusing on hair.

In a course I teach on "The Politics of Sexuality," where we often examine connections between race and sex, we once critically analyzed a *Vanity Fair* cover depicting Diana Ross. Posed on a white background, apparently naked with the exception of white cloth draped loosely around her body, the most striking element in the portrait was the long mane of jet black hair cascading down. There was so much hair that it seemed to be consuming her body (which looked frail and anorexic), negating the possibility that this naked flesh could represent active female sexual agency. The white diaper-like cloth reinforced the idea that this was a portrait of an adult female who wanted to be seen as childlike and innocent. Symbolically, the hair that is almost a covering hearkens back to early pictorial images of Eve in the garden. It evokes wildness, a sense of the "natural" world, even as it shrouds the body, repressing it, keeping it from the gaze of a culture that does not invite women to be sexual subjects. Concurrently, this cover contrasts whiteness and blackness. Whiteness dominates the page, obscuring and erasing the possibility of any assertion of black power. The longing that is most visible in this cover is that of the black woman to embody and be encircled by whiteness, personified by the possession of long straight hair. Since the hair is produced as commodity and purchased, it affirms contemporary notions of female beauty and desirability as that which can be acquired.

147

According to postmodern analyses of fashion, this is a time when commodities produce bodies, as this image of Ross suggests. In her essay "Fashion and the Cultural Logic of Postmodernity," Gail Faurshou explains that beauty is no longer seen as a sustained "category of precapitalist culture." Instead, "the colonization and the appropriation of the body as its own production/consumption machine in late capitalism is a fundamental theme of contemporary socialization." This cultural shift enables the bodies of black women to be represented in certain domains of the "beautiful" where they were once denied entry, i.e., high fashion magazines. Reinscribed as spectacle, once again on display, the bodies of black women appearing in these magazines are not there to document the beauty of black skin, of black bodies, but rather to call attention to other concerns. They are represented so readers will notice that the magazine is racially inclusive even though their features are often distorted, their bodies contorted into strange and bizarre postures that make the images appear monstrous or grotesque. They seem to represent an anti-aesthetic, one that mocks the very notion of beauty.

Often black female models appear in portraits that make them look less like humans and more like mannequins or robots. Currently, black models whose hair is not straightened are often photographed wearing straight wigs; this seems to be especially the case if the model's features are unconventional, i.e., if she has large lips or particularly dark skin, which is not often featured in the magazine. The October 1989 issue of *Elle* presented a short profile of designer Azzedine Alaia. He stands at a distance from a black female body holding the sleeves of her dress. Wearing a ridiculous straight hair-do, she appears naked holding the dress in front of her body. The caption reads, "THEY ARE BEAUTIFUL, AREN'T THEY!" His critical gaze is on the model and not the dress. As commentary it suggests that even black women can look beautiful in the right outfit. Of course when you read the piece, this statement is not referring to the model, but is a statement Alaia makes about his clothes. In contemporary postmodern fashion sense, the black female is the best medium for the showing of clothes because her image does not detract from the outfit; it is subordinated.

Years ago, when much fuss was made about the reluctance of fashion magazines to include images of black women, it was assumed that the presence of such representations would in and of themselves challenge racist stereotypes that imply black women are not beautiful. Nowadays, black women are included in magazines in a manner that tends to reinscribe prevailing stereotypes. Darker-skinned models are most likely to appear in photographs where their features are distorted. Bi-racial women tend to appear in sexualized images. Trendy catalogues like Tweeds and J. Crew made use of a racialized subtext in their layout and advertisements. Usually they are emphasizing the connection between a white European and American style. When they began to include darker-skinned models, they chose bi-racial or fair-skinned black women, particularly with blonde or light brown long hair. The non-white models appearing in these catalogues must resemble as closely as possible their white counterparts so as not to detract from the racialized subtext. A recent cover of Tweeds carried this statement:

> Color is, perhaps, one of the most important barometers of character and self-assurance. It is as much a part of the international language of clothes as silhouette. The message colors convey, however, should never overwhelm. They should speak as eloquently and intelligently as the wearer. Whenever colors have that intelligence, subtlety, and nuance we tend to call them European...

Given the racialized terminology evoked in this copy, it follows that when flesh is exposed in attire that is meant to evoke sexual desirability it is worn by a non-white model. As sexist/racist sexual mythology would have it, she is the embodiment of the best of the black female savage tempered by those elements of whiteness that soften this image, giving it an aura of virtue and innocence. In the racialized pornographic imagination, she is the perfect combination of virgin and whore, the ultimate vamp. The impact of this image is so intense that Iman, a highly paid black fashion model who once received worldwide acclaim because she was the perfect black clone of a white ice goddess beauty, has had to change. Postmodern notions that black female beauty is constructed, not innate or inherent, are personified by the career of Iman. Noted in the past for features this culture sees as "Caucasian"—thin nose, lips, and limbs—Iman appears in the October 1989 issue of *Vogue* "made over." Her lips and breasts are suddenly full. Having once had her "look" destroyed by a car accident and then remade, Iman now goes a step further. Displayed as the embodiment of a heightened sexuality, she now looks like the racial/sexual stereotype. In one full-page shot, she is naked, wearing only a pair of brocade boots, looking as though she is ready to stand on any street corner and turn a trick, or worse yet, as though she just walked off one of the pages of *Players* (a porn magazine for blacks). Iman's new image appeals to a culture that is eager to reinscribe the image of black woman as sexual primitive. This new representation is a response to contemporary fascination with an ethnic look, with the exotic Other who promises to fulfill racial and sexual stereotypes, to satisfy longings. This image is but an extension of the edible black tit.

Currently, in the fashion world the new black female icon who is also gaining greater notoriety, as she assumes both the persona of sexually hot "savage" and white-identified black girl, is the Caribbean-born model Naomi Campbell. Imported beauty, she, like Iman, is almost constantly visually portrayed nearly nude against a sexualized background. Abandoning her "natural" hair for blonde wigs or ever-lengthening weaves, she has great crossover appeal. Labeled by fashion critics as the black Brigitte Bardot, she embodies an aesthetic that suggests black women, while appealingly "different," must resemble white women to be considered really beautiful.

Within literature and early film, this sanitized ethnic image was defined as that of the "tragic mulatto." Appearing in film, she was the vamp that white men feared. As Julie Burchill puts it outrageously in *Girls On Film:*

> In the mature Forties, Hollywood decided to get to grips with
> the meaty and messy topic of multiracial romance, but it was
> a morbid business. Even when the girls were gorgeous white
> girls—multiracial romance brought tears, traumas, and sui-
> cide. The message was clear: you intelligent white men suffer
> enough guilt because of what your grandaddy did—you
> want to suffer some more! Keep away from those girls…

Contemporary films portraying bi-racial stars convey this same message. The warning for women is different from that given men—we are given messages about the danger of asserting sexual desire. Clearly the message from *Imitation of Life* was that attempting to define oneself as sexual subject would lead to rejection and abandonment. In the film *Choose Me,* Rae Dawn Chong plays the role of the highly sexual black woman chasing and seducing the white man who does not desire her (as was first implied in *Imitation of Life)* but instead uses her sexually, beats her, then discards her. The bi-racial black woman is constantly "gaslighted" in contemporary film. The message her sexualized image conveys does not change even as she continues to chase the white man as if only he had the power to affirm that she is truly desirable.

European films like *Mephisto* and the more recent *Mona Lisa* also portray the almost white, black woman as tragically sexual. The women in the films can only respond to constructions of their reality created by the more powerful. They are trapped. Mona Lisa's struggle to be sexually self-defining leads her to choose lesbianism, even though she is desired by the white male hero. Yet her choice of a female partner does not mean sexual fulfillment as the object of her lust is a drug-addicted young white woman who is always too messed up to be sexual. Mona Lisa nurses and protects her. Rather than asserting sexual agency, she is once again in the role of mammy.

In a more recent film, *The Virgin Machine,* a white German woman obsessed by the longing to understand desire goes to California where she hopes to find a "paradise of black Amazons." However, when she arrives and checks out the lesbian scene, the black women she encounters are portrayed as mean fat grotesques, lewd and licentious. Contemporary films continue to place black women in two categories, mammy or slut, and occasionally a combination of the two. In *Mona Lisa,* one scene serves as powerful commentary on the way black sexuality is perceived in a racist and imperialist social context. The white male who desires the black prostitute Mona Lisa is depicted as a victim of romantic love who wishes to rescue her from a life of ruin. Yet he is also the conqueror, the colonizer, and this is most evident in the scene where he watches a video wherein she engages in fellatio with the black male pimp who torments her. Both the black man and the black woman are presented as available for the white male's sexual consumption. In the context of postmodern sexual practice, the masturbatory voyeuristic technologically based fulfillment of desire is more exciting than actually possessing any real Other.

There are few films or television shows that attempt to challenge assumptions that sexual relationships between black women and white men are not based solely on power relationships which mirror master/slave paradigms. Years ago, when soap operas first tried to portray romantic/sexual involvement between a black woman and a white man, the station received so many letters of protest from outraged viewers that they dropped this plot. Today many viewers are glued to the television screen watching the soap opera *All My Children* primarily to see if the black woman played by Debbie Morgan will win the white man she so desperately loves. These two lovers are never portrayed in bedroom scenes so common now in daytime soaps. Morgan's character is competing not just with an old white woman flame to get her white man, she is competing with a notion of family. And the story poses the question of whether white male desire for black flesh will prevail over commitments to blood and family loyalty.

151

Despite this plot of interracial sexual romance on the soaps, there is little public discussion of the connections between race and sexuality. In real life, it was the Miss America pageant where a black woman was chosen to represent beauty and therefore desirability which forced a public discussion of race and sex. When it was revealed that Vanessa Williams, the fair-skinned, straightened-hair "beauty," had violated the representation of the Miss America girl as pure and virtuous by having posed nude in a series of photographs showing her engaged in sexual play with a white woman, she lost her crown but gained a different status. After her public "disgrace," she was able to remain in the limelight by appropriating the image of sexualized vamp and playing sexy roles in films. Unmasked by a virtuous white public, she assumed (according to their standards) the rightful erotic place set aside for black women in the popular imagination. The American public that had so brutally critiqued Williams and rejected her had no difficulty accepting and applauding her when she accepted the image of fallen woman. Again, as in the case of Tina Turner, Williams's bid for continued success necessitated her acceptance of conventional racist/sexist representations of black female sexuality.

The contemporary film that has most attempted to address the issue of black female sexual agency is Spike Lee's *She's Gotta Have It*. Sad to say, the black woman does not get "it." By the end of the film, she is still unable to answer the critical question, posed by one of her lovers as he rapes her, "Whose pussy is this?" Reworded, the question might be: How and when will black females assert sexual agency in ways that liberate us from the confines of colonized desire, of racist/sexist imagery and practice? Had Nola Darling been able to claim her sexuality and name its power, the film would have had a very different impact.

There are few films that explore issues of black female sexuality in ways that intervene and disrupt conventional representations. The short film *Dreaming Rivers,* by the British black film collective Sankofa, juxtaposes the idealized representation of black woman as mother with that of sexual subject, showing adult children facing their narrow notions of black female identity. The film highlights the autonomous sexual identity of a mature black woman which exists apart from her role as mother and caregiver. *Passion of Remembrance*, another film by Sankofa, offers exciting new representations of the black female body and black female sexuality. In one playfully erotic scene, two young black women, a lesbian couple, get dressed to go out. As part of their celebratory preparations they dance together, painting their lips, looking at their images in the mirror, exulting in their black female bodies. They shake

152

to a song that repeats the refrain "let's get loose" without conjuring images of a rotgut colonized sexuality on display for the racist/sexist imagination. Their pleasure, the film suggests, emerges in a decolonized erotic context rooted in commitments to feminist and anti-racist politics. When they look in the mirror and focus on specific body parts (their full thick lips and buttocks), the gaze is one of recognition. We see their pleasure and delight in themselves.

Films by African American women filmmakers also offer the most oppositional images of black female sexuality. Seeing for a second time Kathleen Collin's film *Losing Ground*, I was impressed by her daring, the way she portrays black female sexuality in a way that is fresh and exciting. Like *Passion of Remembrance* it is in a domestic setting, where black women face one another (in Collin's film—as mother and daughter), that erotic images of black female sexuality surface outside a context of domination and exploitation. When daughter and mother share a meal, the audience watches as a radical sexual aesthetics emerges as the camera moves from woman to woman, focusing on the shades and textures of their skin, the shapes of their bodies, and the way their delight and pleasure in themselves is evident in their environment. Both black women discreetly flaunt a rich sensual erotic energy that is not directed outward, it is not there to allure or entrap; it is a powerful declaration of black female sexual subjectivity.

When black women relate to our bodies, our sexuality, in ways that place erotic recognition, desire, pleasure, and fulfillment at the center of our efforts to create radical black female subjectivity, we can make new and different representations of ourselves as sexual subjects. To do so we must be willing to transgress traditional boundaries. We must no longer shy away from the critical project of openly interrogating and exploring representations of black female sexuality as they appear everywhere, especially in popular culture. In *The Power of the Image: Essays on Representation and Sexuality*, Annette Kuhn offers a critical manifesto for feminist thinkers who long to explore gender and representation:

> ...in order to challenge dominant representations, it is necessary first of all to understand how they work, and thus where to seek points of possible productive transformation. From such understanding flow various politics and practices of oppositional cultural production, among which may be counted feminist interventions...here is another justification

153

for a feminist analysis of mainstream images of women: may it not teach us to recognize inconsistencies and contradictions within dominant traditions of representation, to identify points of leverage for our own intervention: cracks and fissures through which may be captured glimpses of what in other circumstance might be possible, visions of "a world outside the order not normally seen or thought about"?

This is certainly the challenge facing black women, who must confront the old painful representations of our sexuality as a burden we must suffer, representations still haunting the present. We must make the oppositional space where our sexuality can be named and represented, where we are sexual subjects—no longer bound and trapped.

---

bell hooks is a writer and professor who speaks widely on issues of race, class, and gender. Among her published books are: Outlaw Culture, Talking Back, Art on My Mind: Visual Politics, Bone Black: Memories of Childhood, *and* Reel to Reel: Race, Sex and Class at the Movies.

Judith Baumel

SNOW-DAY

What was it drove me to insist on sleds,
to pull the children out of the playground
and toward the park's much steeper hills, instead
of making angels? I was waist deep and bound
by ice, and they were too. In their eyelashes
was unremovable ice. They crawled and flailed
on snow. The progress of their grudging limbs
slow. Surely memory of snow-fort caches,
the childish city happily derailed,
its hopes of milk and bread and papers dim.

When I was young I came to Boston late
late late one winter night from Baltimore,
The pre-dawn, post blizzard, of 'seventy-eight
glowed in the silent town where dump trucks bore
their loads of snow as through a secret city—
filling and then dumping in the harbor,
filling yet again. I'd just removed
a child from my womb. Well someone else did it
and it was not a child but some small scar
inside. It meant nothing to me, that newt,

that early fetus, and the procedure meant
nothing except perhaps the end of fear
and queasiness. Today how I resent
the way sadness and loss are souvenirs
we're forced to carry with us. Listen—Happy
is the way I felt, and still I feel,
when I can shovel through the euphemisms

of those who speak for me. More happy. Happy
that forever will that speck, that organism
remain forever small and unfulfilled

in contrast to my son who came exactly
ten years after to the day, and to
a woman ready for him. I had wept
returning to my now-lost lover anew,
seeing the streets of Boston being cleaned,
scraped clear of the invading snow
that clung to arteries, that fairly smothered
our chance to try to make a normal flow
of life. That struggle with the midnight gleam:
the wiping, tidying gesture of a mother.

Judith Baumel is the author of two books of poems: The Weight of Numbers, *which won the 1987 Walt Whitman Award of the Academy of American Poets, and* Now. *She is the translator of Italian poet Patrizia Cavalli, and teaches at Adelphi University and City College of New York. She lives in the Bronx.*

Roberta Swann

MOTHER & CHILD

She spent the day feeling frustrated, sipping with ladies who shape their lives around tea cups. One hand held a cigarette. The other played with crumbs on the table. She switched from first to third person and managed to be amiable. When they were gone, she invented her life as it went along.

Jennifer walked in, fresh mud on her knees, ready for a bath. Daughter, so blonde and blue, who saw only a little, but with great intensity. She turned on the bath water and added Jennifer's favorite scent. The child climbed in with a wooden spoon, a rubber frog, and a toothpaste cap. The bath, her plaything, she stayed in long enough to shrivel into a white raisin.

She walked into the bathroom and took off her clothes. Body looked thin, but breasts and ass were firm. He said she looked haggard the last time he picked the child up, but ex-husbands are not reliable sources. She slipped into a kimono and propped herself on a pillow. From inside the bed table, she retrieved a vibrator. Muffling the buzz with her discarded panties, she aimed for target. She began to feel feral, as if her clitoris were a magnetic needle gone wild. And then she felt relief. And then she felt sexier.

Lost in her own fantasies, she didn't notice the child trail in until she felt a damp hand ask a question. Flicking off the switch nervously, she got busy with a towel. Never had a child been so meticulously rubbed and powdered. And kissed—to keep that little mouth closed.

"What were you doing?"

"Oh, just giving myself a massage."

"Can I have one too?"

"No, sillyhead, little girls don't get massages."

"Why not?"

"They don't need them."

"Doesn't it feel good."

"Yes, Jen, it feels very good. Relaxing…"

157

"So, I want to feel good too."

The child touched the mother's arm, waiting.

"O.K. Lie down."

Jennifer cast off the bath towel and dug a comfortable place for herself in the bedcovers. The machine skimmed her small body and flushed Jennifer's creamy skin.

"It makes me feel ticklish."

The mother smiled and encouraged intimacy. Jenny stared at her mother's breasts that had slipped out of the robe and hung free. The child reached up and squeezed the nipple.

"Look, it changed into magic dots."

Jenny fiddled with her tiny nipplets, then pulled a face.

"Nothing happened."

The mother smiled. What else could she do?

"Buzz my cunny."

She scooped the child in an affectionate hug, cradling her head, rocking.

"Buzz me. Buzz me like you did to your cunny."

Seized by the moment, she loomed down at her creation, a miniature of herself with just the right amount of fingers and toes. A Fabergé egg of a body, the mother thought. Not an immaculate conception this, but miraculous. In some atavistic way, she was letting things just happen. She could not deny the sexual current...

"Mommy, you're not remembering what I said. Pleeease."

The black rubber head seemed gigantic, circling the small pubic area, cupping the pink inch. The child shivered, exhaling an audible sigh. Then she curled up and nestled into her mother. The mother felt like there was a party of babies at her breast. The child was still and silent.

In the moment of passing travail, she felt red and white emotions. Jennifer looked up with a sideways motion of her hand and asked, "Mommy, can I touch your hairy place?" She flipped a mental coin, hoping the penny would take a month to fall.

"How about some cookies?"

"Uh, uh. Can I have another turn?" She decided not to babble or bowdlerize, and summoned her adult and maternal resources.

"Jennifer, my sweet, this game is like birthdays or Christmas, not to happen in bunches."

There was a moment of pause in the child's eyes. Then she catapulted from the bed.

"Well then, dress me."

She ran down the steps and into the yard, tripping over her feet, an angel slipping on wings. From the window, the mother watched the child examine a long-toothed leaf and stick it in her shoe. Jennifer pranced around, singing a funny made-up song. The dog sniffed close behind. She turned around and caught him by the tail. She tried to stick the leaf through his collar. The dog protested. The child insisted.

The mother stood looking out the window. A slight shiver ran through her body as she glanced back at the rumpled bed. She watched the child lift off her feet, skipping. Then Jennifer stopped and looked up at the sky, curious about the cirrus that was moving in.

If there was fault to find, let others find it. At that moment, she felt like a monk among his enchantments.

Roberta Swann is co-founder of the American Jazz Orchestra and program director of The Great Hall at Cooper Union in New York City. She is the author of four books, Private Parts, Women the Children the Men, The Model Life, *and* Everything Happens Suddenly. *Her poetry and fiction have appeared in numerous publications and literary journals.*

Diane di Prima

FUCK THE PILL: A DIGRESSION

On his first trip to town, Billy had embarrassedly purchased some Trojans, and he used them on our first night in our cottage—and, at my insistence, never used them again. I understood and appreciated the thought behind them but they were a drag. Up to that time, I had never used any contraceptives at all. In fact, for the first few years of my running around town I never used anything to avoid pregnancy, and never once got pregnant. Some kind of youthful charisma kept the thing going.*

The one time I thought I was knocked up, two weeks late with my period, I took a long walk in the broiling sun (it was a July) with a red-haired maniac junkie named Ambrose, down along West Street, past the trucks and the cobblestones. Came to a ferry landing, and embarked on a ferry for Jersey City, where we were followed and hooted at by a band of youngsters, bought bologna sandwiches at a local delicatessen, and found our way into the town cemetery, where we sat down on tombstones to eat and recite Keats to each other. A huge white dog came out of nowhere and laid his head on my lap like a unicorn in an old tapestry while I sat on the tombstone, and immediately the bleeding started. This is a method of abortion that I highly recommend, though I have never heard of anyone else who tried it, either successfully or unsuccessfully. Only thing was, when it was time to go back to Manhattan, we could find no ferry and were told by the bus driver who took us to the Hudson tube that the ferry hadn't run in several years....

Later, after I moved uptown, I got a diaphragm at the Sanger Clinic, with much trepidation and lying about being married, and I would scramble out

* N.B. 1988—Please, folks, this is not, repeat is *not* an encouragement to avoid condoms now. Flirting with pregnancy is one thing: having a kid can be a great celebration of life; flirting with AIDS is something else: is simply courting a quick and ugly death.

160

of bed in that freezing cold-water flat, and go into the room called the Woodshed, where I would stand, trembling with cold, as I slipped the small rubber disk into place. And by the time I came back, shivering and with cold feet, to the bed, it would be a matter of starting all over again, of somehow *working up to* the passion we had set so easily and naturally going in the first place.

Well, you may flatter yourself, that's all in the past, the lucky girls have the pill now, and they can do what they please, are as free as men, etc., etc. The pill, the pill, the pill! Let me tell you about the pill. It makes you fat, the pill does. It makes you hungry. Gives you sore breasts, slight morning sickness, condemns you, who have avoided pregnancy, to live in a perpetual state of early pregnancy: woozy, and nauseous, and likely to burst into tears. And— crowning irony—it makes you, who have finally achieved the full freedom to fuck, much less likely to want to fuck, cuts down on the sex drive. So much for the pill.

Then there is the cunning little gadget known as the IUD—intra-uterine device. A funny little plastic spring they stick in your womb. Why not? Principle on which it works (they think) is that it drives your womb frantic, trying to get rid of it, and everything inside of you happens that much more quickly: the monthly egg passes through your system in two or three hours, instead of as many days. Only a few little things wrong with the IUD: cramps, intermittent bleeding, a general state of tension. It also has a habit of wandering, and may turn up just about anywhere, or not turn up at all. There are two strings attached to the clever little contraption and sticking out of the neck of your womb, and you are supposed to check, by poking around in your vagina, whether or not the strings are still there. Nobody has told me what you do about it if they aren't. Also, since the IUD does allow nature a narrow margin of functioning, there are a few hours when you *can* get pregnant, and, if you're going to get pregnant, I guess you probably will, in those few hours. Nurse once told me of delivering a baby with a coil embedded in the afterbirth.

What then? What does that leave us? Leaves us ye olde-fashioned diaphragm, and we all know what a drag that is, and ye almost-as-olde creams and foams, which proportedly can be used *without* a diaphragm, and are good for exactly twenty minutes to a half hour after insertion, which means you have to work pretty fast, with one eye on the clock. They also *drip* and run and are unspeakably gooey, and add to the natural joyous gooey-ness of lust a certain chemical texture and taste, which could, I suppose, with determination, become an

161

acquired taste, but is at least slightly unpleasant to the uninitiated. And up you get, if *he* gets his up again, and you insert into all the gooey mess inside you some more foam. Medieval, I'd say.

Or it leaves us having babies. Having babies has certain advantages, not to be gainsaid. One is that you don't have to do anything about it—when you want to fuck, you just fuck. Nothing gooey, nothing tension-making. If you get knocked up, the discomfort of early pregnancy tends to last only two or three months—whereas with the pill it lasts forever. Pregnancy always makes me want to fuck more, too, and I enjoy it more. And in those last months, the delights of ingenuity are added, and many new joys discovered. As for childbirth, having a baby is a matter of lying down and having it. After the first one, nothing could be easier if you forget the rules: forget doctors, hospitals, enemas, shaving of public hair, forget stoicism and "painless childbirth"—simply holler and push the damned thing out. Takes less time, trouble, and thought than any of the so-called "modern methods of birth control." And to support the creature? Get welfare, quit working, stay home, stay stoned, and fuck.

* * *

Being a woman to three men was an interesting trip. Big Bill had eyes for me, but I put him off for a while. I didn't know how Billy would feel about it if I made it with his dad, and I dug him too much to fuck things up.

We finally got together one weekend when Billy and Little John were off on a two-day hike. After supper Big Bill just sat down on the sofa beside me and began to undo my shirt. His deliberation and assurance came on like restraint, and the man-smell of his body—sweat and earth and tobacco—was tremendously exciting to me. Except for being raped by Serge Klebert I had never made it with an older man, and I was pleasantly surprised. Big Bill's body was lean and hard, the muscles well-defined, steel-like under the smooth, mobile skin. His prick, when I drew it from his work pants, was slimmer than Billy's but slightly longer. It had a kind, worldly-wise air about it, as if it had drawn wisdom from all the cunts it had entered. There was a competence and strength in his long fingers as he took hold of me, a skill and understanding in his lips on my breast that was reassuring and delightful. I was about to embark on a voyage with a seasoned sailor, one who knew the trip and every turn of the wind. He made me sense my youth and awkwardness, and see them as something precious, not easily come by.

162

We passed a beautiful night on the couch, fucking and dozing till dawn. And then, when it turned light, we stumbled off to our separate beds for a few hours of sleep.

The scene with Little John was something else. We were too much alike in our littleness, our high energy and our toughness to interest each other. Though we did try making out once or twice experimentally in the afternoon when Big Bill and Billy were off at work and John had not yet gotten a job on the road crew with them, it never went anywhere and we never thought much about it, one way or the other.

Evenings would find the four of us listening to the world on Big Bill's short-wave radio—the outside world that seemed so far away from our farmhouse, but would suddenly loom: close, treacherous and threatening as soon as we turned the knob. Or we would play chess, or read plays together. Big Bill really dug amateur theatricals and his idea of the way to spend a country evening was to do staged readings. He had a good voice and was really fine at it: Shakespeare or Brecht, found Cocteau too thin, boomed lines at us while insects crash-landed by the thousands on the screens, attracted by our late-burning lights.

Yes, it was good, being a chick to three men, and each of them on his own trip, each wanting a different thing, so that the world filled out, and interplay, like a triple-exposed photo, made infinite space. I have since found that it is usually a good thing to be the woman of many men at once, or to be one of many women on one man's scene, or to be one of many women in a household with many men, and the scene between all of you shifting and ambiguous. What is not good, what is claustrophobic and deadening, is the regular one-to-one relationship. OK for a weekend, or a month in the mountains, but not OK for a long-time thing, not OK once you have both told yourselves that this is to be the form of your lives. Then begin endless claims, and jugglings to avoid boredom, and the slow inexorable closing of God's infinite horizon, like the red-hot tightening walls in Poe's "The Pit and the Pendulum," walls that move in inexorably and choke the life out of your world.

In the Middle Ages there was the chastity belt—but that at least could be dealt with, with a hacksaw if nothing else. In our parents' day there was marriage, there sometimes still is, and that is ugly enough, but it is a legal form, and can be dealt with by more of the same, more papers. It is unpleasant, but it is only one form of the monster. The real horror, the nightmare in which most of us are spending our adult lives, is the deep-rooted insidious belief in

163

the one-to-one world. The world of "this is my old man." Live with one man, and you begin to have a claim on him. Live with five, and you have the same claim, but it is spread out, ambiguous, undefined. What is unfilled by one will be filled by another easily, no one hung up guilty and inadequate, no one pushed to the wall by demands that he/she can't meet.

I remember reading in the books of that great woman explorer, Alexandra David-Neel, that in Tibet both polygamy and polyandry were once practiced freely. Would love to know more about that social structure, how it worked, how they got it to work, who lived with whom. In the photos the women are beautiful, strong, free creatures, sufficient to themselves; I read that they owned land and businesses like their menfolk; and the men—well, the men and women together created one of the wildest magics this planet has ever witnessed.

We flourished on our Hudson River farm, functioned for each other. Big Bill took care of my head—his largesse and stability, his confidence made me feel safe and well, as I had never felt in my life, his gallantry made me feel beautiful. Billy was fleshmate and comrade, we were well-matched: I could hold my own with him hiking, or weeding, or fucking; my life-force matched his well. And Little John was brother and friend; I heard my paranoia echoing in his head, he found his secrets spelled out in my poems. Many a stalemate game of chess went down between us.

It was a different life from any that I had known before: the quiet of those long twilights, when we would pass the grass around and mumble warm laconic sentences at each other in the bare, dowdy living room with its worn-out sofa and dumpy chairs. Billy sometimes singing to us; Big Bill reminiscing, telling anecdotes of Woody Guthrie, or running down the wartime rackets in New York City, filling us in; Little John scribbling in notebooks, biting his nails in a corner. I got used to the slow, spaced rhythm of my days and for a while it seemed to me that I had never known any other place than this timeless one, days colored green by the garden, and nights colored gold by the oil lamp. I lost myself in my new-found woman's role, the position defined and revealed by my sex: the baking and mending, the mothering and fucking, the girls' parts in the plays—and I was content.

But slowly, imperceptibly, the days began to shorten, the grass turned brown, and with the first crickets a restlessness stirred in me for the quick combat and hard living of the city, for the play and the strife and the inexhaustible human interchange that was New York to me then. I would catch myself listening for the traffic, or the background of "Bird" being played on a cheap

164

phonograph in the next apartment, and I knew it was time for me to be on my way. So I took my leave of Billy for the time being—he would be back in New York in the Fall—gave him back his baggy Levis and donned my office skirt and blouse. Big Bill drove me to a bus station, and within an hour I was back in New York.

Diane di Prima was born in Brooklyn, New York, a second-generation American of Italian descent. She lived in Manhattan for many years where she was known as one of the most important writers of the Beat movement. During that time, she co-founded the New York Poets Theatre, and founded the Poet's Press, which published many writers of the period. Together with Amiri Baraka she edited the literary newsletter The Floating Bear. *For the past thirty years she has lived and worked in northern California, where she was one of the co-founders and teachers of the San Francisco Institute of Magical and Healing Arts. Her recent work includes* Pieces of a Song: Selected Poems *and* Seminary Poems.

Philip Roth

from PORTNOY'S COMPLAINT

Then came adolescence—half my waking life spent locked behind the bathroom door, firing my wad down the toilet bowl, or into the soiled clothes in the laundry hamper, or *splat*, up against the medicine-chest mirror, before which I stood in my dropped drawers so I could see how it looked coming out. Or else I was doubled over my flying fist, eyes pressed closed by mouth wide open, to take that sticky sauce of buttermilk and Clorox on my own tongue and teeth—though not infrequently, in my blindness and ecstasy, I got it all in the pompadour, like a blast of Wildroot Cream Oil. Through a world of matted handkerchiefs and crumpled Kleenex and stained pajamas, I moved my raw and swollen penis, perpetually in dread that my loathsomeness would be discovered by someone stealing upon me just as I was in the frenzy of dropping my load. Nevertheless, I was wholly incapable of keeping my paws from my dong once it started the climb up my belly. In the middle of a class I would raise a hand to be excused, rush down the corridor to the lavatory, and with ten or fifteen savage strokes, beat off standing up into a urinal. At the Saturday afternoon movie I would leave my friends to go off to the candy machine— and wind up in a distant balcony seat, squirting my seed into the empty wrapper from a Mounds bar. On an outing of our family association, I once cored an apple, and saw to my astonishment (and with the aid of my obsession) what it looked like, and ran off into the woods to fall upon the orifice of the fruit, pretending that the cool and mealy hole was actually between the legs of that mythical being who always called me Big Boy when she pleaded for what no girl in all recorded history had ever had. "Oh shove it in me, Big Boy," cried the cored apple that I banged silly on that picnic. "Big Boy, Big Boy, oh give me all you've got," begged the empty milk bottle that I kept hidden in our storage bin in the basement, to drive wild after school with my vaselined upright. "Come, Big Boy, come," screamed the maddened piece of liver that, in my own insanity, I bought one afternoon at a butcher

166

shop and, believe it or not, violated behind a billboard on the way to a bar mitzvah class.

It was at the end of my freshman year of high school—and freshman year of masturbating—that I discovered on the underside of my penis, just where the shaft meets the head, a little discolored dot that has since been diagnosed as a freckle. Cancer. I had given myself *cancer*. All that pulling and tugging at my own flesh, all that friction, had given me an incurable disease. And not yet fourteen! In bed at night the tears rolled from my eyes. "No!" I sobbed. "I don't want to die! Please—no!" But then, because I would very shortly be a corpse anyway, I went ahead as usual and jerked off into my sock. I had taken to carrying the dirty socks into bed with me at night so as to be able to use one as a receptacle upon retiring, and the other upon waking.

If only I could cut down to one hand-job a day, or hold the line at two, or even three! But with the prospect of oblivion before me, I actually began to set new records for myself. Before meals. After meals. *During* meals. Jumping up from the dinner table, I tragically clutch at my belly—diarrhea! I cry, I have been stricken with diarrhea!—and once behind the locked bathroom door, slip over my head a pair of underpants that I have stolen from my sister's dresser and carry rolled in a handkerchief in my pocket. So galvanic is the effect of cotton panties against my mouth—so galvanic is the *word* "panties"—that the trajectory of my ejaculation reaches startling new heights: leaving my joint like a rocket it makes right for the light bulb overhead, where to my wonderment and horror, it hits and it hangs. Wildly in the first moment I cover my head, expecting an explosion of glass, a burst of flames—disaster, you see, is never far from my mind. Then quietly as I can I climb the radiator and remove the sizzling gob with a wad of toilet paper. I begin a scrupulous search of the shower curtain, the tub, the tile floor, the four toothbrushes—God forbid!—and just as I am about to unlock the door, imagining I have covered my tracks, my heart lurches at the sight of what is hanging like snot to the toe of my shoe. I am the Raskolnikov of jerking off—the sticky evidence is everywhere! Is it on my cuffs too? in my *hair?* my *ear?* All this I wonder even as I come back to the kitchen table, scowling and cranky, to grumble self-righteously at my father when he opens his mouth full of red jello and says, "I don't understand what you have to lock the door about. That to me is beyond comprehension. What is this, a home or a Grand Central station?" "...privacy...a human being...around here *never*," I reply, then push aside my dessert to scream, "I don't feel well—*will everybody leave me alone?*"

After dessert—which I finish because I happen to like jello, even if I detest them—after dessert I am back in the bathroom again. I burrow through the week's laundry until I uncover one of my sister's soiled brassieres. I string one shoulder strap over the knob of the bathroom door and the other on the knob of the linen closet: a scarecrow to bring on more dreams. "Oh beat it, Big Boy, beat it to a red-hot pulp—" so I am being urged by the little cups of Hannah's brassiere, when a rolled-up newspaper smacks at the door. And sends me and my handful an inch off the toilet seat. "—Come on, give somebody else a crack at that bowl, will you?" my father says. "I haven't moved my bowels in a week."

I recover my equilibrium, as is my talent, with a burst of hurt feelings. "I have a terrible case of diarrhea! Doesn't that mean anything to anyone in this house?"—in the meantime resuming the stroke, indeed quickening the tempo as my cancerous organ miraculously begins to quiver again from the inside out.

Then Hannah's brassiere *begins to move*. To swing to and fro! I veil my eyes, and behold!—Lenore Lapidus! who has the biggest pair in my class, running for the bus after school, her great untouchable load shifting weightily inside her blouse, oh I urge them up from their cups, and over, LENORE LAPIDUS'S ACTUAL TITS, and realize in the same split second that my mother is vigorously shaking the doorknob. Of the door I have finally forgotten to lock! I knew it would happen one day! *Caught!* As good as *dead!*

"Open up, Alex. I want you to open up this instant."

It's locked, I'm *not* caught! And I see from what's alive in my hand that I'm not quite dead yet either. Beat on then! beat on! "Lick me, Big Boy—lick me a good hot lick! I'm Lenore Lapidus's big fat red-hot brassiere!"

"Alex, I want an answer from you. Did you eat French fries after school? Is that why you're sick like this?"

"Nuhhh, nuhhh."

"Alex, are you in pain? Do you want me to call the doctor? Are you in pain, or aren't you? I want to know exactly where it hurts. *Answer me.*"

"Yuhh, yuhhh—"

"Alex, I don't want you to flush the toilet," says my mother sternly. "I want to see what you've done in there. I don't like the sound of this at all."

"And me," says my father, touched as he always was by my accomplishments—as much awe as envy—"I haven't moved my bowels in a week," just as I lurch from my perch on the toilet seat, and with the whimper of a whipped animal, deliver three drops of something barely viscous into the tiny piece of cloth where my flat-chested eighteen-year-old sister has laid her nipples, such as they are. It is my fourth orgasm of the day. When will I begin to come blood?

Philip Roth won the 1960 National Book Award for his novel Goodbye, Columbus, *and a few years later published* Portnoy's Complaint, *from which this excerpt is taken. He has been honored by two National Book Critic's Circle awards, one in 1987 for the novel* Counterlife, *and the other in 1992 for his memoir,* Patrimony. *His other novels include the trilogy and epilogue* Zuckerman Bound, Letting Go, My Life as a Man, The Professor of Desire, American Pastoral, *and* Operation Shylock, *which won the 1993 Pen/Faulkner Award for fiction.*

Lloyd Schwartz

PORNOGRAPHY

I. First Couple

On his knees, his back to us: the pale honeydew melons of his
   bare buttocks, the shapely, muscular hemispheres—

the voluptuous center.

His knees push into the worn plush of a velvet cushion
   on the floral Oriental beside her cot.

He twists sideways—*contrapposto*—and bends to put his face
   into her crotch, between her limp legs,

   one hoisted by his right shoulder, the other—more
   like an arm—reaching around his back, her ankle
   resting on his naked hip.

   She's wearing shiny slippers with bows; he has on
   bedroom slippers and socks.

He's got a classic profile: straight nose, sharp chin.
   Cowlick. His hair tapers high on his neck,
   outlines his ear, in the current fashion;
                                    her
   curly bob gives away the date (barely '20s).

His mouth grazes her private hair; lips apart, he
   keeps his tongue to himself.

He's serious: if he were wearing clothes, and she were something
      with pipes, he'd be a plumber's assistant—inspecting,
      studious, intent;
                     nothing erotic in his look, hardly
      aroused at all (a little hard to tell, of course,
      from behind).

Flat on her back, on the dark, fringed spread, gravity
      flattening her breasts, she looks

      uncomfortable, but not unhappy. Her eyes
      check out the camera. Her lips are sealed, yet—

      isn't there?—a trace of smile
      playing around the edges . . .

She stretches out an arm to him, places her palm
      flat on his head—guiding him so lightly, she

      might be blessing him.

II. Second Couple: The Sailor and His Girl

They're hot, half-dressed (upper half only), and they
      can't wait.

      He sports a sailor's midi and a mariner's
      beret (is that a mound of fishing nets
      she's lying back on?)
                     He rests his naked knee
      beside her ample thigh.

Her dress is long—Victorian and striped. If she hadn't
      raised it to her chest, it would be hiding her
      black knee-length stockings and black, mannish shoes,
      (He's also wearing shoes. How did he get his
      pants off?)

No underwear—
                         nothing fallen around her ankles
    to keep her from spreading her legs.

Not quite supine, she strains forward to eye, and
        hold, his bold erection:
                              bat and hardballs—
    major league (his Fenway Frank; his juicy
    all-day-sucker).

He looks down hungrily at her hungry eyes
        and mouth—one hand pressed flush against
        his own naked thigh.
                          He slouches a little (not all of him is
    standing at attention), to make what she wants
    easier for her to reach.

But the photographer is sharp—he keeps his sharpest focus
        on what he's sure we want it on: all the

        fleshy folds, clefts, crevices—the no-longer-
    secret places—of her welcoming flesh.

He knows the costumes negate the spiritual burden
        (and freedom) of pure nakedness—
                              put us *in*
    medias res (things happening, things about
    to happen); in

        on the guilty secret, complicit—one eye
    furtively glancing over a shoulder…

His models rivet their attention on each other (did he
        have to tell them?), so that we can be

    riveted too.

172

Of course, they're only posing—
      but despite the props and costumes, certain

      undeniable details
      suggest that it isn't—it

      can't be—all an act.

III. *Ménage à Trois*

It's the heavy one—the one with the little pot belly, sagging
      breasts, and double chin (practically all we can
      see of her face)—that he's kissing so passionately.

Yet his arms are around them both, he loves them both
      (and of course he couldn't kiss them
      both at the same time).

Naked except for (like them) shoes and stockings, and garters,
      he sits at the edge of an overstuffed easy chair,
      his knees spread wide,
                    his massive cock
      rising like the Leaning Tower from his gut.

      His chest and neck, calves and thighs, have an athlete's
      sculptured musculature:

      exercise keeps all his parts in shape.

Both women are on their knees. She—the heavy one on his
      left (*our* right)—pushes into him, her round belly
      against his knee, her plush, round bottom
      a luxurious counterweight.

      Her fingers clutch his engorged organ, hang
      on to it, almost to steady herself.

173

The other one is slimmer, prettier, she has a pretty
        mouth—a delicate movie-star face.

        She's almost crouching, practically sitting on her
        own high heels; her right hand tenderly envelops
        his testicles.
                        Hard to tell if she's smiling
        up at his face or down at his genitals—probably
        both, in equal admiration, adoration, desire.

His own benign, blissed-out look is
        harder to read, his shadowy profile
        half-buried in the intense kiss.

There's something sweet, *humane*, about them all: not
        innocent—
                        but nothing (well, almost nothing) hard,
        or hardened yet.

        Only the little they have on reminds us how
        openly this was intended to be obscene.

The composition itself is elegant—balanced, symmetrical:
        the sweeping curve of the pretty one's behind
        and back, flowing up and across the curve of the
        man's shoulders and neck,
                                then down again through the
        fuller arcs of the plump one's back and rump—

        a harmonious circle of arms: theirs behind his back
        supporting him; his around them—his hands resting
        on their shoulders; their hands meeting in his lap . . .

It's like some medieval *Descent from the Cross* or *Holy
        Burial*: the slumping Christ between two
        ministering Angels—
                        but inside out, inverted, a negative

174

of the Passion. Passion here only—and nothing
but—passion. Perhaps

not even passion.

This ancient post card: cracked; corners broken; edges
frayed; worn and fragile

from use.

How many has it gratified; disappointed;
hurt? In whose horny fingers has it

been gripped (and did that hand
know what the other was doing)?

Not innocent—

but nothing about them
hard, or hardened yet;

not yet past taking pleasure
in whatever pleasure they

receive, or give.

Lloyd Schwartz is a professor of English and director of the Creative Writing Program at the University of Massachusetts/Boston, Classical Music Editor of The Boston Phoenix, *and a regular commentator on the National Public Radio program* Fresh Air. *He is the author of two books of poems,* These People *and* Goodnight, Gracie, *as well as a book of critical scholarship on Elizabeth Bishop. His reviews, articles, and poems have appeared in* The New Yorker, The New York Times, The Atlantic, Vanity Fair, The New Republic, *and* The Paris Review. *In 1994 he won the Pulitzer Prize for Criticism.*

Dan Savage

TWISTED

The following column, "Savage Love," was nationally syndicated in 1997.

Y ou bioboys think you've got problems....I'm a female-to-male transsexual who, since my accession to sentience, has been wild about boys. For years I tried to be happy as a straight female, but I wasn't a female and I wasn't straight. What I was, and am, is a guy into gay SM/leather as a master/top. I've been on testosterone a year and a half and pass as male, and in daily life my gender is not problematic. I'm small and boyish (think Michael J. Fox), and while I'd like to be taller, lots of big guys get off on being topped by a smaller guy. And since I'm also a drag queen, I like being able to look good when I go out en femme—which is not reverting to female: I mean drag in corsets and fishnets. Deep down, I think I'm a she-male dominatrix trapped in the body of an FTM tranny.

Here's my problem. I can't afford surgery, having been on disability for five years for CFIDS and cancer. I'm working now, but saving is difficult, and my insurance, like most, excludes sex reassignment surgery. Even if it did, the phalloplasty (weenie surgery) sucks: it gives you a nonerectile, usually nonorgasmic flesh-toned garden hose for 70 grand. With the aid of a penis enlarger pump, this leather-Master wannabe has managed to grow himself a 2 5/8-inch dick. I have some hope of being able to afford breast reduction and scrotoplasty (conversion of labia into balls, with testicular implants). But in the foreseeable future, pending advances in genital reconstruction surgery, I am the proverbial needledick.

Now, don't get me wrong, my minidick, a/k/a Little Willy, is a cute, pint-sized version of an uncut dick, head, skin and all, and in sensitivity and orgasmic capacity is an 11 out of a 10. It's just that, in an SM scene, whipping it out and ordering a slave to worship it is sort of anticlimactic. Friends tell me I shouldn't let being phallically challenged interfere with my sense of sexual self, but then they are either FTMs who are bottoms, or bioboys with standard-issue dongs. At this point, I consider myself bi and enjoy topping sub females, and females are much more accept-

ing of physical imperfections. But my primary erotic interest is hot, raunchy, male/male leather sex, and I understand that gay men want a partner with a dick. Hey, I love dicks myself. Any suggestions or observations? —*Dickless in Frisco*

Wow: a female-to-male tranny sadomasochist bisexual dickless drag queen. Just wait 'til pundits George Will (*Newsweek*) and John Leo (*U.S. News and World Report*) hear about you: they're always harping on the divisiveness of gender and identity politics, on how they pull people apart, instead of bringing them together—let's face it, things were ever so much simpler when men stayed men and women stayed women. In your case, however, gender and identity politics are not pulling you apart, it sounds like they're all that's holding you together.

On to your problem: you're an FTM-SM top, with a strong preference for gay leather sex, and gay boys, but you're stuck topping sub females because you don't have the standard-issue dong most SM bottom fag-boys like their Masters to have…. Jesus H. Christ, there isn't even a simple way to restate your problem. But there is a simple solution: even if you can't afford a frankencock—and you're right about those sex reassignment cocks being a waste of money and fatty thigh tissue—who says that the cock that gets worshipped in one of your hot fag leather/SM scenes has to be your own? Many leather/SM relationships are "poly-fidelious," or multipartnered. Hook up with another top, a guy who doesn't care about your puny equipment, and then the two of you get out there and find yourselves a bottom-boy to love, keep and order around together. When the time comes in the scene for cock worship to commence, give the order to your bottom-boyfriend-slave to worship your top-boyfriend-Master's cock. And everybody will be happy. Except, of course, for George Will and John Leo.

Note to Geo and Leo: In case you had a hard time following the acronyms and tranny jargon in the above letter—even I had to read it twice—here's a wee glossary. It may come in handy if you decide to write a column about how shocked, *shocked*, you were to learn of the existence of SM FTM GMs with CFIDS living in SF.

Tranny: A person who's changing or has changed their sex. Why? Cuz they got a bug in their ass about it, I guess—what business is it of yours?

FTM: Female to Male.

MTF: Minsk to Finland.

Little Willy: A heartwarming film about a state employee and the trouser whale she frees—er, flees—from in a hotel room in Arkansas.

IBM: Itchy Bowl Movements.

Bioboy: Boy born boys, as opposed to girls made boys.

CFIDS: Credulous Flakes & Indulgent Doctors Syndrome.

By the way, Geo and Leo, if you want to research FTMs before you slam them, DIF publishes a newsletter for gay/bi FTMs—*TransFagRag* (Elessar Press; 1259 El Camino Real #151; Menlo Park, CA 94025).

I'm a guy who grew up hiding my TV tendencies. Only in the last few years have I experienced going out in women's clothing. I can pass and love to dress very revealingly. I was surprised to discover how excited I became when a man hit on me. We ended up in a secluded spot where I blew him. After some soul-searching, I accepted that I enjoyed it and wanted to experience more. But while men are the majority of people attracted to TVs, I would prefer to build a long-term relationship with a woman. Are there any out there? Am I twisted, or what?

—Wild Side

Twisted? You certainly are, crumb-cake. But your twists could be worse, by which I mean, "more complicated." You could be a female-to-male transsexual sadomasochist dickless drag queen; you could have CFIDS; or you could look like George Will. There's a host of twisty things worse than your relatively simple and straight forward twist: you're a cross-dressing bisexual guy with hetero leanings—what could be simpler?!

As for finding a mate, you do have two options: Find a woman whose sexual tastes are compatible—personal ads, TV/TS organizations. If by some miracle you meet a woman with whom you're emotionally as well as kink-compatible, you're set. Your second option is to find a woman with whom you're emotionally compatible, date, fall in love, get married, etc. Then very, very slowly break her the bad news: you're twisted. Then pray she doesn't divorce your panty-wearin' ass. Good luck.

Dan Savage has been writing "Savage Love," his nationally syndicated sex advice column, since 1992. Savage's approach to sexuality has stirred up debate on gender relations, gay rights, heterosexual dating etiquette, AIDS, and safe sex. Savage is currently writing two book-length works. He is the associate editor of The Stranger, *Seattle's largest weekly newspaper, and lectures at college campuses across the country.*

IV
RITUAL

Drs. Hannah and Abraham Stone

SUGGESTIONS FOR MARITAL SUCCESS

What suggestions would you give a couple about to marry to help them achieve a happy marriage, Doctor?

It is presumptuous for anybody even to attempt to set up specific guideposts to marital happiness, yet I might venture a few suggestions:

One: *Know thyself.* Learn about the workings of the human body, human mind, and human nature. To make a good physical adjustment, acquire knowledge of the processes of sex and reproduction; and to make a good emotional adjustment, acquire insight into your thinking and feeling. The better you know yourself, the better you will know your mate. Such knowledge leads to understanding and awareness, to tolerance and consideration, all of which are essential elements of a successful marriage.

Two: *Cherish your mate.* Marriage is a declaration of interdependence. When you marry you promise to love and to cherish each other "for better or for worse, for richer or for poorer, in sickness and in health." At the basis of your marriage is the love you bear for each other. The joy of love is the bringing of happiness to the beloved. Cherish your mate and build a strong marital tie.

A married couple are bound together by a cord, a silken cord, shall we say. This cord is made up of many strands. The strongest of these is the love and affection they bear for each other. But other strands are also necessary, the strands of mutual interests, mutual experiences, mutual loyalties, a mutual way of life. The more strands you weave into the cord, the firmer your marriage will be. Weave a strong and lasting cord, a cord that never need be severed.

Three: *When you marry, make a unit of yourselves.* "For this," says the Bible, "shall a man leave his father and his mother, and shall cleave unto his wife, and they shall be one flesh." When you marry, do not remain tied to your parents, but form a new bond with your mate. Honor thy father and thy mother, but do not cling to them. Make your own home, and give your marriage a better chance for success.

Four: *Acquire the art of physical love.* A good sexual adjustment makes a strong marital bond. Learn the techniques of love and develop a mutually satisfying physical relationship. In your togetherness, blend sentiment and sensuality. The more harmonious your sex relations are, the greater the chances for a happy marriage.

Five: *Prepare yourself for parenthood.* Acquire information about the basic facts of childbearing and child rearing. They physical and emotional well-being of your child depends largely upon the care you provide for it during its early formative years. The better you are prepared for the care of your children, the more likely they are to grow into healthy and mature adults. Till the soil well and provide a good nurture for the seed. Give your child a good start in life.

A happy home life is a good asset for any child. Children who come from happy families, from homes where the parents are affectionate, congenial and considerate, are better prepared to have a happy marriage themselves. The best preparation for parenthood is a good marriage.

Six: *Plan your family wisely.* Make a good emotional adjustment before you plan your first baby. Acquire knowledge of reliable contraceptive measures and avoid the anxieties of an unplanned conception. Children should come when they are wanted and expected. They should come by choice and not by chance.

Avoid premature parenthood, but do not delay reproduction too long. For physical and psychological reasons it is wiser to start your family early. Space your children in accordance with your needs, and plan to complete your family while both of you are still young.

Seven: *Have tolerance in your marriage.* If you dance alone you may take any steps you fancy; but if you dance with a partner, both of you must harmonize your steps. In the beginning you may step on each other's toes, but after a while, with patience and practice, you learn to adapt yourselves to each other's rhythms. In marriage too it takes time for a satisfactory physical and emotional adjustment; it takes time for two people to adapt to each other's patterns of behavior and ways of living. Tolerance and patience add to your chances of a good marriage.

Patience and tolerance are also needed by the families on both sides. It takes time for an adjustment between a new couple and the members of their respective families. Because a girl falls in love with a young man, it does not mean that she will of necessity love his mother, or that her father will necessarily like her husband. New sons- or daughters-in-law are not quickly incorporated into the inner life of another family. Time and understanding are needed for a satisfactory assimilation.

Eight: *Nurture your marriage.* Like a plant, a marriage has to be cared for and fostered, especially while it is still young. Strengthen its roots by mutual consideration, by the daily attentions and courtesies, the signs of affection and thoughtfulness, which are like the sun and the rain to make marriage grow and flourish.

Be communicative in your expressions of affection. By word and gesture, show your feelings for each other. Love may be deeper than speech, but often it needs to be spoken. Nurture your marriage and make it grow.

The care of a plant requires also occasional weeding. If weeds are permitted to multiply, the plant may be stunted and withered. If they are removed early, the plant will have a good chance to attain its full growth. In marriage too, weed out your difficulties as they come up. Do not allow irritations to accumulate. Talk your problems over, and resolve them as they arise. Give your marriage a chance to grow and develop.

Nine: *When necessary, seek competent counsel.* If you cannot resolve your difficulties yourselves, consult an adviser. Marriage counseling is today emerging as a serious social science and social art. Physicians, ministers, social scientists, educators are training themselves for this new type of social service and practice. A trained counselor can give you understanding and insight, information and guidance, and help you prevent or remedy marital ills.

Neither of you may be aware of the hidden sources that motivate your conflicts. The cause of some disagreements may not be clear. Behind a simple argument may lie a deep sense of insecurity, or a wish for power, or a sexual frustration. If you are unable to deal with the problem yourselves, the aid of a counselor may be helpful. Seek competent guidance and further the success of your marriage.

Ten: *Follow the Golden Rule.* Do unto your mate as you would have your mate do unto you. Be aware of each other's feelings and sensitive to each other's needs. Forgive as you would be forgiven. Avoid domination or condemnation, disrespect or disloyalty, as you would have your mate avoid these toward you. This is a basic rule for all human relations, and if you adopt it also as a basic rule in your marriage relation your marriage will have an excellent chance of success.

In our culture the family is a democratic institution. It is based not on compulsion, not on binding contracts, but on binding affection and loyalty, on an inner unity and harmony between husband and wife. If you assume your mature responsibilities in your interpersonal relations, in your physical union, in planning for parenthood, in the cultivation of your marriage, your marriage will have a good chance of being both happy and successful.

Our sessions have come to and end, but your marriage journey is only at its start. During our discussions, we have charted the basic problems of the marital relation in the light of our present-day biological knowledge and social attitudes. "Married travelers," says Balzac "are in need of a pilot and a compass." Let us hope that our discussions will have served at least to point out the direction of a happy union and to guide you on the voyage to an ideal marriage.

Dr. Hannah Stone and Dr. Abraham Stone were pioneers in the birth control movement. They each served as medical director of the Margaret Sanger Research Bureau in New York. Together they founded the first marriage consultation center in America, and they were widely active as lecturers and writers on marriage, family life, and planned parenthood. A Marriage Manual *was first published in 1935, and revised in 1951. It presents, as the authors said in their foreword to the first edition, "the essential facts of mating and reproduction." In the late 1960s, after the authors' deaths,* A Marriage Manual *was updated by their daughter, Dr. Gloria Stone Aitken, to include new findings in the field of marriage, family planning, and birth control.*

Alex Comfort, M.D.

SLOW MASTURBATION

Prostitutes aren't usually much good at advanced sex: this is about the one old-time bordello trick which is worth trying. To make it work, you need to know how to tie your partner (see *Bondage)* and to have a partner who likes struggling against resistance, but it works for a great many people. Traditionally, the woman does it to the man, but it works in either direction. You need good access and a completely helpless partner, though you can try it without if bondage games turn you off, but the result is quite different and you can't get so far. The knack lies in playing on your partner like an instrument, alternately pushing them forward and frustrating them (compare *Relaxation).*

The woman starts by tying the man to her satisfaction, either staked out, or wrists behind and ankles crossed, knees open, naked and on his back. She then "signs her name" (*le coup de cassolette).* To do this she kneels astride him, facing him, and performs a tasteful striptease as far as her panties. Next, holding his hair in her hand, she rubs his mouth firmly over her armpit and breasts, giving him her body perfume. Then she locks her legs carefully round his neck and presses her covered pussy on his mouth. Finally she strips off and gives him the direct genital kiss (brushing first, then open, taking her time over it), pulls his foreskin well back if he has one, and stands back for a few moments to let him get excited. If she knows her job, he will be unable to move, while the kiss ensures that he won't lose the feel of her. Coming back she does the same all over again, stiffens him by hand and mouth if necessary, and starts in real earnest.

She has two focal points to attend to, his mouth and his penis, and the knack, during this warm-up period, consists in keeping both of them occupied continuously, without pauses and without triggering ejaculation. The possibilities are obvious—hand to each, hand to one, mouth or pussy to the other; varied by a touch of her breasts, her armpit, or even her hair. Between the two poles she will work over his most sensitive areas with her fingertips (*les pattes*

185

d'araignee), her tongue, and her pussy—this last with one hand on his penis and her other palm over his mouth, never letting the rhythm slacken. If his erection begins to go down she stops, tightens him up (this is the moment for thumb-tying if she is strong enough to turn him easily), then re-stiffens him. Then she can begin slow masturbation proper.

This is about the most mind-blowing (and, while it lasts, frustrating) sexual sensation of which most males are capable. (If you still want to know why we say start by tying your lover, try it for a few moments with an unbound partner.) Sit well up on his chest, with your buttocks to his chin, and put each of your ankles inside the crook of one of his knees. Hold the root of his penis with one hand and with the other pull the skin back as far as it will go with finger and thumb, thumb towards you. Then start quick, sharp, nervous strokes—each one quick, that is, but timed at one per second, no faster. After about twenty of these, give about ten very quick strokes. Then resume the slow rhythm. And so on. If from the turmoil under you and the general scene you think he is about to ejaculate, drop the speed (you can sense this with practice). Keep it up as long as you think he can stand it. The excitement is his, but is less one-sided than it sounds; the male response is enough to turn most women on, and you can press your open pussy hard on his breast bone, but don't let your attention wander. Ten minutes is about as much as most males can stand. If he goes limp, put him out of his misery, either by quickly masturbating him to climax, or by mouth, or by turning and riding him. When he does come, get him untied as quickly as possible—delay after orgasm will leave him as stiff as if he'd played a hard ball-game.

This is the Japanese-massage-special-treatment routine—the only bar to making it at home, like sukiyaki, is if you are a big girl. The Japanese are artists at making their knots, like their dishes, look really nice, and Japanese masseuses are small enough to sit on a man's chest without killing him. If you are a Brunnhilde, try tying his legs apart and taking your weight on your knees with your pussy on his mouth: in the story Brunnhilde tied up King Gunther on his wedding night, probably for a similar routine—we've given the small woman version. And let him try the same techniques on you.

The man has three points to concentrate on—mouth, breasts and clitoris. A fairly tight couple of turns round the breasts helps (careful!). He can start as she did, with the *coup de cassolette* (armpit and glans) and then rub his hand over her cassolette and put it over her mouth, to play back her own perfume.

He needs to watch from her sounds and movements how heavy a touch on the clitoris she can stand. He can copy the spinning-out technique and excite

186

her by postponement, but usually he will get better results by simply pushing her as far and as fast as possible. If she is a responsive subject and not frightened of the whole business the reaction will fully test his skill in securing her. He should kneel astride, but not sit on her, nor hold her down—she should be quite helpless anyway. Finally, and with experienced lovers this will be when she is semi-conscious, he will switch to a few moments of tongue work for lubrication, then vigorous intercourse, and make her scale another, still higher range of peaks, taking his own orgasm early on. He should know by the feel of her when to stop—this bears no relation to mewing and struggles, which reach a peak just short of climax. He should then untie her quickly, skillfully and painlessly, so that she comes back to earth lying quietly in his arms.

One unexpected trick is for the lady to tell her partner she's going to give him the time of his life, tie him, and then, when you've made sure he can't get loose or make a sound, make him watch while you masturbate to orgasm. This is more exciting for both of you than it sounds. He, if he's already excited and expecting something else, will go berserk, and his useless struggles will turn her on. Afterwards she can make it up to him—slowly.

Alex Comfort, M. D., a physician and human biologist, has written poetry, novels, and works of philosophy and science in addition to his best-selling The Joy of Sex, More Joy of Sex, *and* The New Joy of Sex, *from which "Slow Masturbation" is taken. Other books include* A Good Age *and* The Facts of Love, *written with his wife, Jane. Dr. Comfort has conducted research on the aging process as a Nuffield Research Fellow and head of a medical research council group at University College, London, and later joined the Neuropsychiatric Institute at the University of California, Los Angeles.*

Philip Appleman

A PRIEST FOREVER

The first time?
So long ago—that brown-eyed boy...
How can I say this, Your Reverences,
so you'll understand? Maybe
it was the tilt of his pretty neck
when he pondered the mysteries—Grace,
the Trinity—the way his lower lip
curled like a petal, the way...
But *you* know what I mean—down
from your high pulpits and into the dirty streets—
you know there are some provocations
the good Lord made no sinew
strong enough to resist. Think
of David and Jonathan, snarled forever
in a tender web as tough as twine—
like that, maybe—like being driven
by flames, deep in the places we hide,
renounce, deny...

No, Monsignor, try to understand—
if your inquest here is meant
to "evaluate" me again, then
you have to feel that fever in the loins
when a child's face looks up
from the wafer-thin body of Christ, innocent eyes
flooding with wonder. You have to see
that the Lord, the good Lord,
has willed something beyond commandments,

beyond dogma, beyond law or custom,
something—irresistible…

All right—the first time—
of course I remember.
It was a smoldering August afternoon,
the hottest day in the history
of this whole state. And there
in the cobweb aftermath
of too many questions—what is mortal sin?
What are the dangers to chastity?—alone,
almost alone in the church, after
my little pupils had all run off
to baseball, ice cream, whatever,
he lingered on, in the dim vestry…

Well, if you insist, I did ask him
to stay—because
after all those catechism lessons, there was still
one urgent question hanging
in the clammy air,
and inch by inch, among the ghostly chasubles,
we found ourselves edging closer to it.
Somehow, then, my anointed hand was blessing
his brown hair, one finger ordained to touch
the petal of that lower lip. And there
in that sweaty room—dear Jesus, how I still
feel the heat—I…We…

Yes, of course—the others. All
the others…But after the first time,
how do you tell them apart?
Let's see—there was a blue-eyed kid
with an angel's tongue—what was his name?
And a cherub with golden hair, who
used his indifference like a tease. And…
Sixty-eight of them, did you say? All
testifying to…

189

What? I? "Ruined their lives"?
Wait a minute, let's get this straight—
my passion *gave* them a life, gave them
something rich and ripe in their green youth,
something to measure all intimate flesh against,
forever. After that,
they ruined their own lives, maybe.
But with me they were full of a love
firmer than anything their meager years
had ever tasted...

Love, you heard me—you
with all your degrees, your tight mouths,
your clinical jargon, don't tell me
you've never had a movement below your belt
that wasn't intestinal. Listen,
this is not in Aquinas,
not in our learned encyclicals. But
there's a force that moves in our marrow,
that slithered there, long before
theology—something with ape in it,
something with the squirm of snakes,
the thrust of rams. And whatever it is,
it knows what it wants...

Ah—your glittering eyes
show me you understand. And your ramrod backs
tell me you'll never admit it.
But I'm not alone here, am I?
We're in this together, the same old
celibate fix—"It's better
to marry than to burn," our little
inside joke. And it all comes down
to one poor sinner in a straight-back chair
entertaining a dozen sanctimonious...

That word is for the record, Monsignor.
Remember the last time we met like this—
how I pleaded time, place, circumstance,
mitigating niceties, anything but the truth.
And how you enjoyed flaying me then—
you nailed me to lust like a rugged cross,
brushed aside my passion, turned your back
on my word made flesh, hoping
that no more boyish voices
would speak its name to daylight…

Yes, Reverends, I learned
a little something then, in all that
groveling—learned that whatever
the meek may wangle in this life,
whatever skimpy joy they manage
to snuggle up to at night, one thing
is certain as graveyards—the meek
will never, in any shy season,
inherit the earth.
So excuse me if I don't
bob and duck this time.
You have your job to do, go ahead,
throw me to the wolves
and pay off my little lovers—
plaintiffs, have it your way—
hush them up with a million bucks
in widows' pennies. Not a bad price
for all that ecstasy…

Oh, I know where I'm headed—
to "therapy," as we always say,
a little paid vacation
with others who loved not wisely
but too young—and also, of course,
with the usual slew of dehydrating
whiskey priests. But don't forget
that when they say I'm "recovered" again,

they'll send me off to another parish,
with more of those little lambs—a priest,
after all, is a priest forever.
Meanwhile, as I bide my time,
and count my beads, and hum to myself
those luscious songs of Solomon,
what I'll be thinking about—
rely on this, Your Reverences—
what I'll be thinking about
is that brown-eyed boy
with the graceful neck, and the lower lip
that curled like a petal.

Philip Appleman has published seven volumes of poetry, including New and Selected Poems, 1956-1996. *Among his many prose books are the novel* Apes and Angels *and the Norton Critical Edition,* Darwin. *His work has been published in many periodicals, such as* Harper's, The Nation, The New Republic, The New York Times, Paris Review, Partisan Review, Poetry, Sewanee Review, *and* Yale Review.

Alice Walker

from POSSESSING THE SECRET OF JOY

Tashi-Evelyn

"The God Amma, it appeared, took a lump of clay, squeezed it in his hand and flung it from him, as he had done with the stars. The clay spread and fell on the north, which is the top, and from there stretched out to the south, which is the bottom, of the world, although the whole movement was horizontal. The earth lies flat, but the north is at the top. It extends east and west with separate members like a fetus in the womb. It is a body, that is to say, a thing with members branching out from a central mass. This body, lying flat, face upwards, in a line from north to south, is feminine. Its sexual organ is an anthill, and its clitoris a termite hill. Amma, being lonely and desirous of intercourse with this creature, approached it. That was the occasion of the first breach of the order of the universe....

"At God's approach the termite hill rose up, barring the passage and displaying its masculinity. It was as strong as the organ of the stranger, and intercourse could not take place. But God is all-powerful. He cut down the termite hill, and had intercourse with the excised earth. But the original incident was destined to affect the course of things forever...."

As Pierre reads I study his face seeking signs of Adam, signs of Lisette. He seems a completely blended person and, as such, new. In him "black" has disappeared; so has "white." His eyes are a dark, lightfilled brown; his forehead is high and tan; his nose broad, a little flat. He has told me he likes men as well as he likes women, which seems only natural, he says, since he is the offspring of two sexes as well as of two races. No one is surprised he is biracial; why should they be surprised he is bisexual? This is an explanation I have never heard and cannot entirely grasp; it seems too logical for my brain. His brother sits across from him as he reads, sunk in admiration. They have stolen many hours to be together, roaming the Berkeley campus and the city's streets, happy to have found each in the other his own best friend.

Now he stops reading, suddenly, and looks at me. This is from a book by a French anthropologist, Marcel Griaule, he says, turning it so I can see its

193

orange cover and read its title, *Conversations with Ogotemmeli*. I am under the influence of a new, mild and quite pleasant drug. It is as if I've smoked marijuana. I have not grasped the meaning of the passage, which Pierre has read to me so earnestly; nor do I completely comprehend how it is he is sitting in my living room reading to me from this strange book. Have I stopped hating him? I gaze at Benny, who looks so happy, and then down into my lap. My eyes sting the way they do when I'm drugged; closing them brings relief. Pierre is reading as if I am listening: "God had further intercourse with his earth-wife, and this time without mishaps of any kind, the excision of the offending member having removed the cause of the former disorder." I feel him stop, rustle the pages, and look over at me. I raise my eyes and attempt a bright look in his direction. I am awake, I say. Indeed, I am listening. However, as he resumes reading, the words, on touching my ear, bounce back into his mouth, as if they're made of India rubber. This is a distracting sight, and I look at Benny to see if he has noticed it. He hasn't. He sits enraptured, his notepad on his lap. Who taught him to write, I ask myself, if he can never remember anything?

"The spirit drew two outlines on the ground, one on top of the other, one male and the other female. The man stretched himself out on these two shadows of himself, and took both of them for his own. The same thing was done for the woman. Thus it came about that each human being from the first was endowed with two souls of different sex, or rather with two principles corresponding to two distinct persons. In the man the female soul was located in the prepuce; in the woman the male soul was in the clitoris."

Here I looked up. Pierre continued: "Man's life was not capable of supporting both beings: each person would have to merge himself in the sex for which he appeared to be best fitted." So, said Pierre, closing the book but keeping his finger between its pages, the man is circumcised to rid him of his femininity; the woman is excised to rid her of her masculinity. In other words, he said, leaning forward in his chair, a very long time ago, men found it necessary to permanently lock people in the category of their obvious sex, even while recognizing sexual duality as a given of nature.

How long ago was this? I ask, my focus somewhat blurred.

Pierre shrugged, and I fancied I saw his mother's body in the fluid ripple of his shoulders.

Even Cleopatra was circumcised, he says. Nefertiti, also. But some people think the people in this book, the Dogon, are from a civilization even older than theirs, and that this civilization spread northward, from central Africa *up*

194

toward ancient Egypt and the Mediterranean. He paused, musing. My mother used to say genital mutilation, which predates all the major religions, was a kind of footbinding.

After he leaves the house to accompany Benny to a basketball game, I am left with the book, whose pages he has thoughtfully marked, and with the puzzle of his last comment. Suddenly I see Lisette very clearly. She is sitting by a window in front of which there is a desk. She is thinking of me as she looks into a thick brown book in front of her, and her white brow is puckered in a frown. She is gazing at a drawing of a tiny, putrid, Chinese woman's foot, and reading the notation that says the rotten smell was an aphrodisiac for the man, who liked to hold both small feet helpless in his large hand, raising them to his nose as he prepared to ravish the woman, who could not run away. This immobility most satisfying to his lust. The pain of her hobbling attempts to escape pure incentive to relish the chase. His mother has been conjured by the odd, un-American movement of Pierre's shoulders, as much as by his words. Why, I wonder, do we assume people who think deeply about us ever die?

As I open the book, my eye falls on a passage Pierre had not read: "The man then had intercourse with the woman, who later bore the first two children of a series of eight, who were to become the ancestors of the Dogon people. In the moment of birth the pain of parturition was concentrated in the woman's clitoris, which was excised by an invisible hand, detached itself and left her, and was changed into the form of a scorpion. The pouch and the sting symbolized the organ: the venom was the water and the blood of the pain."

I read the passage over again, my eye always stopped by the words "an invisible hand." Even so long ago God deserted woman, I thought, staying by her just long enough to illustrate to man the cutting to be done. And what if pain wasn't what she felt at the moment of parturition? After all, pain was what I felt, having given birth, and I did not have a clitoris for it to be concentrated in.

I read further: "The dual soul is a danger; a man should be male, and a woman female. Circumcision and excision are…the remedy."

But who could bear to think of this for long? I closed the book, wandered unsteadily across the room, flopped heavily onto the couch, and lost myself in a rerun of "Hee-Haw" on TV.

Adam

It saddens me that Pierre has never married, and that he seems content to pursue his career as an anthropologist and to spend much of the time he has for himself with Benny. This petit (for a man) curly-haired, teak-colored person is my son! I am as astonished as he approaches middle age as I was when he was

195

two. Though his voice is deep, deeper than mine, a person of color's voice, it still seems at times, because of his accent, the voice of a stranger. I see his mother in him. Lisette, who took so long to die, bravely determined to hold on to her dignity, her self, to the end; her thick, fierce French neck wasting away as she struggled. Only to beg, finally, for morphine and more and more morphine. Seeing her in Pierre makes the memory of my last visits with her bearable, and reactivates happier thoughts of our earlier days.

Pierre laughs at my concern, gracefully refraining from observing aloud that my own marriage has been hellacious.

I am married to my work, he says.

But your work does not produce children, I counter.

He smiles. *Mais oui*, he says, my work *will* produce children! Children who will at least understand why they are afraid. How can a child be a child if she is afraid?

I cannot argue. Since the moment, as a small boy, Pierre heard of Tashi's dark tower and her terror of it, he has never put her suffering out of his mind. Everything he learns, no matter how trivial or in what context or with whom, he brings to bear on her dilemma. The conversations we have as adults predictably include some bit of information that he has stored away to become a part of Tashi's puzzle.

The only girl he ever loved, for instance. A Berkeley student with whom he often went horseback riding.

She rode bareback, always, he tells me, as we sit on a boulder in the park in the middle of an afternoon hike. She experienced orgasm while riding the horse.

Are you sure? I ask.

Yes, he says. She swooned. And when I asked her, she admitted it.

I am speechless at the thought that any woman's pleasure might be found so easily, I stammer; so, in a sense, *carelessly*.

The word you are looking for, says Pierre, is *wantonly. Loosely*. A woman who is sexually "unrestrained," according to the dictionary, is by definition "lascivious, wanton and loose." But why is that? A man who is sexually unrestrained is simply a man.

Well, I say, *was* she loose?

Pierre shifts his weight on the boulder and frowns up at the sky. Now, he says, in the scholarly tone that still strikes me as amusing in one so childlike in size, we can begin to understand something about the insistence, among people in mutilating cultures, that a woman's vagina be tight. By force if nec-

196

essary. If you think of being wanton, being loose, as being able to achieve orgasm easily.

How did this happen? I ask. To your friend, I mean.

She'd been brought up by pagan parents, earth worshippers, on a little island somewhere in Hawaii. She could experience orgasm doing almost anything. She said that at home there were favorite trees she loved that she rubbed against. She could orgasm against warm, smooth boulders, like this one we're sitting on; she could come against the earth itself if it rose a bit to meet her. However, says Pierre, she'd never been with a man. Her parents had taught her early on that it wasn't absolutely necessary, unless she wanted to have children.

And with you? I ask.

I'm afraid my lovemaking had a dampening, no, a *drying* effect, he says. No matter how I tried, it was hard not to approach her from a stance of dominance. When making love with me, she became less and less wet. His face is sad for a moment, then he grins. She went off to India. I think she left me for an elephant she learned to ride, or perhaps for a slow, warm trickle of water from a waterfall, of which there were many amorous ones on her Hawaiian island.

I always thought perhaps it was to make sexual love between women impossible that men destroyed their external sexual organs.

I still think that is partly true, says Pierre. But there is also my experience with Queen Anne.

Queen Anne? Your friend was named after Queen Anne Nzingha, the African warrior?

No, he says. After Queen Anne's lace, the wildflower.

Later on in the hike, stopping at a pipe for water, Pierre still muses. Is it only woman who would make love to everything? he asks. Man too, after all, has external sexual organs. But does man seek oneness with the earth by having sex with it?

You mean Queen Anne wasn't simply masturbating?

No. She said she never masturbated, except with herself. And even then she was making love. Having sex. Her partner just happened to be something other than another human being.

Was it with Queen Anne that you discovered your duality? I ask.

Yes, he says. Until I met her I was never sexually attracted to women. I imagined all women mainly suffered from sex. Meeting her was a great relief. I realized that even bisexuality, of which I'd always felt myself capable but of which I'd had no real experience, was still, like homosexuality and heterosexuality, like lesbianism, only a very limited sexuality. I mean, here was someone who was *pan*sexual. Remember Pan? he asks, laughing. Well, Queen Anne was Pan's great-grandmother!

An image of Pan, the Greek god, merrily playing his flute in the forest rises up. His human head rests on a body composed of the parts of many different animals. Clearly his ancestors had related sexually, at least in imagination, to everything. And before him Queen Anne's ancestors had related sexually to the earth itself. I am really too old to use the expression "wow" gracefully. But "wow" is what I hear myself say. Which makes Pierre laugh again.

But in a moment he has returned to the thread of his thought. In pornography, he says ruefully, this ability of woman's to take pleasure in diverse ways is projected in a perverted way. I have seen films in which she is forced to copulate with donkeys and dogs and guns and other weapons. Oddly shaped vegetables and fruits. Broom handles and Coke bottles. But this is rape. Man is jealous of woman's pleasure, Pierre says after a while, because she does not require him to achieve it. When her outer sex is cut off, and she's left only the smallest, inelastic opening through which to receive pleasure, he can believe it is only his penis that can reach her inner parts and give her what she craves. But it is only his lust for her conquest that makes the effort worthwhile. And then it is literally a battle, with blood flowing on both sides.

Ah, I say, the original battle of the sexes!

Exactly, he replies.

Well, I say, some men turn to animals, and each other. Or they use the woman as if she were a boy.

If you are at all sensitive to another's pain, he says, grimacing, or even cognizant of your own, not to mention the humiliation of forcing yourself inside someone whose very flesh has been made into a barrier against you, what else can you do?

Alice Walker is the author of novels, short stories, essays, poetry, and several children's books. Her recent works include Possessing the Secret of Joy, The Temple of My Familiar, *and* Anything We Love Can Be Saved: A Writer's Activism. *Her novel* The Color Purple *won the Pulitzer Prize and the National Book Award. Walker's books have been translated into more than two dozen languages.*

Angela Himsel

A WOMAN OF VALOR

Victoria puts her hand to her mouth, kisses her fingertips, and presses them against the *mezuzah* on the classroom door. Inside the Orthodox synagogue on the Upper West Side of Manhattan about fifty or so young women stand, talking quietly before the "To Be a Jewish Woman" class begins. Victoria's plum velvet leggings and black vinyl boots are a vivid contrast to the long skirts and modest blouses favored by the other women. She feels momentarily out of place, not just because of her attire but because, with her blonde hair, blue eyes, and Scandinavian-looking face, Victoria is clearly not Jewish.

When everyone is seated, a woman in her late twenties, with long, chestnut ringlets, introduces herself. "My name is Peninah, and welcome." She hands out the syllabus. *Tumah* and *niddah*, states of impurity and purity. Going to the mikvah. Doing a *b'dikah*, a monthly check. Counting the days. Breaking the hymen.

Somehow, she had thought that "To Be a Jewish Woman" would offer a few kosher tricks, perhaps a recipe for brisket or a tip on keeping your meat *cholent* moist. She'd hoped to pick up some idea of what a Jewish man wanted in his Jewish woman. One Jewish man in particular. Ariel.

Two weeks before, in one of their more and more frequent confrontations over the past year, Ariel had told her, "Tory, I saw Leslie the other night."

"Oh?" Victoria stabbed at the asparagus on her plate. Can't make a scene in a restaurant. Can't dump ice water over his head. Leslie was the Jewish ex-girlfriend, the woman Ariel almost married and whom he still saw, now and then. Leslie had, according to Ariel, "broken through the glass ceiling." Having never heard about glass ceilings, Victoria envisioned Leslie rocketing up through a thin sheet of glass and, as it shattered, shards broke off, sprinkling sharp, dangerous pieces in her wake. Growing up in Indiana, Victoria had wanted to work the check-out register at Newberry's. Who knew from corporate ceilings?

"I know we've talked about this before," Ariel had gone on, avoiding her eyes, and frowning, as if the cares of the world were on his shoulder, "and your not being Jewish doesn't affect at all the way I feel about you, but I have to be honest, I'm at the age where I want children. I want a Jewish home and a Jewish life."

"So have it." Was he trying to blackmail her, she'd wondered, and if she didn't provide him with what he wanted, then Leslie would? And anyway, did a woman who shot through glass ceilings have time to stew Saturday's *cholent*?

The day after that discussion, Victoria had called Rabbi Bergman. In the five years she'd lived in New York City, she'd taken Jewish mysticism and prophecy classes with the rabbi and they'd had several illuminating conversations on the virgin birth and Philo. Rabbi Bergman suggested that, before they discuss conversion, she take a course at the synagogue, "To Be a Jewish Woman."

Now, watching these young women sporting big diamond rings and frantically scribbling into their notebooks, Victoria realizes that this is a pre-marriage class designed to teach the "laws of family purity"—when you can have sex and when you can't. Victoria could just *plotz*.

Peninah says, "During your period, you are *timeah*, which does not literally translate as 'unclean.' It is referring to a spiritual impurity, and when you menstruate, we recognize that potential life is lost, resulting in death of a sort, which is a spiritual impurity. When your period ends," Peninah goes on, "every day you do a check, a *b'dikah*." Peninah holds up a small white cloth and wraps it around her middle finger.

"It's very important, when you put it up your vagina, that you are thorough. On one hand, we don't want to encourage blood to come down, otherwise the counting has to start all over, but on the other hand, you can't just swipe at it, either."

Victoria imagines saying to Ariel, "Please be thorough. Don't just swipe at my vagina." She smiles to herself at the thought. The young woman next to her, catching her smile, gives her an odd look, then goes back to her notebook.

Although Victoria spent her junior year of college in Israel and, if pressed, could name all the barren women of the Old Testament, this aspect of Judaism is new to her.

Growing up in a small town in Indiana, she had attended a church which weekly warned, "Brethren, if you plan to be at the Place of Safety, you cannot let your love wax cold! Satan is out there, tempting us daily, sowing discord, and we must be like the wise virgins and bring oil along for our lamps. When Jesus Christ comes, the church as His bride must be ready."

Though no longer a virgin, wise or otherwise, she is nonetheless waiting for her Bridegroom, one way or another. Waiting, to be chosen and transported to the Place of Safety.

The next morning, Ariel calls her at the photography gallery where she works. "Hi, hon," he says. "How was your class?"

"Did you know about *niddah* and *tumah*?" she asks.

"Not personally, no."

She has not seen him in a week. He was in Atlanta for a business meeting, then the evening he came back he said he was just too tired to get together, and last night Victoria was at her class.

"Do you have plans for lunch?" he asks her.

"Not yet."

"Twelve-thirty?" he says.

"Great."

At 12:15, Victoria rushes into the deli to grab a bagel and cream cheese and diet Coke. The headline shrieks, "Gunman Kills Two, Wounds Six." Though the world is not a safe place, she is resolved to stop looking for a Place of Safety.

The cashier punches the cash register with strong lavender nails. "How do you get your nails to grow so long?" Victoria asks.

"Tits," the woman says.

"I beg your pardon?" Self-consciously, her hand goes to her breasts. They are small.

"They're tips." The cashier holds her hand in front of Victoria's face. Five lavender, oval-shaped, perfectly smooth, symmetrical nails flash in front of her eyes.

"Oh. So they're not real?"

"No. See, my nails are growing underneath." The cashier turns her hand over to reveal yellowish nails, gunk collected underneath them. Victoria immediately envisions a series of photographs of both hands, one revealing the painted tips, the other flipped over, exposing the underside.

Would that being Jewish were as simple: pay for it, glue it on, and *voilà*, who's to say you are not who you say you are?

At 12:45, Victoria is in her sparsely furnished apartment in the East Village, planning her confrontation with Ariel. "So you think my time is less important than your time?"

Just when she is ready to grab her coat and go back to the office, the buzzer rings.

"Sorry, honey," Ariel says, "I got caught up in traffic."

She turns her face when his lips come toward hers and the kiss lands on her cheek. "Uh-oh. I'm in trouble," he says. "I'm sorry, Tory."

He is always sorry, and each time he has a legitimate excuse: Can't make dinner, a business meeting came up; sorry I'm late, I didn't realize the time/thought we'd said 7:30/left a message that I was running late. How many times had Leslie been the cause of his broken promises to her? The pattern, no matter what the explanation, was: we'll do it my way, in my time.

But she won't make a big deal out of this, when the real issue between them is if he can accept her as not being Jewish or if she will, indeed, ever convert, and convert Orthodox. Not that Ariel himself, though he grew up in an Orthodox family, keeps kosher or observes Shabbat anymore. However, she understands, only too well, the pull of one's past.

At one o'clock, Ariel shrugs into his pin-striped suit jacket and Victoria looks around for a towel to wipe the semen off her inner thighs, no time for a shower.

"Victoria," Ariel says, "am I to take it, then, that you're serious about this class or are you…"

"Just toying with the idea, having a bit of fun, being superficial?" Stalking into the bathroom, she takes a washcloth and scrubs at her legs. Ariel follows her, looks in the small mirror over the sink to tie his tie. In the center of the mirror a faded sticker, left by the tenants before Victoria, reads, "Life is short. Eternity is long. Hope you know Jesus."

"Tory, I'm trying to talk about this, dammit." Ariel stands in front of her, forcing her to look at him, and she can't believe even now, though she's angry, that her heart still leaps at the sight of him. To her ears, his voice is a caress, and she has to contain the urge to slip her arm around his waist and let their bodies touch. "You've become a part of my life—our relationship is very important to me. I don't want to give it up."

"But…"

"But—nothing. I know you're drawn to Judaism. You told me that church you grew up in celebrated the Jewish holidays."

The church had believed that they were "spiritual Israelites." Though the temple's blood sacrifices were made moot after Jesus' sacrifice, the Jewish laws and holidays, including Yom Kippur and Rosh Hashana, remained in place.

"And you lived in Israel," Ariel continues, "now you're taking this other Jewish class. Is it such a big step to convert? And for the record, I never said

202

you were superficial. You take these issues very seriously. That's one of the things I love about you."

Victoria says nothing. All her life, she's lived poised on the precipice, with Satan and the Lake of Fire on one side, Salvation and the Place of Safety on the other, and Victoria dead center, split up the middle, and though she doesn't go to church anymore, she continues to live her life in fear of the world ending. How can she be ambitious and buy worldly possessions and have children and break through glass ceilings while at the same time taking "no thought for the morrow"?

"What about children?" Ariel persists. His eyes drop to her naked abdomen, as if willing it to expand. It is as if the force of his blue-gray eyes and the set of his mouth would compel her to agree to his needs, his future, a future Victoria is still uncertain of.

"I'm not sure I want children," Victoria says. Who could, in good conscience, bring children into a world doomed to be destroyed? A world that has no future?

Give up Jesus, sacrifice my salvation, and for what? If Ariel could have guaranteed that a *mezuzah* on her doorpost would make the death angel pass over her house, then sure. But what if the angel of life passed over her house because there was a *mezuzah* on the door? Then, when Jesus returned to greet everyone in the sky, everyone else would sit at His feet except her and her Jewish children. It apparently had never occurred to Ariel that he was responsible for her salvation.

"Tory, you're too old to be acting so goddamned noncommittal and independent all the time. Stop being so fucking stubborn! I'm not asking you to be anything you don't want to be—I'm asking you to have a future!"

"Thanks for your unselfish concern."

In the taxi uptown, they are quiet. A residual of Ariel's seed is gummed to the inside of Victoria's thighs. She will scrape it off tonight.

Every week, Victoria considers not going to the "To Be a Jewish Woman" class. After all, it is not sex tips she's looking for.

However, week after week she shows up, bringing her own notebook and scribbling into it.

"Time and place for everything, especially a time…Each month reminds you of the life cycle…Judaism elevates sex to a holy activity. Dichotomy between clean and unclean, pure and impure. *Mikvah* cleanses mind and heart, not just the body."

One evening, Victoria is late. The new show, "Images on Image," photographs of people who've had plastic surgery, is opening this week, and she had to finish typing the little biographies that go under each photograph.

When Victoria walks in, Peninah hands her a xerox of something in Hebrew and English, smiles, and waits for her to take her seat.

"This is a woman whose role is not limited to being a wife and mother," Peninah is saying. "This is a woman who not only attends to her husband's and children's needs, but buys a field, plants a vineyard, and gives to the poor. I've been married eight years, I have four children, and I work part-time as a family therapist and I want to tell you, it's not easy. But it *is* very rewarding."

Victoria hesitates, then raises her hand. "I'm curious," the eyes of all the women are directed at her, "what the man's responsibilities in the marriage are? I mean," she plunges on, "this passage here, it seems to me that women have to do and be everything. I don't know. I guess I'd love to know what the male version of the 'woman of valor' is."

A moment of silence. Peninah smiles. "Good questions. According to the Torah, men are obligated to provide their wives with food, clothing, and their conjugal rights. But there is not, per se, a beautiful passage like you'll find here detailing what a husband is."

What kind of husband would Ariel be? Willing to make sacrifices? What kind of wife would she be? The kind who makes herself over to suit her husband's image?

"But I can't stress enough that women do not need to turn themselves inside out to please their men. We are not inferior, we are not their toys to play with. And we have to respect ourselves and our bodies to get the respect we deserve."

A woman with breast implants in the "Images on Image" show had said, "My boyfriend likes big breasts, and I figured hey, why not." It is not even a small step from false boobs to converting. And what do those men of valor do for us?

When Victoria presses her kissed fingers to the *mezuzah*, she can't help but admire her slick new lime-green nails, nails which seem to belong to someone else.

That evening Peninah gives an overview of the laws, ending with, "After seven white days, you go to the *mikvah*. There will be a checklist there, and the *mikvah* lady will inspect you to make sure there's nothing that can be considered a barrier between you and the water."

Jesus said that it is not that which comes out of man that defiles, but that which is within. These laws will not save you. Jesus's blood will save you.

With these sharp nails, it would be literally taking her life into her hands were she to poke around in her ears or nose or, God forbid, vagina, in search of anything that needs to be removed before she can be purified.

"During those seven days," Peninah is wrapping up, "your husband is aware that he is being deprived of you, and let me tell you, when you come back from the *mikvah*, it is like a honeymoon all over again. If you practice the laws of *taharat hamishpacha*, family purity, your sex life will remain exciting."

Maybe sex had been the problem between Ariel and Leslie. He'd once said that he and Leslie were like "brother and sister." Ariel probably never bobbed for chocolate kisses between Leslie's legs.

"Women need a little break, too," Peninah continues. "We aren't sex machines who have to perform on demand, and the Torah was also thinking of women when these laws were made. Some men, not all men, think that if you're married to them, they own your bodies, anytime, anywhere. Well, these laws are clearly telling men, 'I belong to myself.'"

Victoria is mesmerized by her nails. They don't seem to belong to her. Where will this madness end, she wonders? Breast implants?

A young woman raises her hand. "If you find some blood after you've gone to the *mikvah*, then what do you do?" The girl leans forward, her long, black curly hair making an impenetrable curtain around her as she prepares to write the answer.

"Again, if it's bigger than a dime, and if its color is suspicious, then you should put your underwear in a bag with your phone number on it, and if you don't feel comfortable, have your husband drop it off at the rabbi. He'll get back to you, that night, and tell you if it's okay or not. It's not embarrassing, really, my husband is a rabbi, and it's just a job. It's not nearly as messy as a gynecologist's job!"

Is it just her or do any of the other women find it perversely exciting to imagine the rabbi in direct relationship with their underwear?

"I'd like," Peninah says, "to spend a little more time tonight not on what the law says, but on the spiritual meaning underneath it."

Victoria leans forward. She flashes on the nails within the nails, about how something may appear completely legalistic and ridiculous but have an underlying significance not readily apparent.

"What I want to stress," Peninah continues, "is how important these laws are to a relationship. During the days you can't touch each other, you are forced to talk things out, not to rely on physical contact to communicate, and let me tell you, even the best of men aren't known for their verbal or emotional communication skills."

"You got it!" Victoria mutters, more loudly than she'd intended, and a few heads turn, then look away.

When Victoria scratches her head, it's as if someone else is scratching it. She bets she could rip boxes open without a knife with these nails.

"I'm not trying to say it's easy," Peninah goes on, "but so many things in life that are worthwhile aren't easy. In today's world, where you think you're entitled to anything you want, it's important to be reminded that there are limits."

Sex over lunch? Fine. Can't see me tonight, have to cancel? Okay. Can't come with me to a friend's wedding, I understand. Why had she always thought when you love someone, you give them whatever you can give them, unlimited. The competitive, glass-shattering Leslie was undoubtedly never as nice or accommodating to Ariel. But these nails, already they're inspiring in her a confidence to internalize their artificial, external strength, to step forward and claim them as her own.

At the end of the class, Peninah gives everyone a gift—a supply of *b'dikah* cloths to check for blood during the seven days following their periods. Victoria imagines Jesus's blood mingling with menstrual blood, the past merging with the present. How are these two bloods related, anyway? One saves, one defiles; one saves your spiritual life, one indicates potential physical life has been lost.

"Tips?" Peninah says, as Victoria thanks her and says goodbye.

"Do you like them?" Victoria sticks out her hands.

"I'll tell you a funny story. A woman in our *shul* asked my husband if she had to take her tips off to go to the *mikvah* and my husband needed to find out exactly how they were put on. So he went to the nail salon and the Korean woman answered all of his questions. At the end, she asked him if he was thinking of opening his own shop!"

Victoria laughs with her at the thought of a rabbi running a nail salon. "So do you have to take them off for the *mikvah*?" Victoria asks.

"The polish, yes. But not these particular tips. The kind that you buy in a drugstore that are just glued on you have to take off, but these are considered to adhere to you, like your real nails. They're like a tooth filling, so you wouldn't remove them."

Halakhically, legally, these nails are considered to be her, not separate from her but her. Perhaps if you play a role externally long enough, it will eventually become you, or you will become it, internally.

Peninah reaches up and tugs on her hair. Her entire scalp seems to move. Then Victoria realizes: Peninah's bouncing chestnut curls are, in fact, a *shaytl*, a wig. This should not be a surprise—Peninah is Orthodox—but the curls looked so natural!

"Can I ask you something?" Victoria says, and it crosses her mind to ask, "If I've been sleeping with a Jewish man does that count, Jewish by insemination?"

"Of course. Anything."

"I bought some matzoh meal, and I've tried several recipes for matzoh balls, with seltzer and different oils and everything, but they always come out hard and lumpy. How do you make really fluffy matzoh balls?"

"Streit's," Peninah says.

"What's that?" Victoria asks.

"A mix," she says. "It's my grandmother's secret and if she knew I told you, she'd kill me. Streit's."

Women wear fake nails, fake hair, and use packaged soup mix. Who knew? At last, the tip Victoria had come to the class for.

Late that night, with Ariel's mouth on hers, Victoria sees a quick image of all the sheep following Jesus the herdsman, and herself, left alone on a mountaintop, destined never to marry into the Christ family.

Then the natural rhythm of their lovemaking, a rhythm passed down through the generations via genetic memory, urges them on: *Shma Israel*, stroke her breast once, *Shma Israel*, one more time, bend, dip, *davin*, and she is on her knees, prayerfully, on top of him, then he is on top, his penis poking around, harder and harder, faster, his finger rubbing against her clitoris, he is inside her and out at the same time, her fingers dig into his back.

"Ouch!" he jerks away, interrupting the rhythm.

"Sor-eee!" Victoria moans.

"What did you do to your nails?" Ariel asks later, when they have caught their breath.

"Like them? They're not exactly mine."

"You're dangerous," he says.

"You're just now finding out?"

He laughs and gets out of bed. Ariel tosses a white cloth at her. She swipes at her inner thighs, and realizes she's using the *b'dikah* cloth. It is now stained a suspicious, bright red, its size far bigger than a dime.

Somewhat vague about her cycle, about time in general, a residue of growing up not knowing if there would be a tomorrow or if Jesus would return while she was sleeping "like a thief in the night" to spirit her a way to the Place of Safety, Victoria had forgotten that her period was due.

If her home were indeed a temple, as Peninah said, then it looked as if some small animal has been sacrificed on her altar, on the sheets where their bodies just moments before had been bound, as if invisible prayer phylacteries had trussed them together.

"You've wounded me!" Victoria looks at his bloody penis. Ariel takes her hand in his. "When do these come off?"

She had spent hours having her short, chipped nails painstakingly wrapped, glued and tipped. They had turned out to look natural, and they felt right. Now she should reverse the process, soak off all the layers?

Trailing a bright green nail down Ariel's face, she answers, "Maybe never."

Angela Himsel is a novelist and lives in New York City. Her work has appeared in Tikkun, Partisan Review, BOMB, *and other magazines.*

Junot Díaz

HOW TO DATE A BROWNGIRL, BLACKGIRL, WHITEGIRL, OR HALFIE

Wait for your brother and your mother to leave the apartment. You've already told them that you're feeling too sick to go to Union City to visit that tia who likes to squeeze your nuts. (He's gotten big, she'll say.) And even though your moms knows you ain't sick you stuck to your story until finally she said, Go ahead and stay, malcriado.

Clear the government cheese from the refrigerator. If the girl's from the Terrace stack the boxes behind the milk. If she's from the Park or Society Hill hide the cheese in the cabinet above the oven, way up where she'll never see. Leave yourself a reminder to get it out before morning or your moms will kick your ass. Take down any embarrassing photos of your family in the campo, especially the one with the half-naked kids dragging a goat on a rope leash. The kids are your cousins and by now they're old enough to understand why you're doing what you're doing. Hide the pictures of yourself with an Afro. Make sure the bathroom is presentable. Put the basket with all the crapped-on toilet paper under the sink. Spray the bucket with Lysol, then close the cabinet.

Shower, comb, dress. Sit on the couch and watch TV. If she's an outsider her father will be bringing her, maybe her mother. Neither of them want her seeing any boys from the Terrace—people get stabbed in the Terrace—but she's strong-headed and this time will get her way. If she's a whitegirl you know you'll at least get a hand job.

The directions were in your best handwriting, so her parents won't think you're an idiot. Get up from the couch and check the parking lot. Nothing. If the girl's local, don't sweat it. She'll flow over when she's good and ready. Sometimes she'll run into her other friends and a whole crowd will show up at your apartment and even though that means you ain't getting shit it will be fun anyway and you'll wish these people would come over more often. Sometimes the girl won't flow over at all and the next day in school she'll say sorry, smile and you'll be stupid enough to believe her and ask her out again.

Wait and after an hour go out to your corner. The neighborhood is full of traffic. Give one of your boys a shout and when he says, Are you still waiting on that bitch? say, Hell yeah.

Get back inside. Call her house and ask when her father picks up if she's there. He'll ask, Who is this? Hang up. He sounds like a principal or a police chief, the sort of dude with a big neck, who never has to watch his back. Sit and wait. By the time your stomach's ready to give out on you, a Honda or maybe a Jeep pulls in and she comes.

Hey, you'll say.

Look, she'll say. My mom wants to meet you. She's got herself all worried about nothing.

Don't panic. Say, Hey, no problem. Run a hand through your hair like the whiteboys do even though the only thing that runs easily through your hair is Africa. She will look good. The white ones are the ones you want most, aren't they, but usually the out-of-towners are black, blackgirls who grew up with ballet and Girl Scouts, who have three cars in their driveways. If she's a halfie don't be surprised that her mother is white. Say, Hi. Her moms will say hi and you'll see that you don't scare her, not really. She will say that she needs easier directions to get out and even though she has the best directions in her lap give her new ones. Make her happy.

You have choices. If the girl's from around the way, take her to El Cibao for dinner. Order everything in your busted-up Spanish. Let her correct you if she's Latina and amaze her if she's black. If she's not from around the way, Wendy's will do. As you walk to the restaurant talk about school. A local girl won't need stories about the neighborhood but the other ones might. Supply the story about the loco who'd been storing canisters of tear gas in his basement for years, how one day the canisters cracked and the whole neighborhood got a dose of the military-strength stuff. Don't tell her that your moms knew right away what it was, that she recognized its smell from the year the United States invaded your island.

Hope that you don't run into your nemesis, Howie, the Puerto Rican kid with the two killer mutts. He walks them all over the neighborhood and every now and then the mutts corner themselves a cat and tear it to shreds, Howie laughing as the cat flips up in the air, its neck twisted around like an owl, red meat showing through the soft fur. If his dogs haven't cornered a cat, he will walk behind you and ask, Hey, Yunior, is that your new fuckbuddy?

Let him talk. Howie weighs about two hundred pounds and could eat you if he wanted. At the field he will turn away. He has new sneakers, and doesn't want them muddy. If the girl's an outsider she will hiss now and say, What a fucking asshole. A homegirl would have been yelling back at him the whole time, unless she was shy. Either way don't feel bad that you didn't do anything. Never lose a fight on a first date or that will be the end of it.

Dinner will be tense. You are not good at talking to people you don't know. A halfie will tell you that her parents met in the Movement, will say, Back then people thought it a radical thing to do. It will sound like something her parents made her memorize. Your brother once heard that one and said, Man, that sounds like a whole lot of Uncle Tomming to me. Don't repeat this.

Put down your hamburger and say, It must have been hard.

She will appreciate your interest. She will tell you more. Black people, she will say, treat me real bad. That's why I don't like them. You'll wonder how she feels about Dominicans. Don't ask. Let her speak on it and when you're both finished eating walk back into the neighborhood. The skies will be magnificent. Pollutants have made Jersey sunsets one of the wonders of the world. Point it out. Touch her shoulder and say, That's nice, right?

Get serious. Watch TV but stay alert. Sip some of the Bermudez your father left in the cabinet, which nobody touches. A local girl may have hips and a thick ass but she won't be quick about letting you touch. She has to live in the same neighborhood you do, has to deal with you being all up in her business. She might just chill with you and then go home. She might kiss you and then go, or she might, if she's reckless, give it up, but that's rare. Kissing will suffice. A whitegirl might just give it up right then. Don't stop her. She'll take her gum out of her mouth, stick it to the plastic sofa covers and then will move close to you. You have nice eyes, she might say.

Tell her that you love her hair, that you love her skin, her lips, because, in truth, you love them more than you love your own.

She'll say, I like Spanish guys, and even though you've never been to Spain, say, I like you. You'll sound smooth.

You'll be with her until about eight-thirty and then she will want to wash up. In the bathroom she will hum a song from the radio and her waist will keep the beat against the lip of the sink. Imagine her old lady coming to get her, what she would say if she knew her daughter had just lain under you and blown your name, pronounced with her eighth-grade Spanish, into your ear. While she's in the bathroom call one of your boys and say, Lo hice, loco. Or just sit back on the couch and smile.

But usually it won't work this way. Be prepared. She will not want to kiss you. Just cool it, she'll say. The halfie might lean back, breaking away from

211

you. She will cross her arms, say, I hate my tits. Stroke her hair but she will pull away. I don't like anybody touching my hair, she will say. She will act like somebody you don't know. In school she is known for her attention-grabbing laugh, as high and far-ranging as a gull but here she will worry you. You will not know what to say.

You're the only kind of guy who asks me out, she will say. Your neighbors will start their hyena calls, now that the alcohol is in them. You and the blackboys.

Say nothing. Let her button her shirt, let her comb her hair, the sound of it stretching like a sheet of fire between you. When her father pulls in and beeps, let her go without too much of a good-bye. She won't want it. During the next hour the phone will ring. You will be tempted to pick it up. Don't. Watch the shows you want to watch, without a family around to debate you. Don't go downstairs. Don't fall asleep. It won't help. Put the government cheese back in its place before your moms kills you.

Junot Díaz has published short fiction in Story, The New Yorker, The Paris Review, Best American Short Stories 1996, *and* African Voices. *His work has been collected in the volume,* Drown. *Díaz was born in Santo Domingo, Dominican Republic, and now lives in New York City.*

Joan Larkin

BEATINGS

They beat me different ways.
My mother was standing
in her light summer suit and hat.
She was late; it was my fault.
She was almost sobbing. A cord
was twisted around her breath,
an animal trying to escape
from her throat. Her knuckles land
hard on my shoulders, in my ribs and guts.
Her face was close. She was yelling,
yanking me by the hair, and I saw my brother
standing near us in the hall, watching.
Standing and forgetting why he was there
watching and what he liked about it.

I was younger. I think we were all there,
four or five in the kitchen, father home
for supper between shifts. He lifted me
over his knees to hit me. Belt,
brush, or large hand came down
open and steady on both buttocks, burning
and stinging through thin underpants,
big voice in control, saying *This*
is for your own good, this
hurts us, this is because we love you.
I cannot remember my crime, only my face
against his knees. His hands, his strong
voice telling me I was loved.

When the man beat me later
in the bed in Brooklyn, the kind man
with big lips and hands, the man
who loved me and beat me
with the same voice, when years later
in the same bed, the thin woman with tattooed
wrists told me I couldn't receive
love, thrusting the dildo till I was
sore and crying *Stop*, she laughing,
shouting I couldn't love her—
it wasn't true. I loved the rising
of their voices—his dark, steady one,
sure, in control, and her demented one
rising like my dead mother's wild voice.

Joan Larkin's collections of poetry include Housework, A Long Sound, *and* Cold River. *She is co-translator with Jaime Manrique of Sor Juana's* Love Poems, *and author of a prize-winning play,* The Living. *She lives in Brooklyn, New York.*

Dorothy Allison

PRIVATE RITUALS

was about eight or so when I discovered that my little sister, Reese, was masturbating almost as often as I was. In the middle of the night, I woke up to feel the bed shaking slightly, the big bed where the two of us slept. Instead of sprawling across the bottom of the bed as she usually did with her legs and arms thrown wide, Reese was pulled over to the far edge of the mattress, her body taut and curved away from me. I could hear the sound of her breathing, fast and shallow. I knew immediately what she was doing. I kept still, listening, my own breathing quiet and steady. After a while there was a moment when she held her breath and then the shaking stopped. Very quietly then I slipped my right hand down between my legs and held myself, thinking about what she had been doing. I wanted to do it too, though I couldn't stand the thought that she might hear. But what if she did? What could she say to me after doing it herself? I held my breath, I moved my hand, I almost did not shake the bed at all.

Reese would go back to our bedroom alone every afternoon after we came home from school. When she would come out, I would go in there. Sometimes I even imagined I could smell what she had been doing, but that could not have been so. We were little girls. We smelled like little girls. I pulled my shorts down and made sure of it, carefully washing between my legs with warm soap and water every time I did that thing I knew my little sister was doing too.

One afternoon, I went outside and stood under the bedroom window, listening for the sound of Reese alone in the bedroom. She was quiet, very quiet, but I could hear the rhythm of her breathing as it slowly picked up speed and the soft little grunts she made before it began to slow down again. I liked those grunts. When Reese did it in the middle of the night, she never made any sound at all. But then I was just as careful myself, not letting myself make a sound even when I was safely alone. I wondered if Reese did it differently in the daytime. I wondered if she lay on her back with her legs wide, the way I

215

liked to when I was alone, rather than on her stomach with both hands under her the way she did at night. There was no way I could spy on her to see, no way I could know. But I imagined Reese sometimes while I did it myself, seeing her as she lay across our big bed, rocking only slightly, showing by nothing but her breathing that she was committing a sin.

Reese and I never talked about our private games, our separate hours alone in our room, but then we never let anyone else go in the bedroom when one of us was in there alone.

My stepfather, Daddy Glen, married my mother when I was four and Reese was still running around in rubber pants. He never spanked us that first year, never even raised his voice to yell at us. He touched my mama like she was something fine and fragile, touched us as if we wore the shine of her on our baby skin. But by the time I was five he started beating me, spanking Reese, but beating me, and screaming all the time. He still stared at Mama as if she were something marvelous and strange, and handled Reese carefully, shaking her so that her loose blond hair flew back and forth but never slapping her. Reese looked exactly like Mama's child, with Mama's eyes, Mama's chin, and her sunshine-streaked curls, but she had a sweet-natured passivity that was totally unlike Mama or me. I was Mama's first-born and her favorite, dark, sharp-featured and too often cuddled up close to Mama's side.

"He's jealous of that child," my aunts warned Mama. "A man grown and he's as jealous of that child as if she were a lover."

To spank Reese, Daddy Glen used his hand. On me he used a belt, sometimes lifting me in the air with one knotty fist clamped on my shoulder, pinning me against the wall and beating me as if his life depended on the intensity of my screams. There were shadowy bruises on my thighs and blood spots on the sheets. He announced that I was "arrogant," that I "thought too much of myself," that I was "spoiled" and "talked back" and gave him "hateful looks." I was five. I didn't hate him yet. I hid from him. Daddy Glen would lock me in the bathroom for a while to think before coming in to punish me. He would go on until my screams reached a certain satisfying pitch, or until Mama on the other side of the door began to scream louder than me. In the beginning I think I was too young to matter as much as she did.

When Daddy Glen yelled, Reese would flee. When he shouted my name, I would shudder like a bird, stopped by an arrow in the air. I schooled my face to have no expression. I admitted that I was a bad girl, evil, nasty, willful, stupid, ugly—everything he said, anything he said. Nothing helped. By the time I was seven, I did hate him. I hated him, my sister, my mother, the air that hummed with electricity when he got mad. I was a bowl of hatred, boiling black and thick behind my eyes.

Sometimes I tried not to scream, sometimes I tried not to fight him. It didn't matter at all whether I screamed or fought or held still. There was no heroism in it. There was just being beaten until I was covered with snot and misery. It wasn't until I was almost twelve that I realized Daddy Glen was pinning me against his thigh and beating me until he came in his trousers. It made it worse. It made everything more horrible. There was no reason in it, no justice. It was an animal thing, just him using me. I fell into shame like a suicide throws herself into a river.

I think I was five when I started masturbating. At least I can vaguely remember doing so. What I clearly remember are the daydreams of fire that accompanied doing it, being tied up and put inside a haystack while someone set fire to the dry, stale straw. I would picture it perfectly while rocking on my hand. The daydream was about struggling to get free while the fire burned hotter and closer. I am not sure that I came when the fire reached me, or if I would come, and then imagine escaping it. But I came. I orgasmed on my hand to the dream of fire.

I'm not sure when I got the science kit. I think it belonged to Daddy Glen's brother's children and I actually only got part of it. But I got the important part, the set of three glass test tubes in their little rack. Cold glass tubes, crystalline and gleaming and dangerous. What might happen if you pushed them inside you? What if they broke?

I pushed one inside myself.

In and out. Gradually it became warm.

I pushed the tube at my asshole and told myself it was going to hurt terribly when I actually shoved it in. When I heard myself say that out loud—"It's going in"—I came so hard I thought I'd broken it. Terrified, I hid all of them and ran outside. It was the first time I hid something, but not the last.

I made up stories for myself, changed some of them a little and told them to Reese and my cousins. I was very popular for those stories though my Aunt Raylene got upset when she heard some of them. If she had heard them all she would have beaten me harder than Daddy Glen. I would tell stories in which boys and girls were gruesomely raped and murdered, in which babies were cooked up in pots of boiling beans, stories about vampires and soldiers and long razor-sharp knives. Witches cut off the heads of both children and grown-ups. Gangs of women rode in on motorcycles and set fire to people's houses. I was very popular as a babysitter, the children were always quiet and well behaved while I whispered my stories, their eyes fixed on my face in such a way they made me feel like one of my own witches casting a spell.

I walked in on Reese one afternoon while she was lying on the bed with a pair of Mama's panties pulled over her face. All of her features were outlined under the sheer material but her breath puffed the silk out over her lips. Frantically, she snatched them off and shoved them behind her on the bed. I grabbed up a book I had been reading from the dresser, and pretended I hadn't seen anything.

Reese played out her stories in the woods behind our house. I watched her one afternoon from the top of the tree Mama hung her bird feeder on. Reese hadn't seen me climb up there and didn't know I had a clear view of her as she ran around wearing an old sheet tied to her neck as a cape. It looked like she was fighting off imaginary attackers. Then she dropped to the ground and began rolling around in the grass and wet leaves, shouting, "NO! NO!" The haughty expression on her face was replaced by mock terror, and she threw her head back and forth wildly like the heroine in an adventure movie.

I laughed, hugged myself tightly to the tree and rocked my hips against the trunk. I imagined I was tied to the branches above and below me. Someone had beaten me with dry sticks and put their hands in my clothes. Someone, someone, I imagined. Someone had tied me high up in the tree, gagged me and left me to starve to death while the blackbirds pecked at my ears. I rocked and rocked, pushing my thighs into the rough bark. Below me, Reese pushed her hips into the leaves and made those grunting noises. Someone, someone she imagined, was doing terrible, exciting things to her.

When I was nine, determined to finally have some privacy, I moved myself and all my stuff out into the utility room, setting up Mama's old fold-up bed next to the washing machine. The latch I had put on the door made it possible for me to play the game I had dreamed about for so long. I started tying myself up, using scraps of clothesline and worn belts. I would spread my legs wide and use rope that I had already tied to the bedframe to pin my ankles. I fastened clothesline to the top of the bed and I wrapped the rope around my wrists, pretending I was tied down. The stories I made up while lying like that were so exciting, I felt as if they made me drunk. After a while I would free one hand and slip it down between my legs to play with myself.

It was a sin what I did alone in there. I was a sinner, a bad person. I told myself I would have to stop doing those things, that sooner or later someone might catch me, and then what would happen? Everyone would know. But maybe, secretly, everyone did the same thing, like Reese behind the closed bedroom door. Maybe everyone was committing the same sin, secretly, fearfully. I looked in people's eyes to try and see if something showed. "We have all sinned and fallen short of the glory of God," the preacher intoned. Yes, I thought, probably so.

I don't think Reese ever tied herself up, but I'm not completely sure.

My uncles were big men with wide shoulders, broken teeth and sunken features. They kept dogs trained for hunting and drove old trucks with metal toolboxes bolted to the reinforced wooden sides. They worked in the mills or at the furnace repair business, or sometimes did roofing or construction work, depending on how the industry was going. They did engine work together on the weekends, standing around in the yard sipping whiskey and talking dirty, and kicking at the greasy remains of engines they never finished rebuilding. Their eyes were narrow under sun-bleached eyebrows, and their hands were forever working a blade, or a piece of wood, or oiling some little machine part or other. "You hold a knife like this," they told me. "You work a screwdriver from your shoulder, swing a hammer from your hip, and spread your fingers when you want to hold something safe."

I worshiped my uncles; Uncle Earle, Uncle Lucius, Wade and Butch and Bo. I begged my aunts for their old worn shirts so I could wear them just the way they did, with the front tucked in my shorts and the back tail hanging out. My uncles laughed at me, but affectionately. They raked their callused fingers through my short black hair and played at catching my shirttail as I ran past them, but their hands never hurt me and their pride in me was as bright as the coals on the cigarettes that were always held loosely between their fingers. I followed them around and stole things from them that they didn't really care about—old tools, pieces of chain and broken engine parts. I wanted most of all a knife like the ones they all carried—a buck knife with a brass and stained wood handle or a jackknife decorated with mother-of-pearl. I found a broken jackknife with a shattered handle that I taped back together around the bent steel tang. I carried that knife all the time until my cousin Grey took pity and gave me a better one.

One summer afternoon, I found a broken length of chain from off the tailgate of one of the trucks. I cleaned and polished it and locked it around my hips. Sometimes when I masturbated I would push the links up inside me. I had read in one of Daddy Glen's paperbacks about women who did something like that. I couldn't stop thinking about it. I collected various sizes of chain for it. It took me a long time, however, to learn to run that chain between my labia so that it rubbed from my vagina to my asshole, and the links pulled up tight to press my clit as I moved. But the first time I did it, that chain was sun-warmed and tingly against my little girl's boyish thighs, as shiny as the sweat on my uncle's freckled shoulders, and as exciting as the burning light behind their eyes. Every link on that chain was magic in my hand.

I became ashamed of myself for the things I thought about when I put my hands between my legs, more ashamed for masturbating to the fantasy of being beaten than for being beaten in the first place. I lived in a world of shame. I hid my bruises as if they were evidence of crimes I had committed. I knew I was a sick, disgusting person. I couldn't stop my stepfather from beating me, but *I* was the one who masturbated. *I* did that, and how could I explain to anyone that I hated his beating me, hated being beaten, but still masturbated to the story I told myself about being beaten? I was a child. I could not explain anything.

Sometimes I imagined people watching while Daddy Glen beat me. I imagined this only when it was not happening. The times when he actually beat me, I screamed and kicked and cried like the baby I was. But sometimes when I was safe and alone, I would imagine him beating me, and then I would imagine the ones who watched. Someone had to watch—some girl I admired who barely knew I existed, some girl from church or down the street, or one of my cousins, or even somebody I had seen on TV. Sometimes a whole group of them would be trapped into having to watch—they couldn't help or get away. They had to watch. In my imagination I was proud and defiant. I'd stare back at Daddy Glen in outrage with my teeth set, making no sound at all, no shameful scream, no begging, no crying. Those who watched admired me and hated him. I imagined it that way and put my hands between my legs. It was scarey to think that way, but it was wonderful too. The girl's face that watched me, loved me. It was as if I were being beaten for her. I was someone wonderful in her eyes.

220

I lived a completely schizophrenic life. I was just about the best little girl in South Carolina, made straight A's at school, took care of my little sister, cleaned the house so Mama wouldn't have to worry, told lies to the bill collectors that came to the door, and went to Baptist Sunday School in clean white dresses. But I was a sinner. I knew I was a sinner. I kept switching to different churches every few months, while pretending that I was struggling over whether to take Jesus into my heart. My mama finally caught on to the game I was playing and had me baptized. Church wasn't any fun at all when no one was trying to save your soul, so I quit going after a while.

I stole laxatives out of the medicine chest and swallowed them in large quantities to punish myself. But I couldn't stop telling myself those stories. Instead I promised Jesus I wouldn't put my hands between my legs anymore. I curled my hands up close to my neck. I gritted my teeth and wore thick cotton panties. I even started going to sleep with my arms stretched wide as if tied to the bed frame. In my imagination they were. It was a way not to sin.

Jesus, help me not to sin, I prayed. It was a joke on Jesus and me that I started having orgasms in that position, arms wide out, not touching myself, the movie playing in my head working more efficiently than my fingers ever had.

My favorite of all my uncles was Uncle Earle, known as Black Earle for three counties around. Mama said he was called Black Earle for that black, black hair that fell over his eyes in a great soft curl, but my Aunt Raylene said he was known for his black, black heart. Black Earle Boatwright was a pretty man, pretty and soft-spoken and hardworking. He always had money in his pockets, a job he was just leaving and another one he was about to take up. He always had some tender young girl on his arm—some seventeen-year-old child who watched him like his spine was outlined in pearls and rubies, his teeth with diamonds brighter than the highlights in his shiny black hair. He'd had a wife when he was young, a Catholic wife and three daughters, but she had left him for his running around, and since then he'd made a career of it, taking up with a new young girl every year or so—always young enough to boast about and as madly in love with him as only a young girl could be.

He married them, each of them, in a courthouse wedding over the line into Georgia or North Carolina after getting them to swear they were of legal age. "It's a sin," my aunts declared. "He's never divorced a one." And he didn't. He stayed married to them as if the marriages were more than the law or men could understand, as if that piece of worthless paper had meaning only he and they could put on it.

"Why do you bother?" Mama asked him after he brought the fifth or sixth of his young brides to stay with us for a week.

"Because they want it so bad," he told her where I could hear. "It seems like the least I can do."

I loved my Uncle Earle absolutely, so I decided all those girls were lucky to have had any kind of marriage at all and too stupid to deserve pity anyway. Besides, he always brought them to stay with us sooner or later, and I would find a way to plant myself up against the bedroom door while he honey-mooned loudly on the other side.

"That's sex," I told myself. "They're having sex in there." I hugged myself and listened for every girl's gasp, every thud of my uncle's body against the bed. It had to be something good if they both wanted it so bad.

I became very very afraid someone would find out the kind of stories I was making up for myself. Because of the fear, I stopped telling my stories to other people, except for rare and special girlfriends who first had to win my trust by telling me something scarey about themselves. I knew that people would think it strange that there were no boys in my stories, no men. Probably it too was some kind of sin, the kind of sin people locked you away to purge.

My stories became more detailed, more violent and more complicated. The world I was creating in my mind was full of violence and sex. It was danger-ous and terrible, the women in it powerful and cruel. Sometimes those women would even bring in men to beat and fuck me. Then again, sometimes I would be captured by evil men, tortured for my bravery and then rescued by beautiful women who wrapped me around with their great strong arms. That world was both complicated and simple, a place of dreams, adventure, sex and ritual. I was thankful that no one knew what hid behind my carefully blank or smiling face.

Once or twice a week, regularly as Sunday School, Daddy Glen beat me with one of the same two or three belts he'd set aside just for me. Oiled, smooth and supple as the gristle under chicken fat, those belts hung behind the door of his closet where I could see them when I helped Mama put away his clothes. I would reach up and touch the leather, feel it warm under my palms. There was no magic in it, no mystery, but those belts smelled of him and made me grit my teeth. Sometimes I would make myself go in that closet and wrap my fingers around those belts as if they were something animal that could be tamed.

I don't remember how old I was when Daddy Glen actually got his cock inside me. I don't remember the fucking but I remember exactly how it felt to stand up afterward, the way I hurt and how angry and afraid I was. I remember going outside and watching Reese ride her bicycle around the house. He was shouting my name but I kept heading off across the open fields behind our house. I lay down in the high grass, but I didn't cry. I started telling myself a long elaborate story, a long, long story. I didn't go into the house until it was dark. Mama was mad at me. She had been calling my name. Daddy Glen took me in the bathroom and beat me. I wrapped my hands in the pipes under the sink and watched the black hairs on his legs below his shorts.

I think it was the first time I didn't scream.

It was only in my secret stories that I was able to defy Daddy Glen. Only there that I had any pride. I loved those fantasies, even though I was sure they were a terrible thing. They had to be; they were self-centered and made me have shuddering orgasms. In the fantasy, I was very special. I was triumphant, important. I was not ashamed.

I learned to push a hairbrush handle inside my vagina to masturbate. I pretended someone else was doing it. I wore a belt fastened very tightly around my waist under my clothes where no one could see. I pretended that someone else had put it there and I couldn't take it off.

I enjoyed my other world so much that I began to live in it, plotting it out like a movie in my head, escaping to it whenever I could no longer stand the real life I did not want to be living at all.

Uncle Earle came to stay with us after a construction accident, hobbling around on a cane. I found excuses to spend time with him and get him to tell me stories. He told Mama that all the girls loved him because he looked like Elvis Presley, only skinny and with muscles. In a way he did, but his face was etched with lines and sunburned a deep red-brown. The truth was he had none of Elvis Presley's baby-faced innocence; he had a devilish look to his face and a body Aunt Carr swore was made for sex. He was a big man with a long, lanky body and wide hands seamed with scars. "Earle looks like trouble coming in on greased skids," my Uncle Bo laughed. All the aunts agreed, their cheeks wrinkling around indulgent smiles while their fingers trailed across

Uncle Earle's big shoulders as sweetly and tenderly as the threadlike feet of hummingbirds.

When Uncle Earle talked, I made my eyes wide, so he would think I believed his stories. I laughed at his jokes, even the ones I didn't understand. He would take me riding in his Pontiac with the top down, riding around dirt roads kicking up clouds of dust. He drank whiskey out of a pint bottle and let me sip a little. I would giggle and fall against him, pretending I was dizzier than I really was. I wanted to touch him. I wanted to smell him up close. His voice would get deeper after I fell against him, and he would tell me to sit up straight, that we had to get home. I didn't want to go home. I wanted to feel the muscles in his shoulders. Behind his sideburns and below his ears, the skin of his neck was as soft as if he were a woman. It took a lot of gentle persistence before he would sit still so that I could touch him when I wanted.

He gave me dollar bills for letting him rub against my backside, something I was happy to do. I wanted to turn around and pull his shirt up so I could smell his belly. But he would get nervous if I touched him too much and he got angry the one time I tried to take my pants down so he could see. I felt guilty then, and angry at him. One day when we were out in the country all alone, I pretended to be afraid and ran away from him. I walked around in the heat under the pine trees, imagining a secret installation built under the ground and the mutated, grotesque creatures who lived there. I lay down and looked up blindly into the sunlight. I began to play with myself, rubbing against the pine cones scattered around. A smoky dust came off the dried cones when I rubbed them together, a bitter dust that hung in the slanting sunlight and made me squint. I pushed some of the pine cones down in my pedal pushers before I heard my uncle coming, and quickly sat up.

Uncle Earle didn't say anything. He just sat down beside me and offered me some warm Coke. I could taste the whiskey in it. He told me I was going to be a beautiful woman. I was gonna drive men wild. He rubbed my neck and shoulders and breasts and told me he would never hurt me. Then he got me to roll over and lay down on my belly. His long body came down on top of me, smelling of cigarette smoke and hair grease. My chin was pressed into the pine needles and dirt. His chest was heavy on the back of my neck. I could feel his cock against my ass, steadily rocking against me. Every time he came down the pine cones in my pants ground into me. They were rough and scratchy but felt good to me. I began to rock with him, squirming to push the pine cones around. I got so excited that he must have gotten scared. When he came, he jumped up and ran back toward the car. I ignored him and reached into my pants to shove the pine cones farther down until they were pushing at my labia. I told myself I was going to shove them up inside me, with the dirt and the grass. I came so hard I peed myself.

It took me a long time to get up the nerve to go back to the car. I wanted to tell my uncle that I had been dreaming about him for years, that I had wanted him to do more than what he had done. But I was afraid to say anything. Uncle Earle didn't say anything either. He poured his little bottle of whiskey out the window onto the dry ground. His face looked shadowy and scared, with the shock of his hair hanging limp over his eyes. He never took me out driving again, and his eyes would slide away from me when I watched him across my mama's dinner table. When I came up behind him on the porch and hooked my fingers in his belt, he jerked my hands out roughly and pulled away from me.

"Ain't gonna touch you," he muttered.

I didn't really know if I wanted him to, but I think I did.

Masturbation for me was a mystery, private and terrible, desperate and glorious. Knowing that my sister did it too helped me to believe that I was not alone. Listening to my Uncle Earle with his teenage lovers made me think sex might be worth the price you had to pay for it. Listening to my parents fucking in the night convinced me that it was an inevitable sin. Listening to my aunts' jokes about men and their ways taught me that sex was also a subject of great humor and bitter enjoyment. But still, I believed that what I did was somehow different from anything anyone else had ever done. Maybe it was because Daddy Glen was fucking me. Maybe it was because on some level I could make myself forget that was happening and go on as if life were normal, as if we were just like everyone else.

When I thought about how different I was, it seemed to me that my difference lay in the things I thought that no one else imagined. The things I dreamed of doing with my life, the stories I made up for myself were clearly something I had to keep secret and protect. In my stories, women did things that I knew they were not supposed to do. They carried knives and rode motorcycles and spat in the faces of those that dared to touch them. I played an incredibly complicated game with every book I read, every movie or TV show I saw; I turned it over in my mind. The heroes and active characters became female while the men receded to a vague blur, not really interesting at all. The stories I made up, in which I was captured and tortured to save my girlfriends—the ones I used so successfully to bring myself to orgasm—they were only the smallest piece of what was scarey and dangerous about me.

Finally, I told. One night late while she was babysitting us, I told Cousin Temple that Daddy Glen had "done things" to me. She climbed out of the bed and ran down the hall. When she came back she had a little comic book with cartoon drawings of men lying on top of women, pushing their dicks between the women's legs. "Did he do that?" she asked me. Temple's eyes were pale, pale blue, burning. "No," I whispered. "He does it with me standing up."

Early the next morning my uncles all stomped in the back door, their faces flat, red and dangerous. Temple had told the whole damn world. My uncles took Daddy Glen away and beat him up, the same way they had when I was six and he had whipped me so badly that Aunt Raylene had seen the marks. Mama moved us out to a motel. But after a few weeks, Daddy Glen came over to the motel and cried in Mama's arms until she forgave him. I understood that we had to go back to live with him. I understood that Mama loved him. We went home on a Sunday afternoon and he had a big basket of take-out chicken waiting for dinner. I went for a long walk and kept making up stories for myself, talking out all the roles as I walked for hours. When I went home, Mama had gone to bed exhausted. Daddy Glen was sitting at the kitchen table, staring out the screen, his hands loose on the oilcloth, cigarettes spilling out of a saucer. His blue-black eyes were mirrors in his pale face. I saw myself in his pupils, my own face brown and empty, my own eyes shining like wet glass, reflecting nothing.

I invented a series of new tests and rituals for myself. I put things in my pants and made rules for how long I had to keep them there—pine cones, rocks, a letter opener I stole from the library whose handle I gripped with my buttocks, little ceramic figures from my aunt's dresser. I added details to my fantasy world, pretending I was required to carry messages tucked in locked containers that the enemies would try to steal from me. I experimented with actually pushing things up inside me. My test tubes were long lost. I graduated to screwdriver handles, my mama's potato masher, various vegetables and most of the tools in my stepfather's toolcase.

My uncle had left his cane. It was blond wood with a knobby top about the size of a closed fist. I discovered that if I put it between my legs it was just about a half inch higher than my cunt. I tied a clean washcloth over the head of it and used masking tape and rope to fasten it between my legs. I walked back and forth with it riding high up against my clit, stumbling painfully. I made myself promise that I would walk back and forth across the room ten times before I could stop. Even if I should come, I promised, I would not let myself stop. When I actually did come and could not finish the required laps, I made a vow that I would have to do it all over again, and double the number of times I would have to cross the room. Doubled again and again, no matter how I sweated and limped, riding that cane like a wooden horse on a merry-go-round, I never caught up, never met my vow. Expiation was impossible. Sin was endless.

I was thirteen. Uncle Earle had moved to Florida. I was rummaging through the house, restless, irritable, looking for something new. In my sister's room, I started opening drawers, pulling out boxes, looking through her things. In Reese's bottom drawer there was a box with a cord tied around it in a complicated series of knots. Slowly I picked it apart, keeping the pattern of the knots in mind so I could tie it back together the way it had been. The process took a long time and calmed me down. When I had it completely untied, I sat still for a moment with the box in my lap. I could hear a lawn mower in the distance, a radio, and someone yelling. I opened the box. Silk panties, an old pair of my mama's. I lifted them carefully. Underneath was one of Daddy Glen's handkerchiefs, loosely wrapping a long smooth ivory handle that looked as if it had once been fixed to a mirror. It fit my hand solidly and felt almost soft cool and yellowed as if it had absorbed years of sweet oil. I lifted it to my mouth wanting to run my tongue over it, but the smell stopped me. I knew that smell. It was my smell, girl smell, sex smell, heady yeast and piss smell. I breathed deeply and grinned, put that handle in my mouth.
"Little sister." I giggled. "Little sister..." I sucked the handle into my mouth, pushed my fingers down in my jeans for a little of the juice from between my legs. Carefully I rubbed it into the ivory before wrapping it back up and tying the knots all over again. "Little sister." I kept laughing, almost singing. "Little sister, just like me!"
It was true then. All of us hid the same thing behind our eyes. I went and got my chain, locked it around my hips, took my uncle's knobby-headed cane and ran out into the thick summer heat. My stepfather was unloading boxes out of Mama's gray Chevy. My Uncle Wade was helping him.
"Come on over here," they yelled at me.
I planted that cane in the damp grass in front of me, and stood rock still,

227

rock steady, memory rolling up like an endless, powerful story. Fire behind my eyes, light and shine, chain in the dark, whiskey taste beneath the Coke, my little sister's face through the back window of the car, Daddy Glen's forearms ridged in muscle, my uncle's eyes narrowed under thick brows—I put my head back and smiled. The chain on my hips moved under my jeans. I was locked away and safe. What I really was could not be touched. What I really wanted was not yet imagined. I looked down at my hands on my uncle's cane, remembering the fear and excitement in his eyes. Somewhere far away a child was screaming, but right then, it was not me.

Dorothy Allison is a poet and novelist. Her first novel, Bastard out of Carolina, *was a finalist for the 1992 National Book Award. "Private Rituals" is derived from passages originally excised from that novel. Her other works include* Cavedweller, *a novel;* Trash, *a collection of short stories; and* The Women Who Hate Me, *a collection of poems. She is also the author of a book of essays,* Skin: Talking About Sex, Class & Literature, *and the memoir,* Two or Three Things I Know for Sure. *Allison was born in Greenville, South Carolina, and now lives in northern California.*

Gretchen Elkins

DOES THIS HURT?

First, the four swimmers—at loose ends because of the canceled swim meet—stole a Port-O-San from a construction site and placed it on the Robertsons' large green lawn. Todd's joy at the sight made him punch Joel in the arm; they mock-wrestled for a couple of minutes, and Joel pretended he was going to pour his beer over Todd's head. Then Todd crooked an arm around Joel's neck, pulling his head down, and at the same time grabbed at Joel's chest through his shirt, pinching and twisting the flesh around the circle of the nipple and saying, *Does this hurt, dude? Does this hurt?* Joel finally twisted away from Todd and laughed along with the rest of them, although the sting from his chest brought water to his eyes. Todd's face was red and Joel wondered if his own was too; anyway, why had Todd seized on him to punch in the first place?

They all jumped back into Todd's pickup, Todd and Mike in the cab, the other two braced in the back, and sped back to Todd's house. *I'm hoome,* Todd growled, in a not very good Jack Nicholson imitation, then kicked the genteel white wooden door open, and led the way in as the brass knocker whacked back and forth. Joel shut the door behind them. Todd's parents were in the Bahamas, his sisters were at the Greenville-Centennial football game, and so they alone were in possession of the house. Todd was widely known for his large collection of videotapes, both regular movies and porno, and it was in this house, remembered Joel, uncomfortably, that he'd seen a video that he'd had to work hard to forget—news footage strung together featuring nauseating images of people burning, falling, dying. *Faces of Death,* that's what it had been called. He hadn't spent much time with Todd since then, until they'd both made the swim team. Mike, Todd's new best friend, rummaged in the kitchen cupboards like he lived in the house, and found over half a bottle of vodka in the freezer; enough for two shots each. They broke open the case of beer, and, exhilarated, buzzed, lounging on the huge leather couches, passed around a bag of potato chips while they

229

watched a movie and talked about "The Great Port-O-Potty Caper."

Joel lay back on the couch with his feet up on the coffee table. Gregg was sitting by him, slightly hunched over on the edge of the couch, forearms resting on his knees. Gregg had transferred to Centennial High just that year, and Joel often found himself watching Gregg, wondering what he was thinking about all this, wondering whether Gregg thought they were all jerks, or just Todd, because Todd *was* kind of a jerk.

He turned his attention back to the video. The movie was not *Road Warrior*, but in the same genre, and was good enough that they watched the whole thing, but still kind of bad, so they all made sarcastic comments during the whole movie except during a few chase scenes. In one scene of the movie, the hero threw himself through a window into a house where a man and a woman were fucking doggy-style with funny costumes on. The guy wore a tutu and ballet slippers, and the woman was dressed like a Nazi. The hero looked at the guy and said, *Nice shoes,* then ran out the back door of the house. Todd rewound this scene and played it over a couple of times while they all discussed the finer nuances of the coupling.

Todd had a girlfriend that he said he slept with all the time, although he did say that he'd never done it like that. Joel said he and Marcy had never done it like that either.

All the guys thought Joel's friend Marcy was his girlfriend, and that they were sleeping together. Marcy had gone out of her way to lie to them when one day she told Mike she respected Joel because he was smart and didn't bitch about using condoms. That was what was so cool about Marcy. She didn't care if people thought they were having sex, but she would have been totally embarrassed if people thought they weren't using condoms. It would have been like eating a whale-burger or throwing trash out the window of a car. Marcy was a crusader, and every other editorial she wrote for the school paper was about safe sex. The guys would have made fun of her, except they thought that she was some kind of free-love, safe-sex hippie and that she and Joel had sex all the time.

In fact, Joel and Marcy had never had sex. She was willing, but the idea made Joel anxious. He worried that he wouldn't get an erection. She thought it was more likely that neither of them would feel sexy, and that they'd both practically die laughing, but she always said she'd be willing to try, since they were best friends.

Once Joel had asked her, *What keeps the tampon from, just, you know, getting lost up inside you?*

Women aren't like Hoovers, you asshole, she'd said with disgust.

After that, in a fake British accent, he'd say things like, *Marcy, dear, could you Hoover up these crumbs for me?*

Todd said there was a country and western bar in Greenville that didn't check I.D.'s, so they decided to drive over there. Joel and Gregg were again in the back of the truck. They sat huddled up to the cab of the truck with a blanket over their knees. Gregg's leg was pressed against Joel's leg. Joel was conscious that the muscles in his leg were rigid, and they started to hurt, because he was clenching them so tightly. They could hear Todd and Mike in the cab of the truck shouting and laughing.

When they stopped at lights, they could hear them better, and Mike shouted *Here come the synchronized shitters*, and, *Will Joel Matthews, gold medalist in the synchronized shit contest, please pick up a white courtesy telephone?* They started laughing, and Joel moved his leg away from Gregg's warm leg.

They were about halfway to the bar, when the pickup turned off the main road onto a little gravel one. Joel thought Todd must know some back-road short-cut to the bar. The truck was going slower now, and it was better because it wasn't as cold. They were the only ones on the road, and Joel liked that too. It seemed as if it was just the four of them in the cold and the wind, shouting and laughing. They came to a wide place in the road, Todd stamped on the brakes and the pickup slewed sideways on the gravel, then fishtailed back straight. They slowed down, then the pickup pulled off the road onto the grassy edge and stopped. It was quiet and again Joel could hear the guys in the cab laughing. There was a short honk on the truck's horn and then the door opened.

Pissin' time, Todd said, as he got out and walked over to the fence by the side of the road.

Pissin' time, Mike echoed Todd—

—*Like a moron*, thought Joel.

He heard the steady thrum of Todd's urine hitting the ground. The clouds in the sky glowed with the orange lights from the city behind them. The street lights of the suburban hills were strung in lines, and Joel could see the headlights of a car miles away, driving down a road on the side of the hill.

They heard a low moan, and goosebumps swept over Joel's skin and a shiver traveled from the base of his spine up through the back of his head.

Fuckin' Aaaay.... Mike's voice dropped off in a grumbled echo of the moan they had heard. They heard it again, and Joel heard Todd giggling nervously at the same time as Joel sorted out what the sound was, and separated the black

231

and white shape out of the black humped mass of trees and bushes behind it.

The cow mooed again.

Joel leaned back against the pickup truck, laughing silently. Gregg was leaning beside him, and put his hand up for Joel to slap in a high five.

Fuck off cow! Todd was mad at the cow. He picked up a rock, and threw it into the black field. Joel heard the thud as the rock hit the ground. Then Todd came back and got a beer.

I'm gonna ride that cow. I'm gonna drink this beer, then I'm gonna ride that cow.

Gregg stood with one army boot on the lowest strand of barbed wire, pulled up the next highest strand, and bowed them all through. They ducked through the fence—Joel held it apart for Gregg—and started walking across the field. Joel thought the cow would run away, but it stood completely still. Joel and Gregg were the last to walk up and complete the rough circle around the animal.

Joel heard Todd say something to Mike in a low voice. Mike put his arm around the cow's neck, as if he were doing a half-nelson on it. Todd walked up to the back of the cow and put one hand on it while he undid his pants with the other.

Joel was angry, thinking, *Why is he going to pee on the cow?*

Gregg was muttering beside him, *He's gonna fuck the cow, he's gonna fuck the cow.*

Joel thought Todd must be faking it, so he walked over to the cow, pretending he was going to help Mike hold it. When he walked past Todd, he saw out of the corner of his eye that Todd really did have an erection. Todd was looking downward at his penis in his hand, and doing a comical little shuffle with his feet, as the cow shifted slowly from hoof to hoof. Then Todd was pressed up close against the cow's hindquarters and had his eyes screwed shut, muttering.

Come on baby, come on, fuck me. He went faster, and talked a little louder.

He knows we're all watching him, thought Joel, leaning with his hands on the cow. The cow was moving its big head a little bit, looking at Joel every now and then over its shoulder. Todd gave a dramatic moan, then he pulled out his dick and wiped it off with a bandanna.

Mike stepped around to the cow's tail, and unbuckled his belt.

Joel's hands were stiffly splayed out on the cow's warm bristle-haired back. He was looking up at the sky. He saw a cloud that looked like a gray brain, with pink curves and bumps—the lights of the city reflected up onto the

232

cloud—*That's why it's pink*, he thought. He could see Mike's dark head moving slightly from side to side, and could hear the catch in his breathing as he came silently.

You go now, said Todd to Joel. *Come on stud, fuck her like you do Marcy.*

Joel didn't move.

Uh, that's okay, I jerked off once already today, he said, listening to his voice waver.

What are you? A fag? Mike was staring at him. They were all looking at him.

Come on, don't be such a pussy, said Todd.

Lemme at that cow, he said finally, pulling open his jeans with one hand.

He held his dick in his right hand so they couldn't see that it wasn't completely stiff, and he pressed his hand, clutching his dick, into the cow's warm vagina. He imagined Gregg behind him, watching him. He thought that maybe Gregg was watching his ass, and he began to exaggerate the back and forth movement of his hips. Todd and Mike were on each side of the cow, holding it where it was—not that it was moving—by leaning inwards on their arms. Joel's left hand slid over onto Todd's hand. Todd didn't even notice, but Joel jerked his hand away. He closed his eyes and concentrated on the thought of Gregg watching him, then on the curve of the back of a dancer in an MTV video that he liked. He imagined his hands on the guy's shoulders and he came, his body stiffening and feeling Gregg's eyes on his back, his lips on the back of the man's neck, then felt his penis sliding out of the wetness of the cow.

Way to go stud dude, said Todd, and threw his bandanna at Joel. Gregg stepped up behind the cow.

Joel tucked himself into his pants, then pretended he was drunker than he really was by lurching across the field to the truck and opening another beer. He went around the truck where no one could see him and poured some beer over his dick and wiped it off on the tail of his shirt.

What is cowpox, anyway? He sat down on the truck's tail-gate and stared at the lights on the hills.

In the morning, Joel spat out toothpaste and looked in the bathroom mirror at his naked chest. It was cold in the tiled bathroom, and he shivered as he looked into the wide brown eyes of the white figure in the mirror.

You cowfucker. It seemed weak. The words wallowed out of his white-rimmed mouth. He tried again.

Pigfucker! That was better. But of course it would have been much worse to have to fuck a pig. Only they probably wouldn't have been able to fuck a pig; he had the vague idea that pigs were more irritable, that a pig would have squealed and run away. Maybe tried to bite.

Faggot. Cocksucker. It was possible to inject those words with the force he thought they deserved.

He watched himself in the mirror as his hand pinched and twisted his nipple. *Does this hurt?* he muttered—*does this hurt?*

Gretchen Elkins writes both poetry and fiction and lives in New York City. She recently received her M.F.A. from New York University, where she was awarded a New York Times *fellowship.*

V
AN EPILOGUE
Let's Talk About Sex

New York Teens on Sex and Sexuality

We wanted to hear what teenagers talk about when they talk about sex. With the help of Sasha Whyte, a seventeen-year-old high school senior, we devised a survey and asked her to interview her peers. In the spirit of Dr. Alfred Kinsey's research, all interviewees were asked the same set of questions in the same order. The final sample of New York teenagers came from diverse ethnic, racial, and economic backgrounds. Additional interviews were conducted by nineteen-year-old Dana La Forey. Real names were used unless indicated by an asterisk.

Q: *What is your definition of sex?*
Bobbi Jo, 15: A man and a woman or a woman and a woman or a man and a man getting off.

Sadiki, 17: I think it's for mainly reproduction, but people abuse it for satisfaction.

Erica, 17: Sex is—whether its male-female or male-male or female-female—when they have intercourse, or not even, when they're kissing, hugging, oral sex. Any kind of activity that has to do with touching is considered sex.

Q: *How important is sex in your life?*
Chad, 17: Sex is a very important part of my life. I enjoy having sex. I'm seventeen, basically in my prime, my sexual peak or whatever you want to call it. Things can happen during the day that will make me think about sex. When a pretty girl walks by or, you know, some kind of sexual matter.

Erica: It depends if I'm in a relationship or if I'm just messing with someone, meaning I'm just talking to a person and just trying to get to know a person. I wouldn't have sex with somebody I'm just getting to know, but if I'm in a relationship I expect that, maybe not in the beginning. It's a pretty big part of getting to know someone, and understanding who you are and who that person is.

*Reality, 16: I lost my virginity at fifteen, which was about a year ago and it's because I loved him and I guess I wanted to keep him or whatever. I was hot way before that, but I was trying to wait. I held it for a little while, but then things happened and we ended up having sex. To me, I guess you could call it a nympho or whatever you want to call it, but I need sex every day, I need sex when I wake up. I'm like addicted.

*Moet, 18: Sex isn't that important to my life. I always feel that you have to be in a relationship before you start having sex with somebody. Maybe when I get older I'll find it important, maybe I'll need it, but right now I don't have needs all the time. I don't know why I think about it a lot, but don't want it a lot.

*John, 17: Sex is not important at all in my life. Since I'm a male, I'd say maybe I think about it three dozen times a day. In the environment I live in there is no sexual pressure. There's more academic pressure than sexual pressure. My parents, I'm pretty sure they don't have sex. In general, Asian and Chinese culture is more conservative and they really stress not having sex. I probably wouldn't have sex until after marriage.

Q: *Do you practice safe sex?*
Chad: That's the thing today—safe sex. It's just an obvious thing if you know anything about AIDS or any other diseases. It doesn't take much to realize that a condom is the best way to go.

Moet: I do practice safe sex. I had a child when I was sixteen so I wasn't always practicing safe sex, but now I do. I know about safe sex as far as condoms and other contraceptives. I learned about it basically from school and my parents, television, the doctors, friends. I waited for two years after having my daughter before having sex again. I was scared to have sex. I was more in touch with diseases and pregnancy. I was more in fear than I was before. Now, I just want to make sure I'm with someone who's about to put that ring on my finger, okay, we don't necessarily have to be getting married, but I want to see that it's going somewhere.

Since I had my daughter I want sex a whole lot more, I don't necessarily have sex a lot more. I think I found out more about myself sexually, things I can do for myself. After having a child, there are things I'm more willing to do now. My fantasies are more graphic and I'm more willing to do things than I was before. I'm not as conservative.

Erica: Safe sex is really important because you want to stay alive, but there's a difference between saying it and actually doing it. There've been times that I didn't and I trusted the person and it backfired on me. I've never been pregnant, but I thought I was. Actually, they told me I was and I went to have an abortion. I was on the table with my clothes off. I put on a robe, they took out a big stick and the nurse was like, "I don't see anything on the screen." I said, "You have to see something because they told me I was pregnant." She says I don't see anything. So they got me dressed again and sent me home. But I was like so devastated. I was only thirteen and it was with my first partner.

Solomon, 18: I was an AIDS coordinator and educator in high school. We went around to other schools giving demonstrations on why it was important to practice safe sex, how to use a condom, how to know the signs of other sexually transmitted diseases like chlamydia, gonorrhea and herpes. The only STD I've ever had is crabs.

The first time I had unprotected sex had to do with love. That was probably a mistake because it made me scared and it made me nervous. The first time I swallowed come also had to do with love. I did that because I felt like it added to the intimacy that we shared together.

*Samantha, 16: By my definition of sex, which is intercourse, I have had protected intercourse every time. My friend yelled at me because…this is really embarrassing, but…to some people oral sex means sex and it doesn't to me, which means it's just not as serious so I don't use protection. My friend yelled at me. I just don't take it that seriously and I don't see it as dangerous.

Reality: The only one I'm with is with my man and sometimes when I have my period and stuff, we'll use a condom, but other than that I don't use it. But if I'm not monogamous I'll use a condom.

Q: *Do you talk to your friends about sex?*
Erica: All the time. I think girls are just as bad as guys. Guys are usually like, "Yeah, I hit that, I had sex." Girls do the same thing. I keep my business to myself, but if I have really good friends I tell them. I don't tell them how it was, but I tell them I did it. We talk about things like past partners we had and how bad they were and how good they were. We compare. I'll see a guy in the hallway and I'll know my friend had sex with him and I'll be like "Oh I know, you're small there."

Moet: I talk to my friends about sex because they talk to me about it. It's not something I always bring up cause sometimes I feel uncomfortable speaking about it with other people. Sometimes the conversations can get a little too

239

explicit and I become kind of embarrassed. We do talk about safe sex and if I think my friends are going to have sex, like if I have friends who are virgins, I'll kind of tell them what my experiences were like. I don't say this is what your experience is going to be like, but I say that was mine.

*Trini, 17: We talk about how good it was, who we did it with, where and how much fun it was. The basics, you know, like how long did he take to come, was he holding onto the sheets.

Q: *Do you talk about masturbation with your friends?*
Sadiki: I don't talk about masturbation with my friends because they're embarrassed. People think, "Oh, you masturbate, that's personal. I don't want to know that you beat your meat, choke your chicken, spank your monkey." You just picture somebody doing that—it's embarrassing.

Samantha: I joke about it with guys, like, "Oh, you must jerk off all the time." Guys say, "I don't have a girlfriend so I have to jerk off four times a week." I think it's different if I was with a bunch of black and Hispanic guys—they wouldn't talk about masturbation.

I'm not saying girls don't masturbate, they just don't talk about it. Most girls don't. Most of my friends don't masturbate. They say so. These are the same girls that talk about the different guys they've blown so I don't think they're exactly shy. I think it's just harder to masturbate if you're a girl. Girls' orgasms don't come as easily as they do for guys. The penis is more immediate, it's there so they masturbate. Girls aren't taught that your sexuality is an immediate need. So you kind of ignore it.

Moet: I don't have a problem about people masturbating, I have a problem with myself masturbating. I always feel like there's this watchful eye over me that's going to tell me, "No, that's a really bad thing to do, you shouldn't sexually pleasure yourself."

Q: *Do you feel you have to compete on a sexual level with your friends or peers?*
Chad: In some cases I feel like, "Oh, yeah, I haven't had enough sex, I haven't been with enough girls." Then when I compare myself to some of my friends, I feel like I've had tons of sex with tons of girls and just think I'm the Mac. You want to have more girls and more sex than your friends. You can call that competition, but it's also personal desires. Like you want more pretty girls and you want to have more sex with pretty girls.

Samantha: I feel like my track record is bad. I feel as if I can't get cute guys like my friends can, that they get guys who want to be their boyfriends and I can't.

240

Solomon: I have a friend Nick who I compete with. One night we went to a series of gay bars and at the last one we went to I started dancing with this guy and the minute I started dancing with this guy, he found someone else. The guy I was dancing with gave me his number, I gave him my number and he left. Nick was making out in the corner with this guy. So I turned around and there was a guy there who was about my height, a little bit thinner with blond hair, blue eyes, thick lips. We didn't have much conversation, we just started making out and then I went to his hotel room. On the train ride home, I met another guy and we went back to my dorm room to have sex. So I won out that night, I beat Nick two to one.

Q: *Have you ever experienced sexual violence?*
Samantha: My grandfather used to touch me. I think he did, but I don't know. It's one of those things that can be misinterpreted. It goes by how I feel, and how I feel is I was touched in a way that made me feel uncomfortable. The last time it happened I was in Jamaica with him. I was eleven. I told my aunt that he gets weird with me and she said "What do you mean by weird?" I told her and she just laughed at me. She was like, "That's nothing, you misinterpret things, you read too many books." I know what happened and I know it made me feel uncomfortable sexually and it scared me.

Reality: I used to be in a home, like in foster care, and you know how that goes, you know, problems. I mean it was never actually taken from me, but I guess that's why I'm addicted to sex like I am now, cause I used to take classes where people would tell me that either I'd be addicted to sex or I'd be scared of sex.

Moet: I did experience sexual violence one time. It wasn't a rape or anything, but a guy thought we should have sex and he was…I could have been raped. We were in his house and he kind of jumped up on me and started busting on me. But we both were clothed. He was drunk. I was crying and I was very upset, but I never reported it cause I just felt it wasn't rape and we haven't spoken since.

Q: *What was the first thing you ever heard about sex?*
Erica: My mom was real open about sex and explained it to me when I first became a young lady. She told me that now I can have children and I have to be careful and not to let anyone touch me. She said I'm allowed to have sex when I'm of age, which is eighteen or over, because then I could understand and be able to handle it and whatever comes after it.

Samantha: My mother never gave me straight answers about anything. I wondered as I got older and more kids were born in my family, why everyone else had their father's last name except for me. My mother would tell stories to get herself out of it. She told me I was born by immaculate conception. She said it with a straight face. End of story. I went to Catholic school, I had no reason not to believe her.

I actually learned about intercourse through this book by Judy Blume called *Forever.* That's one of the greatest books ever created. I think that's how fifty percent of junior high school girls learn about sex. There was this other book me and my friend got out of the library, *Love and Sex in any Language,* and it got into intercourse and what the person does and it sounded bizarre. I think if you can't visualize it, it sounds like a pretty bizarre thing to do but I guess nature did a good job.

Moet: The first thing I ever knew about sex. I just knew that that's how you had children and that you had to have a penis and a vagina come together in order to have children and that's the circumstances under which I knew about sex.

Rya, 17: The first thing anyone ever told me about sex was my mother telling me make sure you get a lot of things before you have sex. Probably that affected me, what she said. You feel that guys owe you something.

Q: *Is sex easier for young men or young women?*
Moet: Sex may be easier for young men because it's more accepted for young men to be having a lot of sex. But if a girl is having sex and enjoying sex and does it a lot, she's thought of as a whore, whereas it seems like guys are encouraged to have as much sex as they can while they're young.

Sadiki: I think it's easier for young women because the woman is the main source behind sex because it's what men want. It's easier for women to get sex. Men for their age group most of the time they've got to find somebody who's willing to do it. But women can be with older men, so they've got two categories.

Solomon: I have a theory on this: Women have a hard time being promiscuous because we sort of glorify the womb in our society. It's so special, it's the agent of creation and women are taught that their vagina is very important, very special and sacred, then also at the same time that it's dirty and evil and bad. So to let their vagina be open for the world to see is a lot different from a man who from the time he's twelve has probably been jerking off and really

242

when most men have sex they're not doing much more than jerking off. So yes, it's easier for young men.

Erica: I think the male race is so closed-minded. I think men just go in there and do it just to say "I did it." For a man sex is sex. Like, "See you later," and it's on to the next one. Women associate love and sex together. We are built different. We're women. We're like fragile, it's true. When you're having sex, that's giving a part of your body. Even if you're getting to know a person, women need to have feelings, well, I need to have a feeling for someone if I'm going to have sex with them. I can't just have sex with a male hooker and act like nothing happened. Men could do that. Men could have sex with a prostitute and act like there's no feeling. I don't understand that.

*Hennissy, 17: It's always the woman that decides whether or not sex is going to be had. The man can put his little suggestions in, but it's always going to be the woman who finally says, let's just do this. And if the woman doesn't want to do it, then it's not going to be done.

Q: *Define the word orgasm.*
Moet: I would say an orgasm was when you have reached your peak and you are just sexually satisfied. When somebody has touched your clitoris and it feels very, very good.

Chad: I guess that's the peak of pleasure during sex, like when someone gets to the point which they wanted to throughout having sex. They get to the point where it's just so pleasurable that once that's over it's not as good anymore. That's the best part of sex.

Solomon: It's the contraction and release of certain muscles stimulating certain nerve endings to make a physical response, usually ending in a discharge of seminal fluid in a man and vaginal fluid in a woman.

Erica: Orgasm is when you get off. When you finally got to your peak of excitement. It's like a roller-coaster ride and when you're about to go down and then you go down and that's it.

Q: *Are orgasms necessary to have good sex?*
Jamie, 17: I don't think so because I don't feel that sex is just...it's also like being with another person, you know, like just being there with that other person that you love or you like so much or whatever, so it's not just the actual act, but the whole idea and everything.

Chad: To have fulfilling sex, yeah, orgasm's a main part. For guys, if you don't have an orgasm you're basically going to get blue balls and then be in pain later on, but a girl could definitely have good sex and not have an orgasm, but not great sex.

Bobbi-Jo: I think it's more about movement and the person who's with you. My friends tell me that you know this person didn't make me come, but he was a good fuck because of the way he moves, he knew how to move.

Erica: I don't think orgasms are necessary for good sex. I hardly ever catch one and it's like when I do get one I hold on to it.

Solomon: There's a lot more to good sex than just an orgasm. Especially for a man because an orgasm's really fast. An orgasm is usually better when the sex has been really good. I think that if a woman hasn't had an orgasm then the sex probably hasn't been as good as it could have been. If the sex is going to be good for a woman it implies a partner taking the time to have her climax. As a man, I prefer to climax. I mean, I've had some really great sex where neither of us came, or only one of us came.

Q: *Are orgasms different for men and women?*
Chad: I think girls have better orgasms than guys just because it's harder for them to have an orgasm. So that must mean they're better. Orgasms for guys, I mean they're good, but I can definitely tell you that they're not as special as when a girl has an orgasm. I can just see it on the girl's faces—they've enjoyed their orgasms a lot more than me.

Sadiki: A woman needs an orgasm most of the time. She wants to get satisfied. Men, they could still get off without even coming to an orgasm. They don't feel complete, but you can get feeling the whole time, but women you could be in there feeling good, but they want to come to an orgasm.

Erica: If a guy doesn't catch an orgasm you're there for hours. It's strange because a guy could come to orgasm and he's done, but what about the girl? It would be nice if you could both catch it at the same time, but it doesn't happen that way. I've had sex a lot of times and I haven't had orgasms, but it's been great. It's great because after you reach orgasm, you're not in the mood anymore so it's good for me because I'm always in the mood. If he gets up again later on it's okay cause I'm still hyped up.

Samantha: Guys can be selfish and when you might be coming close, a guy will stop to do something that will get him off. It makes me very mad. But when you're in a sexual situation, you don't want to come off as too aggressive.

244

You don't want to say, "Hey you keep doing that." To be politically correct would be to take charge of my sexuality, but I guess that's where the pressure comes up of being a girl and you have to be just a little submissive.

Reality: To be honest with you, it's a lot easier for a man to have an orgasm than it is for a woman. A man could have sex or fuck or whatever you want to call it, and if he comes, he comes. But a female it takes a lot of work and all that pushing and all that touching and all that heat.

Hennissy: See, women got it better than guys. Yo. All guys have is this flaccid piece of skin that gets hard and comes every now and again. It's just a piece of tissue. Women got this muscular system, they got mad different parts to it that you can touch. I mean, there's the clit, there's the lips here, the lips there. You do your thing, you gonna make a girl come more than three times, yo. I'm telling you, if I was a woman, yo, I'd get my shit eaten every day.

Q: *What frightens you most about having sex?*
Solomon: What frightens me most about sex is taking my clothes off. I know I have a bad body image. I'm anorexic and have been bulimic and I don't think that people will find me physically attractive. Mentally, I know that I am physically attractive, so it's just an emotional thing. I sit there and go "Oh, he's not going to like me because I'm too fat today," or "My hair's probably too curly or too puffy."

Samantha: Being penetrated by something frightens me. It's like someone invading your body with their body part. When I was younger it sounded like a violent act. I visualized it after seeing a porno movie and it just looked so incredibly violent and scary and dirty. But that's a cool thing about it because it's kind of dirty, kind of wild. That's what intrigues me about it too, the concept of someone entering your body, giving someone permission to enter your body.

Moet: I am most frightened about diseases, AIDS and things like that because those are deadly things. I don't want to die if I'm too young and I haven't had sex worth dying for yet.

Q: *Fifty years ago, Alfred Kinsey created a scale of sexual preferences. Zero means you're really, really het, six means you're homosexual exclusively, and three means you're in between. Where would you rate yourself?*
Jamie: I've never felt sexually attracted to another girl, but I like looking at bodies whether they're male or female so I'd be a half.

Bobbi-Jo: A two. Yeah, I guess because women are attractive, not as attractive as men to me, but I do like my friend Jane sometimes when I'm in a drunken stupor.

Chad: I'm a negative ten on the heterosexual side. I've never ever had a desire to be with another man whatsoever. I'll admit some men are good-looking because I can tell an ugly person from a good-looking person, but I've never had any sexual desire towards men.

Erica: Three. I'm heterosexual, but I'm open to experiences and new ideas or whatever it is depending on the situation.

Samantha: Two and a half. I've had the inclination to kiss girls sometimes but I'll probably never do it. I'm just too chicken. The feelings I have for girls are just really scary to me. They creep me out and I don't know why. It was so good when I was younger. I was masturbating all the time and I thought girls looked so cute in short skirts, it was just the best. But I had to get older and I had to stop liking girls, I had to stop masturbating. I had to start liking guys. I always liked guys, but all these pressures just increase when you get older. I don't want the bisexual label. I don't want to be known as confused or a freak. Not like it's bad to be a freak, but I don't want to be that. Maybe when I get to college things will be different, maybe I'll be getting with girls all the time. I'm kind of introverted, and introverted girls don't kiss other girls.

John: Between two and three. I think that everyone is bisexual in a way. Sometimes you can get attracted to the same sex, but I'm like 99.5 percent heterosexual, but sometimes you just think maybe, but then you're like, Nah… I've thought about it maybe once or twice in my life.

Q: *Complete the following sentence: I will have good sex when…*
Chad: I'm having good sex now. I'm sure I'll have better sex than any I've ever had when I get older or find the right girl. When you feel more comfortable with the girl or the person you're with that makes the sex better. It all depends on the situation.

Erica: I have good sex all the time, well, not all the time, because there's been times when it's been horrible. I will have good sex when I know I'm really committed and I know I really love that person and I know I want to spend the rest of my life with that person and I won't be afraid to show my body or show who I am.

Solomon: I will have good sex when I've had twelve hours of sleep the night before and I've drank lots of water during the day.

Rya: I will have good sex when guys stop being so fucking boring. They're boring. You could close your eyes and know everything they're going to do.

Samantha: I will have sex when I stop fucking. Okay, maybe fucking won't be bad when I get older, but one day I want to make love with someone I can share emotion with.

Moet: I will have good sex when I am living by myself and have found out everything that stimulates me.

Hennissy: I will have good sex when the girl knows what she's doing all the time.

Reality: I will have good sex as soon as I get home.

ABOUT GLOBAL CITY AND THE EDITORS

Global City was founded in 1993 by novelist Linsey Abrams, under the auspices of the Simon H. Rifkind Center for the Humanties at the City College of New York. Its books, as well as the annual *Global City Review*, are edited by various members of a collective of women writers and women who work in mainstream publishing. The collective focuses on issues of race, gender, sexual politics, and women's experience. *Too Darn Hot: Writing About Sex Since Kinsey* is the third anthology edited by members of Global City.

Judy Bloomfield is at work on a collection of poems, *What I Blame the Palm Reader For*. Her poetry has been published in literary reviews and anthologies. She has an M.F.A. in Creative Writing from Sarah Lawrence College and a B.A. in journalism from Indiana University, Bloomington. She lives in Berkeley, California.

Mary McGrail is working on a collection of short stories entitled *Steel Beach*. She has an M.A. in creative writing from City College of New York, where she was a *New York Times* Fellow, and a B.A. in English from the University of Massachusetts, Boston, where she won the Creative Writing Book Prize. She lives in New York City.

Lauren Sanders is a writer and editor who lives in New York City. Her nonfiction writing has appeared in *The American Book Review* and numerous magazines. She has an M.A. in creative writing from City College of New York and is a graduate of Columbia University's School of Journalism. She is currently at work on her second novel, *With or Without You.*

The editors gratefully acknowledge the authors and publishers who granted permission to publish the pieces in this collection.

Dorothy Allison. "Private Rituals" was originally published in *High Risk: An Anthology of Forbidden Writings* (Dutton). Copyright © 1991 by Dorothy Allison. Reprinted by permission of the author.

Philip Appleman. "A Priest Forever" from *New and Selected Poems, 1956-1996* (University of Arkansas Press, 1996). Copyright © 1996 by Philip Appleman. Reprinted by permission of the author.

Judith Baumel. "Snow-Day." Copyright © 1998 by Judith Baumel.

Celia Bland. "As You Speak." Copyright © 1998 by Celia Bland.

William S. Burroughs and Allen Ginsberg conversation. Reprinted by permission of Obie Benz, President, Fossil Films, and the Allen Ginsberg Trust.

Chrystos. "I Bought a New Red" from *In Her I Am* by Chrystos. Copyright © 1993 by Chrystos. Reprinted by permission of Press Gang Publishers.

Sandra J. Chu. "Unmarked." Copyright © 1998 by Sandra J. Chu.

Alex Comfort. "Slow Masturbation" from *The New Joy of Sex*. Copyright © 1991 by Alex Comfort. Reprinted by permission of Crown Publishers.

Junot Díaz, "How to Date a Browngirl, Blackgirl, Whitegirl, or Halfie," from *Drown* by Junot Díaz. Copyright © 1996 by Junot Díaz. Reprinted by permission of Riverhead Books, a Division of the Putnam Publishing Group.

Diane di Prima. "Fuck the Pill: A Digression" from *Memoirs of a Beatnik*. Copyright © 1969, 1988 by Diane di Prima. Reprinted by permission of Penguin, USA, a division of Penguin Books, USA, Inc.

Rita Dove. "Adolescence—II" from *The Yellow House on the Corner: Selected Poems* by Rita Dove. Copyright © 1980 by Rita Dove. Reprinted by permission of Pantheon Books, a division of Random House, Inc.